Organizational Integrity

ALSO BY TORIN M. FINSER, PH.D.

Silence Is Complicity
A Call to Let Teachers Improve Our Schools
through Action Research — Not NCLB

In Search of Ethical Leadership
If not now, when?

School Renewal
A Spiritual Journey for Change

School as a Journey:
The Eight-Year Odyssey of a Waldorf Teacher and His Class

ORGANIZATIONAL
INTEGRITY

How to Apply the Wisdom of the Body
to Develop Healthy Organizations

TORIN M. FINSER, PH.D.

STEINERBOOKS

2007

SteinerBooks

WWW.STEINERBOOKS.ORG
An imprint of Anthroposophic Press, Inc.
610 Main Street, Suite 1
Great Barrington, MA, 01230

COVER AND BOOK DESIGN: WILLIAM JENS JENSEN
COVER IMAGE: CHARLES ANDRADE, WWW.LAZURE.COM

COLOR PLATES: WATERCOLORS © BY KARINE MUNK FINSER, FALL 2006
KARINE@TELLINK.NET

Library of Congress Cataloging-in-Publication Data

Finser, Torin M., 1956–
    Organizational integrity : how to apply the wisdom of the body to develop healthy organizations / Torin M. Finser.
        p. cm.
    Includes bibliographical references.
    ISBN 978-0-88010-578-1 (PB)
    ISBN 978-0-88010-582-8 (HB)
    1. Organizational behavior. 2. Business ethics. 3. Industrial management—Moral and ethical aspects. 4. Communication in organizations. I. Title.

HD58.7.F564 2007
174'.4—DC22

2007000836

CONTENTS

ACKNOWLEDGMENTS

PERHAPS MORE THAN any of my other books, this has been a collaborative effort, as reflected in the long list of friends and colleagues who need to be recognized at the opening of what has been a two year project.

Some time ago I visited one day of a Renewal Course offered by the Center for Anthroposophy which inspired the basic idea of this book, namely using the organs of the body to better understand organizational dynamics. The course involved the dynamics of the heart, lung, liver and kidneys through storytelling and painting, and was taught by Nancy Mellon and Karine Munk Finser. Since then we have continued the dialogue, and Nancy has also gone on to write further about the organs in regard to storytelling.

My colleague at Antioch, Arthur Auer, was the one who first suggested the term "organ-izations" in one of our many conversations. He has been particularly helpful in supplying me with numerous books and articles, especially on the brain, including some wonderful texts by European authors. Thank you, Arthur!

In a conversation some years ago, Bruce Wieland, a Waldorf high-school teacher in Chapel Hill, expressed interest in my idea for a new book and has continued to give me fresh ideas, encouragement, and support. He believed in the concept before it was even born, thus demonstrating that individual initiative can help transform our world through released capacities.

As always, Nicky Heron has served as my partner in editing, encouraging, probing, asking for more examples and drawing forth more than I thought I could offer. She is simply the best.

I would like to thank Robin Johnson, at this writing, a senior at High Mowing, for her wonderful black and white drawings of the organs.

My gratitude is here also given to my long-standing colleague Douglas Gerwin, Director of the Center for Anthroposophy, who kindly gave feedback on the chapter dealing with vocation and adolescent matters.

My deep appreciation also goes to Kim John Payne for his work in our Collaborative Counseling Program at Antioch University, our common questions, ongoing conversations and some of his original material found in this book.

I had the extreme good fortune of having a wise medical doctor literally down the street here in Temple who patiently read each of the chapters on the major organs for medical accuracy. I enthusiastically thank Dr. Bertram von Zabern.

Finally, I need to end where I began. My dear wife, Karine, has once again been my travel companion on this journey. But more than any previous project, because of her expertise as an art therapist, she has been able to offer many insights and get me fired up again when I needed re-inspiration. But best of all, she agreed to do four color plates for this book, something most authors only dream about. She is the heart person in my life. To learn what is meant by this reference, the reader will have to turn to part II.

To those in the workplace who have at times struggled
with organizational oppression in one form or another.

May the life and vitality you bring to your work
be met by organic organizations
that truly support your efforts
and the innate genius of human initiative.

PREFACE

E ACH WRITING PROJECT is a journey. The ending loop of one odyssey often serves as the beginning of the next. Themes that run through several projects begin to have a life of their own and the writer starts to ask—where do these questions come from? Am I writing these pages or is something simply working itself out through me? How do these ideas relate to my destiny, my life tasks? Or to what degree are my efforts a reflection of conversations with others—the bubbling forth of many small instances of synchronicity in the complex web we call life? All I know for sure is that the creative process is one of the world's greatest mysteries.

School as a Journey began as the story of one group of children and ended by prompting me to look more carefully at the sources of joy and renewal in the lives of teachers and schools. This led to *School Renewal* with the story of Sarah and her search for personal and organizational renewal. It ended with a call for leadership and a new kind of community, which began the research process culminating in the book *In Search of Ethical Leadership: If not now, When?*

Along the way, I have continued my work as director of the Waldorf teacher education program at Antioch University, which continues to take me to schools around the world. For instance, in May of 2006 I visited South Korea for the first time. I had been invited to help them celebrate the Korean translation of *School as a Journey*. During book signings and workshops, I was asked many questions about leadership and governance in schools, how to adapt Waldorf education to their culture, and how to foster greater collaboration between parents and teachers. Not only in Korea, but in fact everywhere I go, people are asking for new, nonhierarchical forms of governance. Many people raised in traditional school structures and now working in businesses that squeeze as much out of employees as possible in the name of profit are thirsting for a new paradigm for organizations. There is a vague unease about the status quo and at the same time a questioning. What are we looking for?

For many years I have worked with the inspirations of the Austrian philosopher, scientist and educator, Rudolf Steiner. He provided a methodology for working with questions, a path of inquiry that has helped with challenges in many professions, such as assisting farmers to adopt biodynamic farming, offering new ideas to doctors working with cancer patients and encouraging artists looking for new inspiration in music, movement and drama. So when I heard increasing calls for a new paradigm in working with organizations, I began to reflect on the holistic approach used with children in Waldorf schools and how it could be applied to our work in organizations and groups. What constitutes a healthy organization? So much time and effort is spent sorting out the difficulties and challenges that arise when people come together. We have long meetings, people attend training workshops, we bring in outside consultants, and yet organizations often continue to be "high-maintenance" endeavors. How can we achieve a higher level of performance, a greater condition of health in our organizations?

I remembered a scene from my childhood in New York City. Every few weeks our apartment on West 83rd street would be stuffed with cartons of fresh produce. Walking down the hallway I would pass bags of potatoes, boxes of organic apple juice, bunches of carrots, etc., all part of the latest shipment for the family-owned health food store. Selling organic food was a radical notion in the 1950s, and the business did not last long. Now, fifty years later, almost every town has a health food store, and Whole Foods, Trader Joe's, and other enterprises have capitalized on our collective wish for healthy alternatives. "Organic" has become a mainstream notion, fully accepted and a part of what many consider healthy living. The paradigm shift around nutrition mirrors what I want to promote with organizations. I would like to help move us from a mechanistic, performance-driven model of organizations to one that works with living systems such as those found in the human body. Rather than having good people succeed despite their organization, I would like to change how we work together so that people succeed because of the support they receive from their organizations. Rather than see our structures as dead, two-dimensional diagrams, I want people to see the living, pulsating qualities in groups that reflect circulation, breathing, digestion and other life functions.

In short, my research and professional practice has led me to call for organic organizations.

This new organizational paradigm asks for an orientation towards health rather than a focus on dysfunction. Can we learn from the human body, this miraculous, complex organism we carry around with us every day, and see what works in our bodies often without our even knowing why? Is there a language of health in human physiology that can be applied to organizations?

In my consultations with schools over the past few years, I have found that health is an elusive thing. People come and go, and as they do, the work needs to be done again, or at least renewed annually. Many school leaders ask me for a "model" or form that can be transplanted into their organization so that everything will magically work as we live happily ever after. However transplants have real problems, such as rejection, reoccurrence and identity change, as has been experienced with donor organs like the heart. Organizations need to grow their way to health, and this too is a gradual, organic process. A facilitator can help, but in the end, as with personal health, one has to accept one's responsibility for change to be effective.

This metaphor of growth and personal health has led me to increasing fascination with the notion that the fundamentals of human wellness can be used for achieving organizational health. The human being, when seen as a complete entity of body, soul and spirit, contains crucial secrets of whole systems health. Alternative medical practitioners have long used substances from nature—the source of life—to treat illness. Just as natural substances re-balance and reunite that which has become separated, so organic organizations can use living processes found in physiology to promote health in the work place. This book is an alternative medical approach to organizational dynamics. If the genius behind the creation of the human organism can be applied to organizations, then the very "systems" that sustain us as human beings—circulation and respiration and others—can be applied to our schools and businesses as long as their inherent wisdom is understood and practiced.

For example, I began to observe communication in organizations as essentially a breathing process, one that interacts with the outside world yet requires forms that support and renew, similar to the air and carbon dioxide cycle in the lungs. Aberrations, such as asthma can be found in situations where there is a blockage, and what is held within cannot be released or vice versa. Asthmatic organizations have frequent crises since the natural flow of communication is arrested until there is an outcry or protest from one constituent group or another. A deficit crisis in an organization may have a root cause related to the arrested breathing function or lack of communication of the organism. In crises like these people have tried all sorts of organizational "fixes," but if the solution does not incorporate the fundamental wisdom of the human being, physiological as well as spiritual, it is unlikely to succeed or be sustainable in the long run. One example is the tendency to "hire" some one to perform the function that is deficient in the system, such as a "communications director." Breathing is a fundamental human process that is needed in healthy organizations and cannot be outsourced or delegated.

These observations led me to research human physiology as a template for organizational dynamics, and I was amazed at what I found. We have organizations that are all eyes and ears but lacking in heart and soul. There are liver or kidney organizations, and the secrets contained in these organs help us understand how to heal and move forward in a new way. As a consultant, I have sometimes been called in when there is a "heart attack" in progress, and have found that the causes go far back to the organizational lifestyle of those now in crisis. Re-balancing and healing in these situations involves restoring good circulation and understanding the working of the human heart. In short, our body has the answers if we are able to listen, observe and fittingly apply our learning.

It was in one of those miraculous moments of synchronicity that my colleague Arthur Auer one day used the term *Organ-izations*. He gave word to the ideas that had been building inside me for many months!

What has evolved over two years is a book of exploration that is structured in a way that reinforces the organic theme. Imagine a New England apple tree, as a picture of the organizational structure:

The seed, the idea of the book: the preface.
The soil that nourishes the root system—basic elements of
    Rudolf Steiner's Anthroposophy as a foundation for physiology and organizational development: part I (chapters 1–4).

The branches—examples of various human organs as related to
the basic theme of organic organizations, which is the trunk:
part two (chapters 5–11).
The leaves—the senses, patterns, and pigments: part three
(chapters 12–14).
The environment—planetary influences, whole systems: part
four (chapters 15–18).
The fruit—healthy organizations and more: part five (chapters
19–21).

I am not a medical doctor, although I have consulted some. Nor
am I a therapist, although I married one; my wife Karine has on occasion called me an organizational therapist. My life experience has
brought me to the place where I can appreciate fully the inexplicable,
the mystery in the simple things in life, such as the old apple tree on
our front lawn that continues to live despite many New Hampshire
winters. Likewise, the human body contains ancient wisdom that is
God given. In apprehending this wisdom, we have our best chance yet
to help organizations prosper. The work has just begun.

PART I

FOUNDATION STUDIES
IN ANTHROPOSOPHY

1. THE COMPLETE HUMAN BEING

ORGANIC FARMING BEGINS with good soil, as does an organic organization. To begin the process of organic farming, a farmer will often let the fields lie fallow for a year or two and take the time to assess the whole picture of the farm through the seasons and in relation to the surrounding environment. In this way the farmer can begin the task of breaking down the various elements needed to return the fields to health in an organic manner. So it is for our purposes of a healthy organization. We will look first at the complete human being in order to gain an understanding of the elements of the whole.

Many of our present social challenges arise from our failure to understand the essential nature of the human being, such as seeing the physical body without the emotional or spiritual aspects. Often people see the parts but not the whole—only bits of the problem but not the context. For example, thanks to simplistic portrayals in the media, many Americans view Islam through the lens of fundamentalism and see car bombers rather than people whose lives have been framed through the historical and religious context of the Qur'an. Americans demonize a perceived enemy, while glorifying sports and fashion models based mainly on physical characteristics. The image of the human being is distorted by the entertainment industry and in the wider media, with the result that our perceptions are altered, our expectations are manipulated and we act without adequate understanding of a full person. We see many results of this distorted view of humanity in a variety of social challenges.

For example, if we value one part of the human being, say the brain, and ignore emotional intelligence and other aspects of learning, we create standards like those found in the "No Child Left Behind" educational program. With the active sponsorship of President Bush and the endorsement of Congress, this legislation has set specific standards for school achievement regardless of the real people or locations of the many schools across the United States. The standards are mainly academic, meaning that the non-cognitive aspects of children that will be so essential in later life, such as imagination, creativity, and social skills, among others, are undervalued or ignored. The abstract standard of what a few people consider adequate education is imposed on the many, and along the way teachers are stressed out and children fail. What are we doing to our schools?

If we value the physical aspect of the human being more than the spiritual, then solutions to conflict will be war rather than negotiation and force rather than dialogue. Our experiences in life today are calling upon us to go deeper, beyond the physical "veil" of existence, to see past the outer phenomena. For example, war in the Middle East is often explained by referring to the scarcity of oil. However, simply subduing other nations and drilling for more oil is not a long-term solution to the energy crisis. Without corresponding lifestyle changes in something as simple as our driving habits, a solution will not be found. Forced solutions usually do not hold. Destroying buildings, museums, and human lives in war is a tragic outcome of a fundamental failure in our human interactions of communication, problem solving and understanding of different cultures. How great does the pain need to get before we see the alternatives? For some people, the wake-up call to change is a serious illness, for others it is the loss of a job. Nevertheless, do we have to wait for life events to intercede or can we wake up to these social challenges of our own accord? Can we begin to see the whole human being?

Similarly, if we see illness merely on the level of outer, physical symptoms, then the pharmaceutical industry will continue to produce more pills that often have questionable effects on the human body. Most physical symptoms of illness are merely the outer expression of deeper lifestyle issues and habits that rest in the fabric of a person's life forces. When will we have the courage to examine and treat the root causes of illness rather than just the outer symptoms? If indeed we live in a complex web of interconnections, then our personal health is certainly related to environmental conservation, to the decisions made in corporations and other organizations, and to the passive-aggressive actions of governments.

One example of this interconnection is that many of the products we buy are manufactured in places where workers earn substandard wages with no health care, and some of these businesses still use child labor. Every time we purchase a product made in such places we are stimulating more of the same, voting for social injustice through our choices. When will people reconcile their values with their use of money?

A further example of this interconnection is that we have been slipping ever further backward in our care of the environment. Standards for clean air and water are being relaxed, National parks are opened for logging, and the Arctic is now fair game for oil drilling. Even some that profess to value clean air drive a polluting Hummer. When will people see that the health of the human being is inextricably bound up with the health of our environment? Just as my choice of fertilizer will affect the fruit trees in my yard as well as the soil for years to come, so also the decisions made in a company have a ripple effect throughout the economy, the workplace, and the community. We can retreat with an attitude of "this is all too big for me," or "I'll just worry about myself," or we can resolve to make conscious choices about which products to buy for gardening and which companies to support as a consumer. Furthermore, the very act of responsible stewardship gives each human being making these choices a sense of well being and inner certainty. Ethical decision-making promotes social, environmental, and personal health.

There are many other social symptoms, but in my view of the world, most of them have one common denominator—the human being. It is people who create organizations, who use natural resources, who make policy decisions in government and who use our medical facilities. How people interact depends largely on how they value one another and their environment.

I would like to suggest a holistic approach to human interactions and the organizations they form rather than the reductionist, mechanical constructs used in so many places today. Only by seeing the human being as a varied, multidimensional entity can we hope to evolve more sophisticated solutions to current world challenges. Just as filmmaking took a huge step forward in sophistication when it went from black and white to full Technicolor, so we need to develop a more nuanced approach to understanding human nature.

First, I would like to share a few perceptions of how human beings relate to the world and then go into more depth on this new orientation to the essential nature of humankind. This overview will provide the foundation for examining in later chapters how specific organs in the human body inform our search for organizational health.

In our relationship to the world around us, we see objects, such as furniture, houses and trees. We learn about these things through our senses—touch, hearing, seeing, etc. These objects make an impression on us; we might like or dislike a certain chair, or we might react sympathetically or be repelled by a certain bush. These impressions are highly personal, as someone else might like the very thing we dislike. Finally, over time we acquire knowledge about the objects around us. They tell us about how they work, their secrets or essence. "Chair" has a quality that is essentially different from "table." We come to know the essence of a thing.

This relational work is important, in that one right away begins to see the layering of human experience. As described by Rudolf Steiner, we are bound up with the world in three different ways:

1. The things we encounter and accept as *facts*.
2. The world as something that concerns us and has personal significance as *feelings*.
3. Through life experience we strive to know the *essence* of things, thus giving us permanence in knowledge.[1]

Just as we all have distinctive learning styles, people also tend to prefer one or another of the above pathways to relating to the world. One can simply listen to the language people use to discover the prevalence of the following renditions of these three levels: "Just tell me *what* happened?" "I *felt* excited, and I *felt* that something was about to happen." "I have heard many people express the *idea* of holding a separate meeting." In one case the world is a place of facts; in the second, a place of emotional reactions; and in the third instance, things are distilled into ideas and concepts. How we see the world then informs how we interact and communicate.

For example, in countless situations working with human relationships in organizations, I have found that separating issues and learning into these three levels is most helpful. Therefore, if a group is trying to decide whether to continue with a certain fundraising event, I might ask for the facts. Then, after they are all out on the table, I would ask for their impressions of the last fundraiser. Finally, I'll ask what, for them, was the essence of the experience, as well as for those they spoke with during the fundraiser. This can be as simple as each person selecting one word that describes the essence. When placed out there, facts, feelings and essence inform us by providing a larger context to a decision. Groups that use this process tend to move from pure subjectivity to a more objective place. They are then better able to serve. For service is the act of giving over some of our personal agenda for the sake of the client, child, patient or community. Service objectifies, in that we move beyond ourselves. This is one of three reasons, by the way, why I would like to see organizations that work in this manner describe themselves as service organizations rather than using the more common term *not-for-profit*. Rather than putting things in the negative—we don't make money for personal or corporate gain—I would like to see a more explicit, proactive stance in favor of service and community development.

These three levels also honor the threefold view of the human being as articulated by Rudolf Steiner. Facts tend to inform us of the physical "body" of things. Feelings relate more to the "soul" that lives within each of us. And the essence as described above has intrinsic value in itself just as does the human "spirit." This threefold aspect to the human being is a basic tenet of Anthroposophy and will be referred to repeatedly in developing other themes in this book. They are used in this context as a way of seeing the complete human being in order to assess how to bring about organic organizations.

Our physical bodies are built of natural substances; they can grow, reproduce, and perceive objects in the world around us. Minerals and other substances play an important part in making this aspect of the human body quantifiable and visible to others. When one stops to examine the construction of the hand, the composition of the eye, the miracle of the heart, one is amazed at the perfection achieved in the human form. One senses that the body has been worked on over ages of time, and that what we have inherited is far greater than any scientist could invent. The body is much like a temple, a dwelling place for the human individuality. The body belongs to the first element, that of fact.

Within this temple we call a body we each have a private, inner world that is purely our own. Only I know my feelings, sensations, and thoughts unless I chose to share them with others. For example, after a long winter in New Hampshire we long for the first flowers—the snow drops, crocuses, daffodils and tulips. For me, the yellow daffodils with the tinged orange centers are the most exciting. They make me feel happy, refreshed, joyful, and young. Especially when naturalized along borders and stone walls, they seem to bring hope to the most sodden earth environment. Other members of my family react differently to the first spring flowers. Some are in love with the snowdrops, others love the white daffodils. Even though we all see the same flowers, our responses are different. Our sensations and our experiences vary. We have our own feelings, we form our own mental images of the flowers to carry away with us, and we perform actions according to personal impulses—in some cases, planting more of the flowers we love most. The soul constructs an inner world through perception, reflection, feeling, and willing. This is a reflection of the second stage of fact, that of feeling.

As we think about our experiences, we gradually come to understand things in a new way. The very act of writing is for me a way of learning, even when writing about flowers. By thinking about our sensations, images and actions, we create a rational coherence to our lives. When we enter into active thinking, we become part of a higher order, a spiritual order.[2] Rather than just experiencing and reacting, which is what many are inclined to do in this fast-paced world, self-reflection on life events shows us the inherent meaning in things. In reflecting and thinking, we lift ourselves to the spiritual realm, to the essence of things, the third essential aspect described at the beginning of this section.

As I look around me on a daily basis, I see much that speaks to the bodily functions of human beings in new technology and entertainment features that are intended to make life more comfortable and enjoyable and give pleasure to the physical aspect described above. In turn, people respond with likes and dislikes as sensations and feelings are stimulated. However, the third aspect, the reflective aspect of human striving, seems to be woefully neglected. One cannot always be sure, but often when I listen to people speaking, it seems that their thoughts are jumbled. Thinking is a strenuous activity if done well, and it seems to be in limited supply in some quarters. In short, the spiritual expression in humans is often indistinct, the soul experiences are mushy, and the body is worshiped above all. Our fitness centers are our new community centers, in some cases drawing larger crowds than either churches or educational lectures. I believe in exercise and I use a recreational facility, but I believe that we also need to cultivate the inner life of feeling and thought as well if we are to retain our essential humanity.

Before moving on, I would like to mention the importance of balance rather than preferring one of the three to the others. Mystics see the world as spirit, or see the essence of things, without fully appreciating matter, while materialists place physical things in first place. Romantics place sentiment and feelings first and foremost. In Anthroposophy, all aspects of human nature are valued, and the search for appropriate application and balance is seen as a central task of one's life journey. This balanced, threefold approach will prove vital to our later work with whole systems and organic organizations. Just as the farmer's fields must have a balance of elements in providing organic cultivation, we must use a balanced approach to cultivate organic groups and organizations.

I would like to look more closely at the essential nature of the human being. I would like to see if we can deepen our understanding of how people can live and work better together by using this three-folding methodology, which is essentially a method of research. In the following paragraphs we will explore the four basic aspects that make up the constitution of the human being.

We will begin with the physical body. Our physical nature tends to divide us. My body is separate from yours, just as two crystals may rest side by side on the mantel. This separateness is true of most things in the material world around us. We can be weighed, measured, and scrutinized. Modern science has learned an amazing amount of information concerning the human physical body. Nevertheless, few can understand fully the nature of life, which animates our body and provides growth. This is the second aspect of the essential nature of the human being. In a certain branch of Eastern philosophy, they speak of *qi*, or life force, which is with us from birth to death. A physical body without life force is a corpse. *Qi* is real, yet cannot be perceived with the ordinary senses. All we can see are its manifestations during life, such as in the ruddy face of a child or the recuperative power of the body. This is because we are permeated by life force through an etheric body that works along side our physical nature. The etheric body replenishes, restores and renews our physical body.

To understand the nature of the etheric body, consider that plants are a good example of both the physical and the life force working together. Plants are nourished by more than the minerals of the soil; they grow and reproduce with great vitality, even in extreme climates and under vastly different conditions. They also have the ability to self heal, as seen in the branch that is broken from a tree during a winter storm. Sap, or life force, flows; the wound is gradually surrounded and the tree continues its upward growth toward the sun. Thanks to these life forces, if human beings are not too destructive to their environment, nature can do much self-healing, given enough time.

Animals are a good example of the nature of the sentient soul, because they are also able to experience sensations, especially those of joy, sorrow, hunger, and fear. They are especially attuned to the feelings of others—the joy or pain of a dog's master or the suffering of other creatures.

Whereas many animals simply experience and respond instinctively, human beings respond to sensations with a higher degree of awareness. Feelings of pleasure or displeasure arising from our bodily nature become conscious and we can choose how to respond. When we think about our sensations we form thoughts that help us explain the outer world to ourselves. This is a good example of the mind soul, an additional part of the third, or soul aspect. Rather than blindly following our passions and desires, we are capable of becoming more self aware and creating opportunities, which we can decide to follow or not. Much of modern technology is designed to gratify the sentient needs of human beings. The attempt to make life more pleasurable is a huge driving force in today's economy. This includes everything from the Lazy Boy recliner, to the remote control, to the automatic ice dispenser. All these inventions are possible thanks to thought power—the mind soul that conceives things that will be useful.

Beyond the daily functioning of one's body, sensations, and mind, as human beings we often strive for more, and this is where the consciousness soul comes into play. We seek to understand the things we go through in life; we want to find meaning and purpose in our work. As we begin to use our thinking more actively, we start to see truths that speak across the divides of space and time. I can also grasp an idea once articulated by Aristotle, especially if I have been active in cognizing. There is an eternal sprit that can illuminate my being through space and time; an idea can be kindled that is like a light that refuses to go out. This eternal light that shines within us can be called the consciousness soul.

As described earlier, sensations of everyday life work their way upward from the body—for example, through hunger, pleasure, and pain. These sensations enter the soul of the human being and affect our relationship to others by limiting our responses to some degree. For example, if I am freezing cold, this condition affects my soul and my ability to function mentally as well as physically. However, spirituality works from above downward to expand our soul capacities to get along with others.[3] Through this soul expansion we become more inclusive.

For example, picture a person with many layers of clothing. In the winter, my son Ionas wears underwear, pants, shirt, sweater, snow pants, extra socks, scarf, hat, and mittens. Imagining all these layers on a child, one can then conceive of the aspects of the human being as described above in the same way. We have a physical body clothed in a life force, a sentient soul, a mind soul and a consciousness soul. The latter three are further articulations of the third aspect of the human being generally referred to as "soul," as described so well in best-sellers such as Thomas Moore's *Care of the Soul*. What is at the very core of the human being? Is it the body? The brain?

In the words of the philosopher Jean Paul, "I am an 'I.'"[4] This means that when I refer to myself, I mean me, and no other person on this earth. I am an independent being face to face with the rest of the world. In moving through life, I become more and more conscious of my self, the total experience of my human existence. As Rudolf Steiner noted, "Body and soul are the vehicles of the 'I,' it works for them. Just as the physical body has its center in the brain, so the soul has its center in the 'I.'"[5] Our "I," our actual individual essence, is invisible. The body and soul are the garments in which we live; they are the servants of the "I."

One goal in life is to achieve ever-greater mastery over our bodies and souls. Rather than simply living as a responding mechanism and acting according to outer stimuli, we can become gradually more conscious of our responses and make choices. Over time, the "I" can begin to make choices, support free thinking, and thus begin to transform the everyday aspects of our responses. When our feelings and sensations are transformed we can find our spirit self, a revelation of the spiritual world within the "I."

Inside our spiritual "skin" we are fully alive, permeated by life forces that nourish and sustain our self-development. The truths of the spiritual world reveal themselves with increasing frequency and our intuition increases. Over time, this spiritual substance becomes our own; it lives as an independent spiritual entity within us. We realize our spirit being. This spiritual essence is akin to the vision of an organization, as it forms the driving force, the essential motivation for growth and future development.

Let us consider the layers of the multidimensional picture of the human being as follows:

The physical body

The etheric body, or life force, restores the physical human body;

The astral body, or dawning of consciousness, relates to our feelings and emotions;

The sentient soul relates to our experience of sensations;

The intellectual soul relates to our ability to comprehend sensations;

The consciousness soul relates to our desire to seek for greater understanding;

The "I," or personal identity, relates to the kernel of our spirit nature.

When a human being embarks upon a path of conscious self-development, the "I" can transform the aspects just described into spiritual capacities dedicated to serve the world. Later, in chapter 11, we will discuss in more detail the brain (the *corpus callosum* and the *neurocortex*) so that we can understand how this might occur. Many of the world's great teachers or initiates, such as Buddha, Zarathustra, Hermes, and others are examples of beings that transformed themselves into servants of humanity.

How does all this help us work together on a more mundane level, in our jobs, for instance? Imagine two kinds of meetings. In the first, people are reacting, making side comments, rolling their eyes and talking past each other. There is a tone of disrespect and cynicism in the room. The meeting adjourns on a disquieting note; everyone is weighed down with the experience. Afterward, participants meet in twos and threes to discuss "another one of those meetings." They go home tired and discouraged.

In the second meeting, there is much lively interest in what is said. Participants listen with open minds, build on each other's comments, follow the train of thought, and work toward solutions that serve their community. Ideas are summarized and the group feels lifted by the clear thinking and good will of all present. They leave the meeting with a sense of accomplishment. Since they have already reviewed the session together, no one needs to huddle in small groups. They go home ready to be with friends and family.

What causes the vast difference between the two meetings described above? I have been in both situations, and at times the subject or content under consideration is the same in both instances. It is not the content that makes the difference. It is the people in the room. In the first case, they were working out of the "lower members" of human nature—physicality, sentient reactions, and heaviness—as evidenced by attitudes of dejection, negativity, and subjectivity. In the second meeting, there is a group of self-aware people who are practicing the personal work of transforming themselves toward serving higher aims. One has a sense that each person in the second meeting is a self-aware "I," inwardly active and fully conscious. In one form or another, each member has a spiritual practice that enlivens their inner being and leads to joy and success in their human interactions.

When we stand outside in the wind we may not see it as the thing we call wind; but, depending upon its strength, we can certainly feel it on our face, or we can see how it blows through the trees. Wind is a natural force, and our environment is full of natural forces of all kinds. Whether speaking of the shoreline and its erosion or the contours of a riverbed, we can observe the effects of natural forces all around us, shaping, forming, creating and destroying life. We, too, are part of a living whole, not just as "bodies" on the earth but with all the unseen forces that affect us as soul and spirit beings who work, laugh and play together.

Living systems, like human beings, are full of movement, but when it comes to humans these movements are more subtle than wind and waves; in some cases the movements affecting humans are invisible to the naked eye. Invisibility, however, does not render a thing irrelevant. To the contrary, in terms of human physiology, these subtle movements are fundamental to organizational dynamics. For example, someone in a group refers in passing to a recent loss, and the depth of her sorrow is quickly felt by others whose eyes tear up in response; thus a sympathetic movement of empathy ripples around the room.

The human body and organizational structures in general are created out of movement. For example, there is the stream of life forces that works in general from right to left, while the physical stream moves from left to right (see the diagram next page from Rudolf

Steiner's *Psychology of Body, Soul, and Spirit*). This may sound nonsensical, but just consider the growth pattern of plants and the wonderful spiral pattern referred to as the Fibonacci series involving the leaves along a plant's stem. Fibonacci, a great mathematicians of the Middle Ages, observed a sequence of 1, 1, 2, 3, 5, 8, 13, and so on in which the two previous numbers in the sequence form the next as found in numerous spiral formations in nature. Alternatively, consider the swirl of water as it runs down the drain, moving in a different direction in the Northern from that in the Southern Hemisphere. Some movements flow clockwise while others go counterclockwise. In the meeting of these two forces, form is created. One simple way to imagine this is to observe that when wind and water movements come together, waves are created.

Form arises from the meeting of two or more movements in space. This has tremendous implications for how we imagine social forms. Rather than trying to implement an abstract structure conceived by someone in management, participants can create and then name "forms" by observing movement and interactions between people. How people communicate, designate tasks for one another, and typically interact creates patterns that then can be recognized and used to form organizational structures. Even language illustrates the meeting of these elements, as when the external gestural qualities of consonants interact with the internally expressive qualities of vowels to form the structure of words. Organic organizations work with the life forces of language, movement and human interaction to create structures that breathe and pulsate with life.

In a similar way to this directional movement, the emotions or astral body of the human being, as described by Steiner, tend to swell upward from below, while the intentionality of the "I" tends to flow downward. For example we have all experienced how emotions "well up" at times, taking hold of us in our limbs, our diaphragm, our breathing and finally bursting forth in words as they rise to the head. Likewise, as we try to reassert self-control, the guidance of one's ego, or "I," as described earlier, works from above downward. Then we resolve in our thoughts to calm down and take a deep breath; our stomach muscles can then begin to relax again and our toes can uncurl. These are real life processes that are natural cyclical phenomena much like the movement of water over a waterfall.[6]

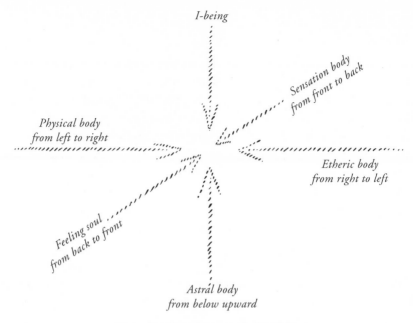

I-being

Sensation body
from front to back

Physical body
from left to right

Etheric body
from right to left

Feeling soul
from back to front

Astral body
from below upward

After a blackboard drawing by Rudolf Steiner:
A Psychology of Body, Soul, and Spirit *(p. 43)*

These movement patterns—and there are more—have tremendous implications for organizational dynamics. Consider an example from one of my classes at Antioch University. We often do something we call the "carousel." Essentially this is a way of working with small groups in which each one is given a "station" represented by a table with paper and markers. Each small group works on an aspect of an issue and then the entire group moves on to another station. This is an inclusive, time-effective way to involve everyone's best thinking, while using a small-group format that encourages participation. Most facilitators set this up and then circulate in a coaching mode. With the above movement insight to work with, I have tried the simple experiment of sometimes having the groups go from left to right or at other times from right to left around the room. One can actually observe the difference. The "life stream" right-to-left movement evokes more animated conversation, laughter, and visual artistic creativity, while the left-to-right "physical stream" tends to focus people, with results that are often more concrete and factual. Once I had observed the validity of this movement psychology, I happened to recall recent research on left and right brain functioning, especially as documented in Carla

Hannaford's book *Smart Moves.* The human being is a microcosm of larger natural processes.

Understanding the multidimensional human being is a backdrop for later chapters on the organs and their vital role in organ-izational health. The four aspects of the human being—the physical body, the etheric (or life force), the soul aspects (sentient, intellectual, and con-sciousness as previously noted) summarized as *astral,* and the kernel of our spirit nature, the "I"—each play a role in how the organs func-tion. In certain parts of the body, the physical principle predominates, in others the etheric or the astral. When there is too much of one or a displacement of one of the four principles, an illness can occur. For example, when the physical element is too strong in the kidneys— which otherwise are more comfortable with the astral element—then the overabundance of physicality shows itself in kidney stones, min-erals that would otherwise be of better use in human bones. The four aspects of the human being play with each other in the human organs like color across the evening sky. Just as each evening is slightly dif-ferent, so is the constitution of each human being.

Life gets very interesting when you put it all together, and when people come together in groups. Given a common task, one person may want to work with the diverse feelings in the group, while another will want to form and structure the assignment to get things done. One can-not say that the one or the other (astral or physical) is right or wrong. Rather, the science of organizational dynamics is a holistic approach intended to harness the resources available in collaborative work. I feel that this can no longer be assumed; it needs conscious attention.

If we can study the morphology of organ development and under-stand human physiology in new ways, we have a chance to capture the inherent wisdom of the body in our living organizations. Natural processes are at work, speaking of larger archetypes that can inform and guide our actions.

Having examined the essential nature of the human being as a holistic gestalt, let us continue with the added context of *time* and *des-tiny* in this foundational work leading to the eternal question: What is my place in this world? When we begin to understand our place in the world we have a conscious understanding of how to begin interacting in groups.

2. Beyond Memories

Having described some of the essential characteristics of human beings in general, the next step is to look at some of the qualities that contribute to the individuality of each person. When it comes to working together in organizations, each person's contribution is very much affected by one's individual life path, accumulated experiences, memories, and yearnings. Rather than suppress these individual contributions, organic organizations weave them into the tapestry of the culture.

Looking at a family photo album will bring back memories, some humorous and some poignant, startling, or wistful. The photos spark other mental images, and soon one is reliving past experiences. When the album is finally closed, we are different. Our souls have expanded; our hearts are full. There is a breadth and depth that was not there before. It wasn't just the photos or the images of our children when they were younger, but something new has happened. In remembering, we are recreating past realities. Each of us is a changed person through our remembering.

If one has the courage to look within, one finds a treasure trove of memories that have collected in the soul. Gradually, some of our memories sank below the threshold of daily consciousness, and thus we may not be aware of all that rests there. Such experiences mature over time, and when we decide to draw them forth again, they rise above the threshold of consciousness in a new way. They have become personal resources. For example, I can see things more clearly because my vision has grown over time. This processing of experiences nourished the part of me that is *always* me—my spirit. Consequently, we are often drawn to older people for advice, because they have grown in spirit through the years. The spirit is nourished by the treasures of the past offered up by the soul.

Most people have a vague understanding of this. But let us take a leap forward, beyond memories, so to speak. Could it be that just as memories come to life again when we recall them, the results of our actions have a tendency to come back to us? We all know that memories are just waiting to reappear. But could it be the same with the results of past actions? Perhaps experiences in the outer world come toward us because we need to meet them. Regarding such experiences, Steiner asks, "Are they waiting to approach the soul from the outside, just as a memory waits for a reason to approach from the inside?" [7]

This is worth examining. Let us say, for example, that one goes to a certain university. There one meets one's sweetheart, the person with whom one ends up spending many happy years together. On a superficial level, we can say that this meeting was the result of another action, namely the move to the particular university or college. But if such a meeting has happened in your life, a little self-awareness will show that the reality of the experience is far greater than geography or mere chance. When one meets a life partner, there is an overwhelming sense that this is of far greater importance than we can realize in the moment. A voice inside says: What have I done to deserve this? What has destiny brought me?

If my spirit is truly eternal, then the joys and sorrows, the things that happen to me in this life, and the people I meet may depend on actions and interactions that precede this life. Rudolf Steiner stated this concept in his book *Theosophy*: "In this way, we can become able to recognize an experience of destiny as a past action of the soul finding its way to the 'I'.... What we experience as destiny in one lifetime is related to our actions in previous earthly lives." [8]

Thus every action has its consequences. Throwing a stone into a pond near our house delights our son Ionas with a kerplunk, a splash, and ripples. This is a clear example of how phenomena proceed from our every action. Some create ripples that go beyond the confines of one sojourn on Earth. In the case of past actions from other lifetimes, the consequences often come to meet us from without in the form of the people, events, and experiences we encounter.

Why is this so? It has to do with an action's very nature—its anatomy, so to speak. When something is performed as an action, the need to carry out its consequence is impressed on the soul. For instance, if I were to hurt someone, my soul immediately begins to work with the possible consequences. Even when not fully aware of it, we recoil inwardly at what we have done. Some of this soul processing may be unconscious, but it is nevertheless real. It is of course best if one can right away make amends for hurting someone, but this is not always possible. There are situations in which a hurt lingers on, and consequently a yearning grows in the soul to redress the situation. It is inherent in human nature to reclaim equilibrium, to make peace with a situation. Because life is messy and much happens over the years, some things have to wait for another incarnation.[9]

My soul in one lifetime "educates" my spirit to find opportunities for rebalancing in the next life. I then seek out the people and situations that will give me a chance to make amends. This is not just true in the case of negative experiences but also holds true for positive experiences from the past. Good deeds also have consequences. For example, I have often wondered whether the partner we find in this life who brings us joy may have something to do with the quality of interaction we had in a past life.

Thus, in the complex web of destiny, we find ourselves in fascinating situations, go through all sorts of experiences and "chance" encounters, all by way of placing before us the opportunities our souls have desired. Through our past actions the human spirit prepares its own destiny. In a great web of connection, we are linked to each other through multiple lifetimes. Along the way, the spirit grows. What the soul has preserved as memories of life experiences the spirit transforms. Through this, new capacities are developed. Over time we are better able to meet situations with clarity, poise and compassionate understanding. We are in a better place to help others when we have done our own transformative work.

All this has many implications for our work together in organizations. Do we just bring our baggage to the workplace and dump it on others, or are we personally working with our past experiences so they can be transformed into new capacities for service? Those who have been through the most, have suffered more than others, or have lived life fully in both joy and sorrow often have the most to contribute when a challenge arises at work. Character is formed on the anvil of life.

What we do at work also shapes our character. If one spends years as a nurse or a teacher, a mechanic or an electrician, the nature of the work influences how we fit in to the world around us. We not only see other people through the eyes of a teacher or nurse, but we also become more and more of that role. I can usually spot retired public school teachers before they introduce themselves as such, due to their manner of interacting with my children. Some people are fortunate to have a career, a calling in life, while others are not. This leads us to look more carefully at vocation and the organizational implications of how people find themselves through work.

3. VOCATION

WHY LOOK AT vocation in relation to organizational dynamics? There are several reasons that come to mind. First, many people I meet these days are trapped in their jobs. One person said to me just recently: "My company is paying me too well for me to quit." I took the meaning to be that the family is dependent on the income and that doing something else, something more meaningful would not be possible. Others may not be making quite enough income but are trapped in the benefit plan and are not willing to risk losing the health insurance coverage. No matter what form this takes, the result is that one is unable to listen to the inner stirrings, the call for a new arena of work, and life continues in the same, predictable fashion.

Another reason to study vocation is that many people feel caught in the classic struggle between freedom and necessity. The call of freedom may mean starting a new career, moving to a new location, opening a business or becoming a teacher. The outer form is not as important as the way in which the inner voice prompts us to begin anew. Necessity is that elemental force that binds us to the harsh realities of life, binds us as products of heredity, race and geographical location among other things. This can take various outer forms, including the notion that the family business requires my continued participation. If I leave, the costs are too high. I am bound by good reasons and bad, my love of family and the necessity of continuing with work now become bittersweet. Those caught in the clutches of necessity often have a love/hate relationship to their work; for if it were all bad, one would be more likely to switch.

Likewise, there are those who wander through life, never really finding their true calling. I spoke with someone in her fifties recently who described this situation. Children have been raised; jobs have been worked; yet there has always been the question: "What am I supposed to do when I grow up?"

Then there are those who have forged ahead, found new careers, even invented new occupations. These folks tend to have one thing in common—they listened to an inner stirring, they took the plunge, and they are so excited about what they are doing that everything else falls into place. Sacrifices are made, loved ones usually stay connected and may even be intimately involved, and a new career unfolds. For some people this may mean opening a restaurant; for others it may mean working with children or inventing new technology. There is a sense of adventure and joy. Where did this new direction come from? How can others gain access to this elixir?

Finally, there are those who want to live several lifetimes at once. Personally, I would do many more things if only there were more hours in the day. Parenting and partnering are often full-time, immensely rewarding occupations. Then there is my love of teaching, the joy of connecting with the wonderful people attracted to Antioch University and the Center for Anthroposophy here in New Hampshire. The field work with schools, collaborative leadership training and consulting, give me raw material out of which I learn to understand the dynamics of groups and organizations. Then there is my thirst for research and writing. If only one had more time for all of the above.

Every moment of the day we are compelled to make choices. Will the outer demands always hold sway? Are there times when we listen to the inner voice as well? With each of the various aspects of life, there is both a reactive and a proactive way of working. Learning to know one's vocation and heeding the call of life can be a tremendous help in achieving success.

When I do workshops on vocation, I often begin by asking participants to list the physical characteristics that they have inherited from their parents. These may include everything from hair color to height, from facial expressions to health. Once a few people share their lists, I then talk about our connection to heredity. We are given certain physical characteristics thanks to our parents. One's race, birthplace, nationality, culture, physical health, and predisposition to certain illness all arise from heredity. This is a fact.

The next question is subtler. What can be "read" in the demeanor and physical expression that is you and not someone else? Are there certain facial expressions, gestures and habits that you have acquired? Each person has a slightly different way of walking if one takes the time to observe. If we look carefully, we can see the whole personality simply in the way someone walks. Posture is also significant. Here we are not just talking about physical aspects, but the life (etheric) forces that have shaped us. This can be seen in some of the smallest details.

For example, most babies like to "pull in" with a bottle, pacifier or some thumb sucking. As the biological father of three sons I have observed vastly different behaviors just in this small detail. One liked to suck the two middle fingers of his left hand while twiddling his hair with the other hand. Another was a classic thumb sucker, while Ionas, our youngest, caressed his stomach while drinking his bottle. Each gesture was so individual. Even at age four Ionas would complain if I cut his nails too short because then he could not "touch my stomach." The important thing about such observations is to let the phenomena sink in without looking for an immediate interpretation. In regard to these three fellows, what do these gestures tell me? For each distinctive gesture is a window into the soul and the emerging personality.

The third step in the workshop process is to look at the list of physical characteristics and the typical gestures and ask, what has been transformed? Each of us works with life and over time things change. What has been given from parents or early mannerisms that change as the years go by? It is helpful to see what has been transformed. Let's say a child grows up in a large household with many loud voices competing for attention at mealtimes. The parents argue, even shout at times, yet they clearly love one another deeply. Years later, the child in question has become a quiet, mild-mannered person known for respectful listening. Clearly these changes were self-initiated. This is an example of the third step in the vocational exercise.

Finally, I ask the group to look at biography. What have I done with my life thus far? Can I identify major turning points? This constitutes the last preparatory step before taking on the issue of vocation directly. For in the four steps covered in the above exercises, attention has been given to four aspects of the human being as described in chapter 1:

1. Physical: heredity, earthly, the given life situation.
2. Etheric: life forces, that which has formed us, given us characteristic gestures, habits, inner disposition.
3. Astral: overcoming emotional and personal challenges, conscious attempts at transformation, change, making my life my own.
4. "I," or ego: my unfolding story, my individuality, my unique self.

These four aspects are interrelated. For example, the physical aspect creates life situations and the "I" transforms these life situations into life's story. Along the way we enter into relationships with people and these connections influence our work, our vocation. Likewise, the etheric forms our inner peculiarities that then show themselves in demeanor, gesture and posture. This is especially true in the "formative" years of seven to fourteen, when the etheric works most strongly. An example is the rich imaginative life many children have at this age; they can easily accept their characters in a dramatic production with minimal use of costume or makeup. This direct ability to grasp the pictorial and imaginable immediately is the etheric life force at work.

But in the seven-year period that follows, which is the development of the physical into the emotional, the astral body is released and a great struggle ensues. Will I continue in just the way my parents want me to be or can I become something that is just me? The movie *Failure to Launch* treats an exaggerated form of this issue when two aging parents hire a young woman to lure their son, age thirty-five, into finally moving out of their house. Usually, this separation from heredity happens in the teenage years, but our society has in many ways prolonged adolescence. During these transition years the past and future struggle within the young person, with occasional outbursts of rejection and reconnection.

Thus, etheric life forces and the astral of the above four aspects are related, as are the physical and the "I." But there is more to this story. If you place this view of the human being in a time line that stretches far back, even prior to birth, you can begin to appreciate a remarkable statement by Rudolf Steiner when speaking of the characteristic gestures, posture and demeanor of the child, "A great part of what thus appears in the developing child is derived from karma and is the effect of the vocation of his preceding incarnation."[10] If I understand this correctly, the particular characteristics of a child in this life are a result of a past vocation. That which occupied many of the working hours of a person in one life has been carried forward into formative elements in the present life. Let us say a person was a blacksmith in the Middle Ages, spending hours on end working with metal, fire and physical exertion. This so impressed itself on the soul of the person, that when reincarnated, the gestures of the new life bear the imprint as it were of the vocation of the past life. The past work lived on in the etheric and is now imprinted in the person's physical attributes. We are shaped by our work in many unimagined ways.

Then, in the teenage battle to assert "who I am," the vocational karma of the past—such as in my example of the blacksmith—is countered by an equally pressing demand to transform what has been given into something new. One could say that puberty is our only legitimate "crisis." Depending on how this struggle is resolved, the young person will find a new vocation for this life, remain mired in the ambivalence of indecision, or accept a handed down career or job.

Many of our high schools and colleges do not take into account this epic struggle for vocation in the years fourteen to twenty-one. Often, students are expected to declare a major and take courses that specialize in theoretical content areas that have little validity in terms of the search for vocation. Many professors are trained in their subject areas but have minimal understanding of adolescent development.

Waldorf high schools come closer than any place I know in working with the emerging emotional life as well as the ripening intellect. It is when they truly engage the will, be it in a naturalist program, taking apart a car in physics or building a canoe in preparation for a field trip, that the adolescent really takes hold of life. I remember when my son Thomas came home one night after a class on permutations and combinations with Connie Gerwin, the math teacher and his advisor at High Mowing School during that time. They had sampled a sumptuous meal together—ten students working on all the possible permutations and combinations of the multicourse feast. He has never forgotten that learning experience. When students are provided with such rich opportunities in high school, they are more likely to connect with the world and future career possibilities.

There are those students whose vocational interest happens to fall into a prescribed content area, and they may consequently become enthusiastic engineering students or pre-med majors as an example. These students can thrive in college and public universities. Other than in the Waldorf high schools with which I am familiar, our higher educational institutions do not do so well with those struggling to find themselves, especially for those who want to explore "out of the box." Some students experiment with different jobs and lifestyles during their twenties, and perhaps in the face of pressure they even submit to study in an academic institution. Those with healthy instincts often take time off between high school and college, or do a year abroad during the university years.

From a vocational perspective, I advocate for a "thirteenth year" of development transition between twelfth grade high school and college. Recognizing the need to experience different ways of living and learning, students can spend time learning by doing, working with different professionals in the field, trying things out and learning from life. If they undertake academic work, it should be based upon natural interest and a wish to make sense of experiences. The focus could be service learning. Some will find a thirteenth year challenging, but adversity also educates. With improved training for college advisors, we can better help our eighteen-year-olds. Freshmen, especially the boys I have known at college, are usually at a loss as to know what to do with their sudden freedom. So often our youth have high ideals that are then shattered when they come up against the realities of the world. Coming up against oneself in the workplace, even encountering a certain amount of adversity, schools the soul and ignites the spirit flame of our own unique individuality. In this schooling of life, vocation is uncovered, drawn forth from the clutches of karma. Our subsequent career choices would then more likely be in response to a true calling.

Getting a right vocation is not only important for future career success and family happiness, but has implications for personal health and well-being. Many illnesses today are bred in the hot house of stress. Even though stress is part of everyone's life today, for some, the discrepancy between inner calling and "must-do" work is too great. If you have to go day after day to a job that is totally unfulfilling, something starts to die inside. Apathy and stagnation allow predator forces into the castle of self. In contrast, enthusiasm creates vitality and the strength to do the impossible. One modality slays forces in the soul, the other recreates. Doctors and others who work with illness can attest to the effect of stress and dejection on physical health. Lack of vocation is frequently manifest in heart disease. The heart, as will be described in greater detail later, is the "sun" center, the place where our most sacred wishes are housed and nourished. When we cannot circulate in good ways with our vocational work life, our physical circulation can suffer. Our interactions with others and the world in general can either help or hinder our physical health. Living one's passion, heeding the call of vocation, is good for body, soul and spirit. Rudolf Steiner spoke to this connection of vocation and physical health when he said, "If we go more deeply into this, the fact becomes apparent that a person's external career in one incarnation, when it is not merely a career but also an inner vocation, passes over in the next incarnation into the inward shaping of their bodily organs."[11]

Thus, vocation has importance beyond a career path. It can literally shape our organs. Later in this book we will look more closely at the physical organs themselves and what they tell us about working together in groups and organizations. If we can achieve a complete picture of the human being in a state of health, we will find clues for developing and then sustaining organ-izational well-being.

4. The Long Journey

A FTER EXPERIENCING THE natural splendor of Oslo, Norway back in 1923, Rudolf Steiner made the following observation:

> We see marvelous sights when admiring a beautiful landscape; marvelous sights when admiring the starry sky at night in all its splendor. Yet if viewing a human lung, a human liver, not with the anatomist's physical eye, but with the eye of the spirit, we see whole *worlds* compressed into a small space. Apart from the splendor and glory of all the rivers and mountains on the surface of the earth, a still more exalted splendor adorns what lies inside the human skin, even in its merely physical aspect. It is irrelevant that all this is of smaller scale than the seemingly vast world of space. If you survey what lies in a single pulmonary vesicle, it will appear as more grandiose than the whole range of the mighty Alps. For what lies inside the human being is the whole spiritual cosmos in condensed form. In the human inner organism we have an image of the entire cosmos.[12]

Now, I have to admit that I am partial to the Alps—whether flying over their snowy peaks in an airplane or walking their grassy slopes in the summer, I am always impressed with their sparkling beauty. It had never occurred to me to view the inner organs of the human being in the same way. For the most part, in fact, I am unconscious of my organs. It is great when they simply do their work; there are other things to think about. In a way they have been sleeping friends, helping silently and unobtrusively.

Having established in earlier chapters a foundation for viewing the human being in space, and before we move on to specific organs in the human body, this chapter will look at the human being in the context of time. We will examine some of the earliest aspects of evolution as envisioned by Anthroposophy and relate the elements found there to organizational life.

Now that I reflect upon it, there are really three aspects of my consciousness. During the day, for the most part, I am awake and attentive. In this state I see what is around me from the outside. Sense impressions come toward me; I see, hear, touch, and experience the world. This is like knowing the body mainly from the outside—the skin, head, limbs, and so on. Then there is my night consciousness, known as sleep. Here things go along just fine until they are disturbed. I may be aware of my breathing for a while, but for the most part I am oblivious to the regular work of my heart, liver, kidney, and other organs since these organs live in the night consciousness.

Occasionally, I have dreams. When they are remembered, it seems that they come about half way between waking and sleeping. Pictures are created, some perhaps prompted by a noise outside, others arising from an experience in the previous day. Different people have different kinds of dreams and at various times of the night. I am particularly susceptible to the times when the liver (3:00 A.M.) or kidney (4:00 A.M.) begins to stir. Therefore, the organs are generally asleep in us, but sometimes exert an influence that is greater than we think.

Throughout the day things flash through our consciousness, but sometimes we cannot process it all and events and experiences reverberate through us during sleep. Just as the organs are doing their silent work, so also the organs can continue our "digesting" of the day, each in their own way. When we are free enough to dream dreams that go beyond the "captured organ-centered work," then our dreams can be of a different nature, they can be unforgettable; they can at times be messages directly from the spiritual world. These occur rarely, and can be life-changing when we bring them back into consciousness the next day.

Within organizations, we have similar stages of consciousness—sleeping, dreaming, and waking. Most of us flit from one "waking" concept or image to another. We place a high value on the spoken word, what is said in meetings, and what we can see with our own eyes. Indeed, there is much valuable information that can be gleaned in heightening our observational skills. Who is speaking and how much? What is communicated in body language? How does this group interact as opposed to another one in the same organization? Do they share airtime? Who is exercising leadership? There is so much we can learn from careful observation. Indeed, most of our organizational issues and challenges are referred to in this first level of understanding; they are worked in the realm of "day consciousness." as in "lets talk it through."

Sometimes, however, one senses that there is more at work in a group. There are undercurrents, unspoken agendas, and implicit understandings. One can occasionally sense these aspects, but for the most part they remain elusive, as in a dream. Whenever we are vaguely aware of something, with realization that "dawns" over time, we are more in the dream state of consciousness. For example, one leaves a meeting wondering: "what was going on in there between Neal and John?" One senses that there was tension but is aware only of the affect, the general impression. Then a few days later, you might be driving to work and realize, "oh, they are competing for the same position, and even though it had nothing to do with the agenda item, they were showing their tension." A dream consciousness in organizations need not be seen as a bad thing, for if we were all fully awake to every aspect of what was going on in a meeting we might never get everything done. Dream consciousness can serve as a protective blanket in an organization.

Then there is the night consciousness. Like the sleeping organs, there are few clues as to this level of work. There is a kind of primordial influence that is unmistakable once identified. In conventional language, we use the word "culture" to encompass this overarching aspect. It is the difference between IBM and Apple Computer, between the local family restaurant and McDonald's. It is more than the décor, geographic location or the staff. A pervasive but subliminal element informs every action and communication throughout the organization, no matter how large. It is so big that no one could engineer a clone even if they wanted to. The culture of an organization is like a national park, a signature that is both unfathomable and yet unique.

For years, organizational consultants have tried to solve the riddle of "culture" by asking what made a healthy culture and what detracted from it? If there were deep-seated problems within the culture of an organization, how could one stimulate change? I once worked with a school that illustrated this situation perfectly. Outwardly, they wanted better leadership. But underneath the surface, their culture of disrespect had so undermined the fabric of human interactions that no one wanted to lead and those who ventured forth occasionally were immediately cut down. Here was a case where outer solutions and structural changes were not sufficient. Something fundamental had to change, but how?

This is where I became more interested in the organs, the sleeping giants of our bodies. Did they have secrets that could unlock new understandings of how we are organized? Are there "laws" of the human organism that apply to organizations? Margaret Wheately, in her book *A Simpler Way*, and other writers have touched on this in terms of the natural world and living systems in organizations, but I want to take this further by looking first at evolution and then specific aspects of human physiology. What can the heart tell us about organizations? Is there special knowledge that comes from the liver, the kidney, and how can we apply it?

But first I would like to look briefly at an Anthroposophical view of human evolution in relation to organizational dynamics. The descriptions below will give us the backdrop for the specifics of human physiology. Thus, for example, when I later discuss the importance of warmth in relation to certain organs, the reader can recall the evolutionary description of warmth as one of the earliest forces behind the development of the human form. For once again, the macrocosm and microcosm work hand-in-hand.

An Evolution of Consciousness

Those who think just in terms of material processes can trace evolution only from quantifiable artifacts belonging to our ancestors. Even though recent discoveries have continued to push back the supposed origin of human life, there is still great uncertainty as to how it all began. Debate continues between so-called neoclassical evolutionists—those ascribing to cosmic intelligence—and creationism, for example. In his work on evolution, Rudolf Steiner described a revolutionary approach that began with three fundamental points of view:

1. If we wish to fully understand the human being we need to consider evolution, and if we want to better understand evolution, we need to develop a complete view of the human being. Human and cosmic histories are inextricably intertwined.

2. He further affirms that spirit comes before matter. Everything around us has a spiritual origin that gives us the signature, the essence of that which later becomes manifest physically.

Since this is such an important concept for Steiner, let me share an example. The *Mona Lisa,* indeed any work of art, did not come into being because the pigment was moved about from palette to canvas. It cannot be understood based solely upon the quantity or type of oil paints used. The masterpiece arose in Leonardo da Vinci's mind's eye; it was conceived long before the pigment was applied. The inner picture that was to become the *Mona Lisa* was nurtured through countless observations of women, through practice drawings and much reflection. Thanks to *The Da Vinci Code,* many people now have a greater appreciation for the hidden secrets behind the masterpiece, even if one might not agree with all the author's interpretations. In the end, the painter's genius created this work of art. Genius, creativity, and inspiration are all spiritual qualities. Any creation, even human conception, is spirit before matter.

3. A third preliminary point is that when matter appears in human evolution, it does so very gradually, through a process that could be compared to condensation. Just as water condenses out of humid air, the human form materialized gradually though several distinct stages discussed below.

WARMTH

It is hard to imagine the world before anything existed, in a state of nothingness. One has to gradually eliminate everything we have around us: furniture, cars, and clocks—even voices, sounds, visual impressions and us. Even if one successfully blocks out everything, one still has to eliminate our thoughts, feelings and inner stirrings. Even with great effort we can only approximate a state in which nothing existed. Imagine standing at the edge of a great precipice, high up on a mountain. One stands at the edge, with air all around and a great foggy void below. Then imagine letting go and falling. The sensation of falling into the abyss is an experience of nothingness with the fear and dread that comes with it.

Falling into the abyss—a modern, existential experience for some— is a significant part of the evolutionary story, as this negative space calls forth a response, an act of courage. The will to exist arises, and a spiritual dynamic is created. There is a "stir" in the void, and warmth is created. This is not a matter of temperature, but of a soul experience akin to when a parent sees their child successfully perform on stage, or one meets a long-lost friend. Another way to describe this earliest stage is that into the surging sea of nothingness, a courageous sacrifice was made. A spiritually risky event took place, and through this act of sacrifice conditions of alternating warmth arose and the earliest forms that would one day be human began to stir.

Even today, wherever we have sacrifice, we have warmth. Parents will remember the dreaded call in the night, "Mommy, I am sick." Many of us know what is like, when dragged from deep sleep, one has to hold the head of a child as he or she retches over the toilet at two o'clock in the morning. Then there are the sheets that may need changing and finally one falls back into bed. Yet, despite or perhaps because of the sacrifice, one is different. Although still tired, I have often felt inner warmth after such an experience, even more love for our child, and new abundance within. Sacrifice calls forth warmth.

When I walk into a store, school, or restaurant, I often do the "warmth test." Not particularly scientific, it consists of my using any perceptive antennas at my disposal to ascertain the level of warmth in the establishment. How are the people interacting, is the staff friendly, do people matter, are differences integrated into the whole. These are but a few of the things I try to pick up. Generally, I want just the right amount of "warmth;" too much suffocates and too little leaves me disengaged. I find it interesting that although coffee and bread have been around for a long time, it is the ambiance and the creative concept that set Starbucks or Panera apart from the competition. I remember speaking with the CEO of Panera a few years ago and he was emphatic on the notion of having the right creative concept. The rest is "just" execution. Executives and other leaders would be well advised to try the warmth test once in a while. It reveals a lot about the creative potential of human beings.

LIGHT AND AIR

After a period of rest, the evolutionary process continued with the advent of life, not as we know it, but as a creative, or etheric, force (described earlier). Arising from the first stage of warmth, wise spirits, inspired by the sacrifices they witnessed earlier, now start to give of themselves. As Steiner describes it, they ray forth their goodness, their grace. As all giving also involves receiving, other spiritual beings, which could be called Archangels, come into being in order to receive the gifts of wisdom flowing toward them. They hold onto this divine wisdom, yet also reflect some of it back. This reflected wisdom takes the form of light. That which was purely spiritual, now takes on a degree of form in what we today call "light."

In order to understand this concept, take as a meditative exercise the phrase: "Wisdom lives in the light." My favorite way of contemplating these words is in a quiet spot outside, perhaps under a tree with shafts of light streaming through the branches on a late afternoon. I can then unite my whole feeling life into experiencing the reality of wisdom belonging to the light realm. As I surrender to these words, the words eventually disappear and I am left with an essence of "wisdom in the light" which unites me with both inner and outer realities in a single moment of joy.

With the reciprocal actions of giving wisdom and reflecting light, two-dimensional space is born. The inner and the outer exist at the same time. In this space, one now has the movement of air and light, and the human form takes on life. Using terms introduced in the first chapter, we can say that the etheric comes into existence at this stage of evolution as a meeting of life forces in air and light condensed into the early stages of a human form. Only later will the earthly, material aspect of human physiology become manifest. According to this viewpoint we were beings of warmth, light, air and movement before we solidified into physical entities.

In organizations, there are those who do their duty, work for others and perform their tasks as required. And then there are those who are inspired. This is a marvelous moment, when suddenly we light up with a new idea, an inspiration. Perhaps this comes in the midst of a conversation, and we hear ourselves saying something entirely new. Perhaps we see a familiar object and suddenly see it with new eyes. Or perhaps we wake up in the morning with a creative impulse. Inspirations take on all shapes and sizes, but they have in common a "spark." Something new is born. Just as we can speak of "Genesis" in terms of the world's beginning, we can also speak of the genesis of a new idea or innovation.

How can we continue to innovate, change and grow? Organizations can either encourage or hinder human inspiration. Of course one needs form and structures, but if they become too rigid, innovation is stifled. I believe in establishing a common vision and then letting employees be as independent as possible. They should at times feel as if they were "self-employed," with maximum individual responsibility and initiative and minimum "corporate" red tape. If one works with meeting times effectively, it is possible for the inspirations of the periphery to flow into the center and be shared, tested and encouraged. We either innovate or die. Organizations need maximum light (inspiration) and maximum air (circulation). Thus the pathways of innovation in organizations follow some of the same characteristics described in the evolutionary picture of humankind.

Water

As the evolutionary process of condensation continued, the next stage saw the arrival of fluids, both in the atmosphere and in the still developing human organism. At each step of the way, humans become more formed and here we have the early stages of gender differentiation. What was whole now becomes separated. Some spiritual beings renounce their further development in order to aid the progress of evolution. One can see this also as a kind of rebellion, played out on a cosmic plane. When some set themselves apart from others, there is a split, painful at times, but nevertheless a spur for further development. One need only study the history of revolutions around the world to see how these times of opposition, these archetypal splits of dark and light, often, in the end, aid human evolution. In the French Revolution, for example, the violent clash of workers against the aristocracy eventually brought forth a new form of democracy.

Water is a classic example of renunciation. Even today it is one of the most susceptible elements in our environment. It renounces form, flowing according to the dictates of outer structures, in riverbeds and rock formations. It selflessly absorbs foreign substances, including chemicals and other pollutants. It is one of our most precious resources, and yet is most easily abused. *Water is renunciation.* This is a curious notion. In a society where so many try to "get ahead" in terms of careers, material things and even self-development, the idea of renunciation may seem foreign indeed. When was the last time you gave something up that you really wanted?

There is more to this than just foregoing a latte or a new pair of shoes. If one begins to experiment with renunciation, one soon realizes that there are powerful forces at work in this struggle. It is not so much a matter of giving up something one wants, but rather of harnessing the inner resolve to do what is needed in service of others rather than of Self. A teacher who renounces devotes several hours a night to preparation, entering the classroom long before her students arrive to draw a map on the blackboard. Such a teacher is not only prepared, but also has an inner strength that the students will feel. It is a process of concentrating energy and harnessing resources—a form of self-discipline that can affect directly the way her students behave and learn. In contrast, one who is indulgent and skimps on preparation, reusing old material without renewing it, will quickly loose contact with the students; they will drift away, and classroom management can become a problem. It depends on the degree of renunciation one is willing to practice: giving without expectation. In the positive case, there is flow, an exchange that is rich and meaningful, as many have experienced when they give selflessly. In the latter case, the classroom atmosphere becomes "thin," there is little out of which to build constructive learning relationships.

Water plays a role in organizations beyond the proverbial "water cooler" conversations. First of all, there are almost always those who renounce personal interests in favor of the greater good of the company or school. There are often people in groups who keep things flowing with just the right comments, a suggestion of a birthday celebration or a timely acknowledgment of a small success. But there is a more fundamental aspect that goes beyond the informal "flow." Water tends to serve revitalization. Just take polluted water and follow its course over rapids, around bends and over cascading rocks. After many miles, it will have re-oxygenated and will be renewed. The flow forms based on water research under the direction of Jennifer Greene in Blue Hill, Maine, is a clear example of this. Her lab has for years helped purify water by working with natural dynamics in flow forms rather than the use of chemicals.

After hours in the sweltering sun in the deserts of the southwest, one craves water more than anything else. Water is vital to life. It refreshes and renews. In our organizations, we need to attend to the revitalization as well. On a daily basis, many use the dry sands of the intellectual soul for most tasks. People write memos, type e-mails, respond to phone messages, and gradually the "juice" is sucked right out. Water consciousness is an antidote. It works with rhythm, with connecting, with regeneration. In practical terms this means doing some things rhythmically, observing the cycles of the year and living in accordance with nature. Connecting can happen in a good conversation that might happen over lunch or just by accident. The intellectual soul would say "this is not in my calendar for today and I will waste time that should be spent on other things." When there are too many barriers, water stagnates.

Beyond the interpersonal, one can look to the fluidity of organizational structure. Here one wants to attend to the dynamic, the interaction between groups and units to see if there are possibilities for movement, spontaneous exchange and change. Rather than staying with one structure over many years, one can adapt and amend, based upon the changing needs of the people within the structure.

MINERAL

Having passed through stages of warmth, light, air and water, we now arrive at the last stage of evolution according to Anthroposophical indications. In previous phases, human beings made progress in developing life forces and a vague picture consciousness, but the physical body as we know it today was not yet manifest. The organs for outer sense perception were not present. During an interim period, the work of earlier evolution was "recast" so that the emerging human being would be able to develop new faculties, including "object consciousness," an awareness of things more as we know them today.[13]

At this time in evolution the earth was all soul and spirit; matter did not exist. What would become the physical body of the human being was in an astral form, a body of consciousness, according to Steiner. Gradually, through a process of condensation and solidification, the human form passed through states of heat, air, and water and finally took on earthly materiality. The earth actually alternated between two different states as Steiner expresses in *Esoteric Science*, "During one, it was allowed to surround human souls with its substance and clothe them in bodies. During the other, these souls deserted it and only the bodies remained, and both the earth and its human beings were in a state of sleep. We can state quite objectively that at this point in the distant past, the earth was going through periods of night and day."[14] The day period occurred when human beings inhabited that portion of the earth that faced the Sun, while night occurred when humans led a purely soul existence. During these times of night the human body was in a corpse-like state only to come to life again in the next daylight hours. Human consciousness was, so to speak, "on" and then "off" for periods, much as the sun and moon come and go.

The stores, schools and office buildings we inhabit during the day become corpse-like at night. When the lights go out and the last janitor departs, all that remains is the shell of an organization. Without the people living, working and wandering through them, our institutions are dead. So much effort goes into moving money and "things" of this world around all day long, when in fact it all vanishes when human activity is not present. Left on their own, physical things begin to decay and gradually return to the dust of the earth. In contrast, when the children return to a school the next morning, the institution is reborn. They provide the teachers with life forces that become the substance of their mutual work together. The real work of organizations rests in the mutual evolution of the people who come together with common purpose. By mutual evolution I mean that in working together, everyone changes. We are all interconnected, more so if one takes into account some of the spiritual dimensions of warmth, light, sacrifice and renunciation that have been described.

During this stage of earthly evolution, humans gradually lost their intimate connection with the world of spirit and soul as their bodies became more and more solid, and gender separation occurred. As solidification gained momentum, human souls grew less and less able to direct and participate in the organization of their bodies. The divine connection between all things was being severed. As a result, independent human beings that could claim a measure of freedom were ready to emerge.

This set the stage for the development of human organs and the completion of the human form. One can picture a perfectly round sphere that rests at peace in a sea of fluids. Over time, through the influences of the environment, a small indentation occurs (see diagrams below).

This indentation deepens and becomes a pocket, which then gradually closes (opposite page, see third and fourth stages in diagram). Finally, the inner sphere is completely enclosed within the outer sheath, and a human organ is born.

That which was once part of the great whole now remains as a microcosm in the human body. We each have the wisdom of the spheres within our bodily organs. To understand the universe is to understand human nature. To understand the captured wisdom of the organs is to understand mighty universal processes that affect every moment of our lives. A whole-systems approach to organ-izational work begins with seeing the big picture in the particular instance.

In part one, we have examined the soil that nourishes the root system—the basic elements of Rudolf Steiner's Anthroposophy as a foundation for physiology and organizational development. The threefold method of research offers us the opportunity to look at all issues from the viewpoints of fact, feelings and essence. Further, we can see the human being as a whole being with the basic constitution of the physical body, the etheric or life force, the astral or soul aspects and the "I," the kernel of spirit.

In part two we will look at examples of various human organs as related to the basic theme of organic organizations. The health of "the whole" depends upon how we work with the individual organs and our understanding of their language.

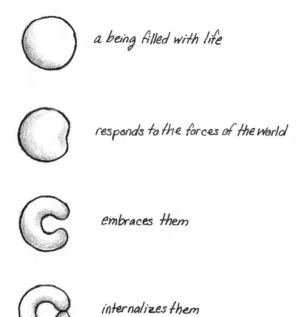

a being filled with life

responds to the forces of the world

embraces them

internalizes them

creates an organ

PART II

ORGANS AND
ORGAN-IZATIONS

5. Heart Knowledge

Having established a foundation for seeing the complete human being in both space and time through the effects of karma and the evolution of consciousness, let us look specifically at the various organs and their metaphor for health in organizations. We will begin with the heart—because it is the heart that balances and harmonizes the whole—and relate that to our work in groups and organizations. As stated earlier, I am not a medical doctor; thus I wish simply to capture a few of the key elements of each organ in ways that relate to everyday life. In some cases, for those who want to go further there will be indications for continued research and study. My aim is to reach into the mysterious realm of the human organs and find meaning that can help us understand human interactions in the workplace.

The Heart Balances and Harmonizes

In every human body, there are multiple processes at work all the time. For instance, the intake and digestion of food is a gradual, continuous process that goes far beyond the act of eating. For the purposes of later contrast I will call this a "lower" activity as it takes place mostly below the midline of the body. Then we have respiration and other "higher" activities. Another way to look at this is to compare deeds and ideas, the below and above. There is so much that continually goes on within us. If one stops to reflect, it is amazing that things don't work at cross-purposes and that we don't have more internal collisions. We owe this good fortune, in part, to the existence of our organs—in this case the heart—which is able to observe our activity and harmonize our internal systems. That which is out of balance is brought back into harmony thanks to the heart. Through its work, the heart makes the organism a unity. It observes the internal interactions, and balances, mediates and harmonizes by adjusting blood and nutrient flow as needed.

The heart not only per-
forms its task on a daily basis,
but also is, as Walter Buhler
describes it, "an organ that
very carefully observes what
is taking place."[1] It is attentive, keeps a watchful eye on
itself, and is in many regards
a sensing organ, one that
continually perceives. The
blood comes from all parts of
the body—liver, head, limbs,
and kidneys—and the heart
"learns" from the blood what
is going on in the rest of the
body. For example, it may
notice that the blood from the

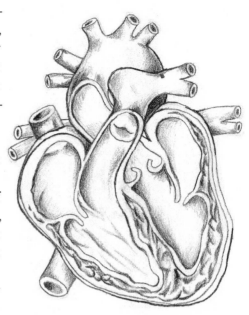

liver and lower body is warmer and the blood from the head is cooler
and begin to balance that out.

Just run up a flight of stairs and you will not only take deeper breaths
but also your heart will beat faster. This faster circulation is a result of
rapid motion, in this case of the legs, and consequently more oxygen is
needed. The heart senses this and immediately adapts. Indeed, every
time we do physical work or exercise, the heart beats faster, showing
us that it pays close attention to the interactions within other parts of
the body.

However, the mystery of the heart is far greater than these preliminary observations. In order to observe, sense, and respond, the
heart brings the movement of the blood to rest. With the help of some
very special valves that allow the blood flow in one direction from the
atrium into the ventricle, the heart brings movement to rest. The heart
holds up the blood and "calls" four times: Stop! stop, stop, stop! The
cardiac valves help the heart arrest the flow of blood long enough to be
observed and sensed.

Imagine throwing a pebble in a pond. As long as there are ripples,
it is hard to see one's reflection. In fact, the surface of the pond needs
to be still in order to see oneself. This quieting of the circulation of
the blood in the human heart is intimately bound up with the forma-

tion of human consciousness. As Buhler states, "Stillness, holding up, and stopping are thus bound up with the sensory-nervous system, the formation of a mirror, and the origination of consciousness."[2] Thus the heart, in this moment of stillness, creates a mirror that allows for reflection and this is necessary for consciousness. In the heart, we have movement, rest, heightened inner consciousness and then renewed movement. This is the essence of life.

How can organizations other than the human body become heart organs? Much of this book is devoted to this question. For now, one can simply observe that the movement, rest, inner activity and renewed movement described above has its wisdom in the flow of information and the interaction of human beings within organizations. The wish to harmonize through contraction and expansion, stop and start, stillness and action, supply and demand, heaviness and upward thrust, are all part of the dynamic of life we call rhythm. Heart organizations are inherently rhythmical. All that detracts from this fundamental rhythm of life breaks an organization apart. Restoring rhythm is to restore life, as will be seen in examples throughout this chapter and beyond.

Pulmonary circulation, the amazing gathering of blood that is sent to the lungs, is also a window into the interface of inner and outer worlds, and another source of life. Through the fresh air given by the lungs, the heart stays in touch with the outer world. As stated above, the blood informs the heart of the condition of the inner world and condition of the other organs of the body. The heart keeps a harmony between the inner and outer, between the stockholders and the board, the parents and the teachers, the environment and the organism. Looking at the heart using our threefold method, we observe that the heart is able to keep harmony through a highly developed sense of empathy, the ability to live into the condition of first one aspect and then into the other. This essence of the heart, the activity of soul from which the heart exists, is feeling—one of the most important ways in which people relate to one another in everyday life.

Leadership in any group or organization can play an important role in supporting or arresting the heart function in an organization, not only by modeling the qualities just discussed, but also by providing the calm within the movement that can so easily sweep us along in the stream of life. Like a heart, a leader needs to observe, sense the big picture, and then be willing to act with renewed energy. Observing does not mean the same to all people. Someone more attuned to the head sees things as reflected images—analyzing, and sensing dispassionately. A person more oriented to the heart is emotionally attuned to the soul life and receives everything openly and freely. These two tendencies have their shadow sides, the former being too "cold" in observing/analyzing, the latter being too "warm" in embracing and then giving everything away. The best form of leadership is one that is able to value and work with both aspects in order to promote health in the group.

THE HEART IS SELFLESS

Most people think that the heart works as a pump and causes circulation. Rudolf Steiner saw it another way: "The most important fact about the heart is that *its activity is not a cause but an effect*."[3] This means that just as we move and therefore develop muscles, so the blood circulation helps form the heart through its movement. One way to understand this concept is to think of the effects of the current of a river on its shore. Just as the movement of water shapes the banks and the sand, the movement of the blood's circulation helps form the organ of the heart. The heart is not just physical; it includes the etheric, life force that is constantly formed and shaped by the movement of circulation. The heart takes nothing from the blood and unlike other organs, gives nothing back. It is like a good friend that helps, but asks for nothing in return. It simply beats, and in so doing, guides and supports. For centuries, people around the world have recognized the connection between the heart and love. It is a place of warmth and infinite generosity.

This is not a passive state, but one of intense activity. A heart person does things with great enthusiasm. Such a person has courage for life. Indeed, heart failure, the fear and tightness that comes with angina pectoris, is an emotional and physical experience of excruciating pain. When the heart ceases to function, even for a few seconds, one experiences a true fear of death. If one is fortunate to come back from such a near death experience, the heart immediately resumes its service with devotion and courage. We can be human as long as we have a heart, and organic organizations work with the heart qualities described in these pages.

The Heart Transforms

When one looks at the gesture and not just the physical functioning of an organ, one uses a feeling apprehension that can help penetrate beyond the phenomena to essential qualities. This approach is evident in the following statement by Karl Konig, "The heart prepares, spiritualizes our every activity, all our deeds, and becomes the repository, so to speak, for everything we do in life."[4] This spiritual function should not be understood as simple storage, but rather as a transformative process in which our actions are refined over time. The heart captures a portion of everything we do and carries it forward in time. Thus we become either "hard-hearted" or "warm-hearted"; we expand with life experience, or we contract. The heart is like a treasure trove of accumulated experiences. From the tapestry of life the heart carries a few key threads forward, some would say, even into the next life. In this way our deeds in one life can become the karma of the next, as described in the chapter on vocation.

Warmth of Personality

In its mediating activity between above and below, inside and out, the heart helps connect our feelings with our thoughts. The outer activity of the lower human being is perceived and transformed in the heart. For example, we take an encounter with another person and process it using heart capacities—the most important of which is warmth and sympathy. When entering a restaurant, how does the host greet a person? One glimpses "the full person" and the other's heart qualities in a few seconds of interaction. As Friedrich Husemann tells us, "The physical basis of this is the passage of blood, through which the heart receives the warmth produced by the "I" in the metabolism. The heart is the organ of warmth par excellence.... Through the heart, the "I" also directs the transformation of the physical into emotional warmth. Emotional warmth then streams into thinking that would otherwise remain abstract and lifeless."[5]

I have found that our encounters with others become more grounded and realistic, and our conceptions of others become enlivened through the heart process of warming. Our new insights are likewise "weighed in the heart" and can be better realized in action that helps society. So the heart helps tremendously both in the "intake" and the "output" side of things. Our deeds are then imbued with emotional and spiritual warmth. A teacher working out of the heart impulse is able to "hold" a class in her consciousness, carry them inwardly, and support them out of her depth of experiences. The "I" is involved in any situation that involves warmth, eye contact, and engagement with other human beings. Two teachers can instruct their students with exactly the same information but one may deliver it mechanically and the other brings it to life.

CONSCIOUSNESS OF THE CENTER

Through our rhythmic system we are able to establish a relationship to the world. This happens on many levels, not just in terms of breathing. We are drawn out in sympathy to people and objects around us, or we are repelled in antipathy. Our circulation and breathing are altered depending upon how we relate, such as through fear, joy, or anger. Without the heart, however, we would loose ourselves in the extremes of experience. The heart centers us and helps establish a more focused connection to earthly life. This happens because an intimate part of us is inextricably connected to the heart. The "I" lives in the warmth of the blood. The "I" helps the heart establish a personal connection to the past, present, and future. We are able to provide context and meaning that informs our feelings, thoughts, and actions. The heart makes it possible for us to respond out of our "center," rather than just react in the moment.[6] Steiner refers to the "I" in the blood in his lecture "The Four Temperaments" and elsewhere. It is a complicated notion to grasp, but we can understand it somewhat through an example: A person who looses too much blood also looses consciousness, as happens when a person faints. The "I" part of that person is loosened from its bodily connection when the blood departs. Conversely, the circulation of the blood heightens our awareness of Self. [7]

This mysterious relationship of the "I" to the blood in human beings is well illustrated by patients who have received heart transplants. Not only was the new organ often rejected, but also it would gradually show the same symptoms as the previous, diseased organ. Dr. Holtzapfel, in his book *The Human Organs,* portrays this account from one of the earlier transplants: "The most alarming feature in patients who have undergone heart transplants are personality changes that can reach even psychotic proportions. The daughter of Dr. Blaiberg reported in an interview after her father's death that, after his heart transplant, a complete personality change occurred, reaching such a dimension that she could hardly recognize him. Observers of other transplant cases report a partial loss in the individual "I" of the patient."[8]

Clearly there is more to the heart than the physical organ. An operation can change the physical reality but not the life forces surrounding the organ. Thus in Anthroposophical medicine, as indeed in most homeopathic remedies, the goal is to treat the underlying causes that often reside in the lifestyle, the habits, the etheric body of the human being. Otherwise there will be repeated occurrences of the same illness. Finally, the change of personality reported in heart transplant patients shows how the heart touches the spiritual core of our being, the "I," and the innermost self. Unlike other organ transplants, the heart is at the center of our individuality, as reflected by the phrase "the heart of the matter."

STRIVING TOWARD EQUILIBRIUM

The exhalation and inhalation of the lungs are accompanied by the systole and diastole of the heart. In the contraction of the systole, we take in, form, and concentrate as in the forming of a thought. In diastole we relax, give in to the digestive process, and let go. In pulmonary circulation, our individual emotions encounter the world around us; we react to events with changes in breathing. These two poles of the heart's activity alternate with each other, respond to each other almost instantaneously. In the slight pauses between systole and diastole, the "I" intervenes to initiate the contrary movement as seen by Dr. Husemann's description of the struggle:

> The heart can be seen as the center of all striving toward equilibrium, the center in which the "I" constantly struggles to balance extremes. As it struggles, however, it creates a larger "inner space" for itself, which it can then fill with greater intensity. Each polarity is thus an opportunity for the "I" to enhance its activity, upon which all personal development is based.[9]

As I understand this observation, we grow and develop owing largely to our expanding heart forces. Such growth happens in the work to bridge the polarities to find equilibrium. Those in our world with a "big heart" are true helpers of humanity.

HEART PROBLEMS

When there is a loss of equilibrium, when the systolic or diastolic is too strong, various aberrations occur in this alternation of "taking in" and "letting go." Some people have such a growing sense of self that it develops into delusions of grandeur. When combined with unbridled will forces that are unleashed upon the world, we have fits of anger. This can sometimes be what is called "righteous anger," a pure outburst based upon accumulated injustices. This is the diastolic tendency in the extreme. Sometimes these attacks of rage actually occur after episodes of heart disease when the stress on the physiological level begins to affect the soul as well. As with all heart issues, body and soul are closely intertwined. But since the heart is a centralizing, rhythmic organ, everything that happens in the rest of the organism tends to find its way to the heart.

In contrast, the extreme manifestation of systolic activity, the "taking in" gesture, is a hardening, a growing "cold" of heart. These people feel threatened by the world and retreat into themselves. You ask them how they are, and they say "fine" with an edge. The omission of anything else speaks volumes. Systole is indeed the physiological basis of fear, an emotion that is truly associated with the heart. These people feel confined, earth bound. Their options are limited and with this they see their individuality slipping away. There may be heightened fears of existential threats, with death being the ultimate result of cardiac fear. Heart depression includes guilt feelings, self-reproach and notions of sinfulness. This has a basis in the liver too, which we discuss in a later chapter, but is intimately connected to the functioning of the heart as the seat of conscience. So we have two extremes: those with feelings of grandeur combined with boundless confidence in future honors and accolades, as opposed to acute depressive types who are convinced that they have done everything wrong and that the world is out to get them. The ultimate exaggeration of the former is madness and the latter leads to stupor.

Another serious imbalance arising from heart functioning is commonly called hypertension or high blood pressure. These people are on the go, and their circulation reflects that. Elevated levels of pulse and circulation are a sign that the will, the active side of our lives has not found sufficient rest. In blood pressure readings, say 120/80, the first number speaks to our state when active, the second to our circulation when at rest. Many people today live in a constant state of overdrive, and this affects the heart most acutely. Some years ago when I was overdoing the travel part of my life, my blood pressure went to 180/105, meaning that both the active and "at rest" numbers were too high. Of the two, the one the doctors worried about most was the resting blood pressure, because it meant that I was losing the ability to slow down. More exercise, higher intake of potassium, and a more balanced, heart-centered lifestyle has helped restore me to health.

Our technological advances, while intended to save time and effort, have often conspired to separate us from our movements. When one walks one is fully involved in movement. When driving, this is less true. Even more extreme is transportation by train or airplane, in which one remains quite passive. Rudolf Steiner said that this passive movement is a main cause of heart disease. As I understand it, when I move physically, I create warmth. Walking down the road I am living in a stream of warmth that is not only internal, but also outside in the surrounding currents of the etheric body, the replenishing life force that restores and renews one's physical body (as discussed in chapter 1). When the movement is passive, as in flying, there is a reflected stream of warmth that is not matched by my inner warmth. This reflected warmth presses in on the heart and it is deformed. The warmth of movement from without is not counteracted and we catch a kind of "cold" in the heart. Since the heart is an organ of warmth, this condition can develop into heart disease over time. We pay a price for our frequent flyer miles.

In general, human beings today need to slow down if they are to reverse the startling increase in heart attacks among both men and women. Carl Honoré caught the attention of many with his book *In Praise of Slowness*, in which he describes the benefits of working less hard, leisure, "slow food," and raising an unhurried child. We need to find real moments of rest, and realize that in our rush to get through the day, we are forgetting to live. We need to find the essential among all the unessentials of life and get back to the "heart of the matter."

Further Organizational Dynamics

What can the wisdom of the heart tell us about how we work together in organizations and groups? This is a challenging assignment, as there are almost as many types of organizations as there are people. I would like to select a few of the characteristics described in the above pages and relate them to organizations with the hope that in striving for more complete understanding we can improve how we work together.

When we meet in large groups, we are dealing in particular with the dynamics of the "heart." Anyone who has been part of a large gathering will remember how the circulation of thoughts and feelings manifest themselves. There is constant movement in a large group, not only in terms of ideas, but also in terms of attendance and attentiveness. Some are engaged and leaning forward, others are circulating out for a time. People come late and leave early. There are high points of interest and then a falling off into random discussion. Most exciting for me is the circulation of ideas and feelings that "pulse" through a meeting. One person will mention something in passing; it disappears as if forgotten, only to surface again in another form with different language. The same essential idea can resurface several times in a meeting, each time taking on a different tone and color in terms of expression. Good meetings work with these "threads" and weave them together in the end into a rich tapestry of accomplishment.

Speaking more specifically, meetings have a systole and diastole, movement in and then out again. For instance, if a proposal to do a retreat is brought forward, there may be many that speak in favor. The positive momentum builds, sympathy for the idea grows and one speaker after another extols the possibilities of having a retreat. A good observer of meetings will note that just as the movement of the blood outward calls for the counter movement, so the positive momentum on the retreat proposal may go too far. Someone, somewhere in the group, will feel called upon to mention that the retreat may cost a lot of money. That then opens the door for others to bring up counter movement comments: Who has the time to organize it? Do we have a site? What if some people can't attend? Thus the momentum has shifted. Nonetheless, just as the heart seeks equilibrium, a good conversation will end with the "balance point" at least within sight. A committee will take up the proposal for a retreat and consider the costs and other details, while planning a dynamic event that will entice full attendance.

The facilitator is often the most visible expression of the heart function in a meeting. This person will make visible what is circulating in the group, sometimes even drawing upon nonverbal clues. Surfacing what lies in the room is a true heart deed, because it should be done selflessly and without personal agendas. "This is what I am hearing" is a facilitator's frequent refrain. Some use a somewhat rigid protocol for facilitation, which can put the heart function into a straightjacket. For instance, a technique called "stacking" requires those who raise their hands to take numbers and wait their turn to speak. This means that the contribution of "number seven" is often old, spent blood, if you will; when spoken ten minutes later, it actually arrests the forward momentum of the discussion. I prefer facilitation with a freer hand, in which the facilitator can respond to the level of interest, connect ideas, and move according to the many different types of "signals" that people give the facilitator in a meeting. Consequently, the best training for a facilitator is the arts. Music, painting, and movement all help develop the intuitive artistic sensibility that constitutes heart-centered facilitation.

A heart organization is one that is warm, friendly, and welcoming. It cannot be defined by architecture or the presence of food, though these aspects can help. The color of the walls and the quality of promotional literature, for example, are all symbols of something that is either present or missing. No glossy brochure can mask for long the absence of genuine heart forces in an organization. Conversely, a school with warmth may thrive even in the absence of some of these outer props. When I am in such a place, I can feel the genuine interest of those around me. They greet me in the hallways, and there are many smiles. There is a sense of intimacy, even in just a few exchanges. The human encounter is seen as more important than the preplanned "business" of the day. There is less rushing around. A heart organization takes care of all its members, especially when one is sick or needy.

There is a more difficult aspect of the organization-as-heart that resists verbal description. This is the aspect described in "consciousness of the center." If the human "I" finds a home in the warmth of the blood, where is the inner sanctum of an organization? Is there such as thing as a "being" of a school? Is there a "core" to Apple Computer? What is the heart of an organization? There are two possible responses. One has to do with the founder(s) and the first key leaders, who frequently exemplify the organization's essence, the qualities that live on after their passing. Having mentioned Apple Computer several times, I will add that there was an interesting interlude when Steve Jobs departed, and the company floundered. This is the case when the "heart" of an organization is tied up with the heart of its founder. There is another, more elusive aspect to this question as well. Just as the blood conspires to form and maintain the heart, so the quality of human relationships within an organization can determine whether there is a central impulse and "genius" is allowed to manifest. When people work in harmony and strive for balance with selfless interest in the larger good, an invisible and etheric yet powerful "heart" is created in the center of the organism. It is the spiritual counterpart to the Oval Office, the surgery in the hospital or the kitchen in a home. When it is there, it spreads goodness and plenty throughout the organization. When it is absent, no amount of external fixes can take the place of this heart function. The central task of a consultant is to help an organization find, and if needed, repair its heart function.

Finally, a few words about heart attacks, hypertension, madness, and stupor in organizations, all of which are heart diseases. My phone often rings after an organizational heart attack; a key employee has been terminated, a conflict has escalated and two groups are threatening mutual destruction, or a financial shortfall has occurred. These outer symptoms usually point to trends that have been some time in the making. There is a difference between triage and organizational development. Many people in the heart attack mode understandably want emergency care. Hypertension in our organizations often occurs from too many meetings, lack of good facilitation, and a diffusion of responsibility. The human organism knows who does what in its physiological actions and for the most part it functions smoothly. Yet in our schools, for instance, in the name of inclusion we seem to draw everyone into almost every issue. People are afraid, do not trust one another, and as a result they insert themselves into everything that happens. The human body is a wonderful example of restraint. The lungs do their thing, the kidneys another. Only in illness do you find, for example, liquid in the lungs. We need to do a much better job at distributing our tasks and letting go of what is not ours. When there is a heart illness in an organization, everyone suffers. It is the flip side of circulation. Once the equilibrium is lost, one can lurch from crisis to crisis, and gradually people drift away.

I am a great believer in rebirth, not only in a religious sense, but also in terms of finding the "heart" once again. This can happen in an extended retreat, in which all the stakeholders come together and begin by working rhythmically, having large group and small group conversations, participating in artistic activity and projects and creating reports among other things. With good facilitation the focus can gradually shift from the periphery to the center. In an activity called "eurythmy in the workplace," we build up an exercise using copper balls. The first stage consists of standing in a circle, facing a partner, and moving "do-si-do" style around the periphery while passing the balls with each encounter with another person. Then, when that is working rhythmically, we are asked to do the same movement but everyone faces the center. Suddenly we become a group, not just a collection of individuals. The last stage, particularly helpful for organizations that want to learn to work better with the community, involves everyone facing the front of the room while continuing the same movement. Now the organization is oriented to the outside world. This is a heart exercise that I have found invaluable in rebirthing. Whatever one uses, the point of a retreat is the human bond that builds worlds. More time and energy needs to be spent valuing and supporting those things in our lives that have a heart quality.

If the heart is valued, even cherished in an organization, there is a chance of receiving a "bonus," an act of grace. This gift is a future-oriented notion that I want to indicate in "seed" form to stimulate some additional pondering. We often hear references to the four chambers of the heart. I would like to suggest that in the future, individuals within organizations may be able to develop their feeling perceptions to such a degree that in addition to atrium and ventricle, there develops a fifth chamber, a delicate, sensitive, nonmaterial space between human beings. Created out of purified ideas and ideals, this space can be entered by those who experience the resonance of true human interaction. Experiences in this space will be momentary, even fleeting, but once having met in the fifth space, humans will be changed, and humanity will have received a gift of the heart.

KEY WORDS FOR THE HEART

Integration, balance, harmony
Movement to rest to movement again
Contraction and expansion
Selfless
Transformation
Warmth of personality
Consciousness of center
Equilibrium
Hypertension
Systole and diastole in meetings
Facilitation as heart function
The fifth space

6. THE KIDNEY

IN THE WELL-KNOWN adventure by Mark Twain, Tom Sawyer and Becky Thatcher were lost in the vast labyrinth and crooked aisles of McDougal's Caves. At first they wandered about with their friends, with many sparks of lighted candles, exploring the myriad passages of the caves. Then, gradually, Tom and Becky descended lower into unexplored territory, finding hidden crevices, terrifying bats, and underground pools of water. In the riveting tale told so imaginatively by Mark Twain, the two children display a host of emotions and share moments of great tenderness toward each other. After many days, they survive the ordeal and emerge through a small opening five miles down the river. They will never be the same after this experience, and the whole town is roused in the middle of the night to celebrate. Only later does it emerge that, along the way, Tom has discovered the lost treasure that he and Huck Finn have long sought. The journey through the caves has made both boys very rich.

Inadvertently perhaps, Mark Twain captured many of the themes that can be covered in a discussion of the human kidney. The journey down through the caves describes the embryological journey of the kidney. In fact, the kidney wanders up and down, back and forth considerably during the nine months of fetal development. Even the eventual physiology of the kidney has remarkable similarities to the terrain covered by Tom and Becky—the tiny cuplike capsules called the *glomeruli* into which fine arteriolar loops enter, the tubules which wind themselves around the *glomeruli*, the hairpin turns, the passage through the medulla, and the eventual exit through the renal pelvis. Along the way there is considerable movement, alternations between rounded and straight directions and a swinging back and forth that we will need to take up again later in this chapter when discussing the "astral" element in organizational dynamics.

Then there are the touching moments between Tom and Becky as they face the extreme possibilities of life or death. They watch with

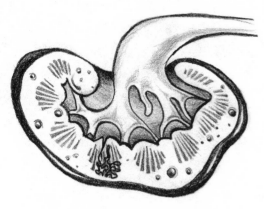

baited breath as their last candle flickers out. Tom blames himself for not putting out more markers along the way, and Becky drifts in and out of sleep. They share their last morsel, a "wedding cake" they had put aside during the recent picnic. These qualities speak to the devotional aspect of the kidneys: a pathway "into" protected areas where reflection and spirit vision can be rekindled.

Again, using the threefold method of looking at the kidney, we see much more than the physiological or factual aspects of this organ. Many jewels of insight can be found in the protected spaces of the kidney. More than just a metaphor, these "secrets" can yield much wisdom. For often the true human spirit is revealed in the darkest places. This might be in the prison cell that held Nelson Mandela, the desolate gulag that was home to Aleksandr Solzhenitsyn, or the cave of doubt that all human beings experience at one time or another. In the hollow places of life we find the real "jewels," the treasure that enables further growth.

There are, of course, also some negatives along the pathway to self-knowledge. We can develop self-pride once we have found our "jewels," or the loneliness of the "cave" can make us depressed. Like the labyrinth in the story of Tom Sawyer, there are so many possible passageways through kidney consciousness that one can become agitated or torn apart by the possibilities. In this perplexity, it is hard to find one's "center" the guiding intention that comes from oneself and not the environment.

Emotions and feelings are closely connected to the kidney and the bladder region. Studies have shown that feelings of annoyance hinder the blood flow through the kidney. A sustained attack of anger, deathly fear, or shock can interrupt kidney function.[10] Long-term stress affects the adrenal gland as well as the kidneys with symptoms such as heightened wakefulness, increased blood pressure and blood sugar as byproducts. The sentient soul, the holder of sense impressions described in the first part of this book, has an intimate relationship to the renal system. Thus our feelings about our sense impressions, affects, and drives are connected to the functioning of our kidneys. In a larger sense, there is always the potential for experiencing sympathy or antipathy, the polarities of one's emotional life. Are we are drawn in to the emotional dynamic of experiences, or are we pushed back?

This emotional dynamic is once again reflected in human physiology in terms of inhalation and exhalation—the lungs—or excretion and incretion—the kidneys. These are physical expressions of the soul polarity of sympathy and antipathy. Even our unconscious desires are active in the human organism—namely, the hunger for oxygen and basic nutrients. There is such a thing as "air hunger" which causes the inner exchanges of gases—namely, our breathing. In fact, the concentration and dilution of substances in the urine by the renal system is also very much a function of the element of air with the characteristic alternation between compressions and rarefactions. Thus, as opposed to popular conceptions, the kidney is very much an air organism.[11] In extreme cases the polarity described above can manifest in soul opposites of enhanced excitability or apathy. Generally, the kidney person is known as quite excitable, lively, flighty, and sanguine. However, impassiveness can set in through a dull, barely conscious state that can reach outright apathy or stupor.

Of all the basic emotions, fear is the one most closely associated with the kidney. On one level there is physical anxiety, a vague feeling rising out of the upper abdomen that makes a person feel trapped. Friedrich Husemann says: "Fear is essentially an obstructed emotion that can turn into or discharge itself in aggression, a fact that becomes particularly apparent in physical anxiety."[12] Once again, as with all kidney "riddles" there is an emotional opposite of fear, and that is addiction. Here we give in to a consuming urge to enjoy the body and the world around us despite the fact that this drive never fully satisfies our inner emptiness. We seek through the satisfaction of our cravings to dissolve physical anxiety and escape our bodily confines, yet the anxiety returns all the more acutely when the intoxication has passed.

For those we are calling kidney types, it is particularly important to work on the assimilation of experiences. We have to absorb more and more these days, and the mere overload of sensory data can strain the kidney. Kidney types occasionally need to retreat into their caves—the home, gazebo, or den—to process and recoup. However, in a more acute fashion, life occasionally gives us larger things to digest, and whereas some people seem to be able to bounce back quickly, the kidney folks need to take the time to process and assimilate. This can be done in a variety of ways, but often they need to be alone to reflect and regroup.

A lifestyle that is on the go all the time injures the kidney, no more so than in the lives of our children. Too many sensory impressions, too much intellectual content at an early age, too little time to process and "play" leads to kidney stress. Again, Husemann explains this: "Intellectual precocity is bought at the price of poor organ maturation."[13] We can't see into the organs directly, but the outer symptoms include emotional excess and antisocial behavior. A kidney under stress acts like a trapped animal; it lashes out without reason.

An extreme example of a kidney disorder that rises to the level of psychosis is the schizoid tendency. Dr. Victor Bott has the following description of how this relates to all that has been discussed in this chapter:

> What was a disturbance of assimilation on the physical plane may become an inability to "digest" or to assimilate certain events. It is not proteins but psychological matters that behave as foreign bodies in the depths of the soul. It is, moreover, not uncommon to find abnormalities of the blood proteins in these patients. The ego no longer occupies the center of the soul, and everything becomes organized, at first very logically, around these 'mental parasites,' which are undigested memories or experiences. We are faced with a condition in which the astral body predominates over the ego, which has become incapable of setting the contents of the psyche in order.[14]

These findings are significant in that they strongly indicate how physiological troubles have psychological ramifications. This provides the "bridge" between our study of the organs and the people who populate our organizations. We carry our inner organs with us to work each day and with them our state of physical and psychological health. Thus, I found it interesting that some medical professionals like Dr. Friedrich Husemann have discovered an increase in schizophrenic syndromes in those third world cultures that have been exposed to Western civilization.[15] We need to expand our scope of perception beyond what the pharmaceutical industry offers in the treatment of specific symptoms to areas such as soul hygiene and education.

If we want to support the healthy function of the kidneys in our children we can encourage imitation of that which is good and beautiful, a respectful relationship to authority, and the emotional intelligence that comes from engagement in the arts, literature, and dinnertime sharing. (See *School as a Journey* and other books on Waldorf education.) Good listening can arise from hearing imaginative storytelling; purposeful movement can arise through eurythmy and Spacial Dynamics; and cooperative learning experiences promote healthy kidneys in children. Just as an infant needs special care, the kidneys need warmth and protection throughout life.

THE ORGANIZATIONAL DYNAMICS OF THE KIDNEY

One characteristic already mentioned in relation to the kidney-bladder system is the formation of separate cavities: the *glomerulus,* then the pelvis of the kidney, and finally, in the bladder itself. Combined with the up-and-down movement of the blood flow through the kidney and the close emotional connection to the flow of urine (at times of personal excitement the bladder fills up more quickly), there is a strong connection between the kidney-bladder and the astral-emotional body (described in chapter 1). This becomes our point of departure for considering various organizational aspects.

Just as the heart was described as fostering integration, so the kidney encourages differentiation. This later aspect happens when organizations form "units" and committees. When one finds many of these smaller departments and less of a "whole-systems" approach, one can hypothesize that one is dealing with a "kidney" organization. Here, a frequently unconscious attempt seems to be to work toward solving issues by taking them apart, sending them to "committee," and excreting the results. There is often a kind of random flow in these organizations that defies rationality. Just like the meandering of Tom and Becky, issues bounce from one committee or unit to another and nowhere does one find the central "presence" that gathers and connects "the dots." Memos may be written and sometimes read, reports are given, and yet somehow the life of the organization is not much affected. This sleepy state is, however, awakened from time to time by an emotional outburst from one person or another. Suddenly in the course of a rather boring meeting someone says something inflammatory and everyone is awake again. This is also characteristic of a kidney organization—emotions are used to gain consciousness.

However, after a while this can become pathological, while governance by personality becomes the norm. People remain passive in this situation, sheltering their real feelings and thoughts and responding in reactive ways when provoked. In these extreme situations it becomes almost impossible for leaders to function since the "I" quality of holding the center is undermined. One example is a deficit or financial loss that results from everyone demanding a "piece of the pie," with no regard for the good of the whole organization. Such fragmentation develops to the point where the overall crisis is so great that survival dictates cooperation. These schools and organizations tend to learn best from crises.

In a positive sense, the kidney/astral quality can be used by organizations to gather resources that feed the whole system. Just as the kidney assists in the transformation of food substances absorbed from the digestive system, so committees and work groups can help prepare the way for organizational growth. This comes about by impregnating an issue with consciousness, working it through so well that clarity is achieved and then offered up to the larger group. A proposal that has been carefully developed, researched, tested and articulated can be absorbed by others with little effort. Differentiating and working in small groups can actually help the healthy functioning of the "whole."

The key to accomplishing this can be seen in the larger context surrounding the role of clarity and the way questions are framed. Is a task taken up as a service for the good of the whole or is it for personal gain? Is the initial question framed as a thin disguise for a personal agenda, or is there a sincere desire to learn? Is there clarity regarding the parameters of the task and the group entrusted to do the work? Here we get to the inherent wisdom of the kidney. The spirit can be revealed in darkness, the jewels can be found in the deepest caves. Will they be hoarded by a "dragon" or brought to the surface of day consciousness to become part of the crown jewels of the organization? Our intentions matter, as they live in the depths of kidney wisdom.

The last quality of the kidneys that I wish to highlight is perhaps the most subtle. It has to do with the inner vision; the active monitoring that goes on continually within the human body. The kidney "sees" potassium and sodium and adjusts and regulates accordingly. In the depths of the human organism, the kidney is able to perceive the light and colors, so to speak, of the various systems at work. As a result of this perception, the kidney is able to regulate the contents of our blood serum.

This perceptive capacity is interesting to look at from an organizational perspective. How do we regulate and self monitor? What are we able to perceive while in the act of doing, or performing tasks? Is it at all possible to self-monitor and regulate? There has been much conversation in recent years about learning organizations, yet often this is placed chiefly on the shoulders of individuals or key leaders as yet another "should" in their job description as opposed to seeing things systemically. I believe that we can learn something from the kidney in terms of regulating ourselves systemically. It involves developing peripheral vision, an awareness of what is happening even while performing one's daily responsibilities. Peripheral vision is seeing the whole circle, being aware of the movement within the system just as the kidney works with the whole movement of fluids through the body. We need to see the whole in the parts, the specific as it relates to the larger context. When we are able to stand firmly on our piece of the ground and still see the horizon, it is possible that each self-monitoring person can adjust and make minor changes when needed. The whole system can change because of this activity. We spend far too much time in our organizations trying to fix other peoples problems, do their work, or change what is really beyond our jurisdiction. Instead, this kidney model can effect major changes by making thousands of minor, "local" adjustments. For example, by simply changing the membership of one committee we can bring new focus into an organization. And it all begins, I feel, by developing new perceptive abilities. The kidney is an organization's inner "eyes and ears."

To access this wisdom one must find stillness. When we listen with sensitivity we gather the wisdom of the stream, the flow within an organization. One of my favorite songs begins: "Peace I ask of thee oh river, peace, peace, peace." When we take the time to listen, answers come from within, out of abiding quiet. But this requires faithfulness in listening; a belief in the wisdom of the "waters" and a silencing of preconceived notions. The kidney then becomes the inner voice of wisdom because of this devotional aspect.

The negative side of the kidney function in organizations involves too much bubbling movement of the waters; too much sanguinity in which nothing ever comes to rest. Here there is too much fleeting consciousness or astrality. Outwardly, one then experiences a kidney person as someone who is nervous, jittery, even torn apart by conflicting currents. When we are involved in too many activities and expose ourselves to sensory overload, the kidney suffers over time. We become perpetually exhausted.

So the kidney holds yet another key to building healthy organizations—being willing to go through the process of transformation in order to find inspiration. This process means being willing to undertake the journey of self-transformation, to make our way down into the caves of our being and to use the wisdom we have gained upon our return. Can we stop awhile to listen for this wisdom?

KEY WORDS FOR THE KIDNEY

Hidden jewels in caves and hollow places
Emotional dynamics
Kidney as air organism
Excitability vs. apathy
Fear, anxiety
Assimilation of experiences
Differentiation
Peripheral vision
Inner eyes and ears

7. The Liver

During the Christmas holidays of 2005, we visited my brother-in-law's family in Brazil. After a few days in Sao Paulo, we took a bus to the beautiful island of Ilhabela, just off the coast. Although not as far north as the Amazon basin, this island nevertheless represented for us northerners an immersion in a tropical climate. The vegetation was succulent, large, and watery, with the most amazing flowers. The colors were so vivid we were tempted to stop and see if they had been painted. The abundant growth everywhere made us feel somewhat insignificant while standing under the lush foliage. When inland, we could walk for a long time without seeing a glimpse of the sky, and even on the beach, we could feel the surge of nature's elemental forces. Even though it did not rain much when we were there, the humidity was so high it sometimes felt as if we were submerged in condensation. Warm, moist, and rich in vegetation, the tropical forest is truly an incubator of life.

In many ways the eco-system just described is a macrocosm of the micro-cosm we all possess on the right side of our abdomen—the liver. It, too, is rich in fluid, containing little more solid matter than the blood itself. It is a heat center with a temperature of over forty degrees centigrade. It is soft and rather lacking in structure. Moreover, like much of the vegetation in the rain

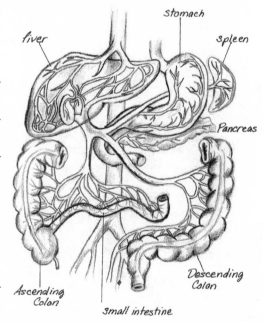

forest, the liver has tremendous regenerative capacities. It can grow back even after as much as eighty percent of it is removed.

The German word *leber* means to live. The French *foie* is derived from ficator, the fig tree, or tree of life. In Russian the liver is called *pyetchen*, which comes from *pyetch*, the stove, which is a central element of the Russian house. Like a stove, the metabolism of fats and the biliary processes are connected with this caloric function. The bile contributes, with the pancreatic lipase to the digestion of fats, substances that are necessary for the maintenance of body temperature.[16] Humidity and heat are also part of the pathology of the liver. Too much water can lead to swelling—*oedema*—while too little fluid can lead to hardening, or *hepatic sclerosis*. Likewise, the level of heat can lead to jaundice or gallstones.

The liver is most known for glycogenesis and glycogenolysis as described in some detail below by Dr. Holtzapfel:

> In glycogenesis, the liver transforms the glucose of the blood into glycogen, an insoluble substance closely related to amidon, which it stores up. In glycogenolysis, the glycogen is transformed again into soluble glucose. These processes, which are a typical example of "cogula" and "solve," alternate according to a precise rhythm, which is independent of mealtimes. Glycogenesis, a process of assimilation, takes place at night, or, more exactly, it starts at 3 P.M. and attains its maximum about 3 A.M. The opposite process of glycogenolysis, which is a process of dissimulation, starts about 3 A.M. and attains its maximum about 3 P.M., and is thus diurnal. It is interesting to note that similar processes are found in the formation of amidon and sugars in plants and this brings us back again to the vegetable kingdom and the tropical forest.[17]

Like the growth producing sap rising in trees, the liver regulates the ebb and flow of energy.

The collection of glycogen in the liver reaches its climax during the nighttime hours of sleep, and the decomposition of the blood that especially leads to the formation of bile reaches its climax during the course of the day. This twenty-four hour rhythm of the liver is alluded to in the Prometheus myth. The god Prometheus, who brought fire from Olympus to humanity, was doomed by Zeus for all time for this transgression. A vulture consumes his liver by day only to have it grow back again by night, and so he must endure his fate again each day. This process of regeneration is an essential component in our vitality or fire of life—our ability to live. It is also very much connected to our consciousness as described by Dr. Holtzapfel:

> The disintegration processes in the liver are instrumental to our day consciousness and therefore mainly take place during the day. We are not conscious of the regeneration process that happens during the night. A changeover of this time rhythm leads to illness. If the up-building phase of the liver metabolism is shifted into daytime, it causes depressions and disturbances in the will sphere, which can be ameliorated by decreasing the time spent in sleeping. If the gall becomes active during the night, gall colics set in which almost always happen by night and which with their attendant pain are experienced with intense consciousness. [18]

As we saw with the kidneys in the last chapter, a physiological process involving the liver influences our psychological state—in this case our consciousness. These disturbances in the rhythm of the liver functions can be caused by the changes in time that many travelers have to undergo as well as the use of artificial sweeteners and alcohol and can have many negative consequences.

But it is in regard to the will that I would like to examine the liver more closely. Rudolf Steiner described the nerve/sense system—the nerves, spinal cord and brain—as a synthesizing process, one in which we collect the various impressions from the world around us and form them into a unity, a complete "whole" so we can understand and make sense of them. In contrast, the organs and the metabolic/limb system, which include our digestion systems, can be characterized as an analyzing process. Here things are kept separate. Another way of putting it is that the head unites the activities of the senses while the organs in the rest of the body hold things apart as a natural part of their biological function. Once again using our threefold method of examination we can see that the head is like a mirror of the outside world whereas the organs are a world unto themselves. The synthesizing activity becomes the basis of thinking, and the analytically built up organs give the foundation for the life of will. Especially with the help of the liver functions, we can transform an idea into action, a thought into accomplishment.

How does this happen? When we resolve to do something, that intention originates in our inner core, our "I." However, just to think something is not enough; it takes much more to realize an intention. It needs to be "warmed up," carried through our organism so to speak, and brought into action through the limbs. Just as the blood courses through the liver, our intentions move through the human organism out into the world. For example, a former colleague resolved to open a community center in Great Barrington, Massachusetts. His intention was so strong that it excited others, and now that community has a wonderful place for recreation and community gatherings. His intention—liver resolve—found expression throughout the town—circulation of the blood in the body. To quote Giovanni Maciocia's knowledge of scholars of Chinese medicine: "energy deriving from the liver can give a person great creative drive and resoluteness.... an indomitable spirit and drive."[19]

In contrast, a defect in the liver often results in irritability, anger, and an especially strange inability to carry out one's intentions. Steiner gives an example of a man who would arrive at the tram station, wait patiently, and then not be able to get on board when it arrived.[20] The will got stuck—it was transfixed. There are many people who just can't seem to do what they said they would do. This is a universal problem, one that needs serious attention as illustrated in the example below.

I once visited a school with a peculiar problem. Every day at recess, the children ran outside and the assigned teachers failed to show up for playground supervision. To solve this seemingly simple staffing issue they first tried to post the names of teachers due out on the playground each day of the week. That didn't work. Then they discussed playground supervision in the faculty meeting and everyone agreed that it was essential that at least two teachers be out there everyday on a rotational basis. That didn't work. Then the administrator began writing reminder notes and putting them in teachers' mailboxes the morning they were to supervise at recess. Not only did this attempt fail, but it also backfired, in that the teachers in question got angry and accused the administrator of highhandedness, of acting like "the boss." Some even asked for an apology. Meanwhile, day after day went by and the playground continued to be inadequately supervised. Eventually some parents noticed the problem and voiced their concerns. The board passed a resolution on supervision, and still many days went by with less than two teachers on the playground. Most agreed it was a collective failure, but few were willing to admit individual responsibility.

The whole situation bordered on the absurd. When I arrived I soon discovered other symptoms of what appeared to be a larger problem. In general, many at that school found it hard to honor agreements of any kind, verbal, contractual, or implicit. Some people came late to meetings; others handed in reports and grades late; and some just did what felt right in the moment, with little regard for the effect on the school as a whole. Only gradually did it dawn on me that this was a "liver challenged school," that they had trouble bringing things into the will, into action. That is why their meetings featured "apparent agreements," and everyone left thinking the problem had been solved only to discover that the playground would once again not be supervised the next day. Good people, with clear intentions, were not able to do what they said they would do.

I have found in subsequent years that this phenomenon is more common than I had thought. Once at a conference in Europe I had a chance to interview an experienced medical doctor on the subject of the liver. Much to my astonishment, she described the liver as the most stressed of all human organs. She detailed how everything we ingest these days is mildly polluted, from our bottled water to many food substances. For example, water that sits in some plastic containers takes on some of the chemicals used in making the plastic. Then there are food additives, artificial sweeteners and the list went on and on. As a consequence, the liver has to work extra hard to overcome all these hindrances. In our culture the liver is on perpetual overtime.

A stressed liver is less able to regenerate, is less able to do its essential work. Add to this the arrhythmic lifestyles of most people these days, and one knocks out the last support, namely the 3 A.M.-to-3 P.M. cycle just described. In short, one's will organ is submerged under the tangle of one's lifestyle jungle. Thus, more and more people are almost physically incapable of doing what they say they will, walking their talk or transforming their intentions into action. As a society, we used to have a natural corrective in physical work. Churning butter, milking cows, weeding, chopping wood and such chores were once essential to survival. With the advent of modern technology, we no longer have to do much in terms of food preparation or the creation of shelter. Stick something in the microwave, turn on the air conditioner or heater, and we can worry about other things. All this has deprived us of a natural training ground for the will.

Some will argue with this point and describe how much they jog each day, how many hours they work along with other activities. Yes, there is some will involved in these other activities but of a different kind. The one that is most helpful for human development is what I call "intentional activity." This means doing something for a purpose rather than as recreation. For example one person will just take a walk, which is fine. However, another person can take the same walk to buy some milk at the store. I maintain that in the second instance, there is intentional activity that serves to harmonize, integrate, and strengthen the will. As Maciocia has pointed out, "The liver is said to impart to us the capacity to plan our life smoothly and wisely."[21]

But the liver does more than help us plan. The root of "organization" is *organe,* meaning to "get things done." Indeed, I found references to the connection between the liver and muscles or sinews as noted by Maciocia, "If Liver-Blood is deficient, the sinews will lack moistening and nourishment which may cause contractions and spasms or impaired extension/flexion, numbness of limbs, muscle cramps, tremors, tetany, or lack of strength of the limbs."[22] In simplest terms, organizations exist to help people get things done that they could not do alone. Therefore, the above discussion on the liver as the organ of will and resoluteness is crucial to the performance of our organizations. If people cannot experience the effectiveness of their workplace, their organization may become irrelevant.

Disturbances in the liver provide a basis for two psychological extremes—anger and brooding. Anger is related to the "fire" element of the liver as mentioned earlier, and brooding has more to do with phlegmatic types, as Dr. Husemann says:

> Who, in addition to being calm, are also serious and overly conscientious. In such people, the tendency to mull things over becomes an inability to let go of the memory of troubling...experiences. This sets the stage for an internally conditioned, endogenous depression...In severe cases, sometimes clearly subsequent to upsetting experiences, symptoms of a hepatobiliary disorder will frequently occur, including sensations of pressure and fullness around the liver, bitter tastes in the mouth, nausea, intolerance to fatty foods,

and (less often) increased thirst or biliary colics. Sometimes the disorders underlying these symptoms can develop into actual liver disease, such as hepatitis.[23]

I found it extremely interesting that some of these endogenous depressions and disorders are linked to unresolved conflicts that have settled into the physical realm. We all know that conflict is a part of life, sometimes resulting in the "fire" response of anger, other times tending more toward simmering resentment and withdrawal. Many organizations have established protocols for dealing with the more overt types of conflict, with expectations of mediation for example. It is the long-simmering; depressive types of conflict that I feel need more attention, especially in light of liver knowledge.

"The congestive tendency of the liver may be assumed to culminate in the retention of bile, which directly affects the will. The ancient designation "melancholia" (illness from black bile) points to this, and physicians as early as Hippocrates conceived of bile as thickening in a very real, material sense. The "I," which stimulates and activates the will, cannot penetrate a congested biliary system.[24] The watery system has become congested and hardened. The rhythmic movement that restores health is arrested and as in conflict, there is a hardening of positions.

When conflict is not overt and visible but takes the subterranean route, it is more difficult to deal with. Wounds are nursed over time, people brood over perceived wrongs. When accompanied by strong liver tendencies, this brooding shows that the soul is gradually becoming overwhelmed by organic processes. This is analogous to the soporific effect of eating a Thanksgiving dinner; the bodily processes can take over. Disturbing experiences are not confronted and they harden and fester, thus further oppressing the liver, which is the organ of mature emotional life.

Another response to conflict is the superficial route, in which things are brushed off. This can be due to the natural tendency to avoid conflict, or an irresolute inner life that does not wish to take hold of experiences. In a curious "dance of conflict," I have found that sometimes the two parties of the disagreement display opposite responses. One may take the brooding, inner route and the other tries to repeatedly brush it off and dismiss even the notion that there is conflict. Combined, these two partners perform the perfect "dance," in that their behavior becomes mutually reinforcing.

One healing tool in working with groups, especially those experiencing conflict, is the agent of time. Our sense of working with time has been challenged due to our technological advances, yet for those who try and bring healing to organizations, the time agent becomes a great physician. So for example, in the case of the liver issues discussed above, one way of beginning is to identify those who are paralyzed in the past, who continually relive and recount things that happened in the past. These depressive types tend to bury themselves hopelessly in past lights and occurrences that may have lost all meaning to anyone else. Then there are the superficial ones who bounce from the present into the future with little regard to what has just happened. Those who have the symptoms of stagnation and hardening tend to feel the weight of the past most often in the early morning; the others may be oblivious to daily rhythm.

So how does one work with time in organizational development? This question deserves a book of its own. All I can do here is give a few hints that I have on my path of action research. If for instance we are dealing with liver related conflict as described above, then the time of day selected for a mediation conversation can be crucial. For example I tend to avoid early mornings and late afternoons. Time releases its genius through rhythm, and it can help to give attention to the cycle of sessions, the questions that are posed at the end of a session, and the length of conversation time. When I did my mediation training, I was particularly intrigued with the technique that involves meeting with the parties separately and then together. The individual meetings serve not only for fact-finding, but also for validation. However, it is in the group sessions that one really starts to work on the tapestry of resolution. One of the key moments is when the parties start to talk to each other and not just through the mediator. These phenomena are all related to the wisdom of time, the synchronicity of the unplanned "when" and both parties look at each other and begin direct dialogue.

The obvious theme concerning the liver is the importance of rest and regeneration. So much that challenges us in working together is due to the state of perpetual exhaustion that characterizes many people today. Chronic sleeplessness, sensory over stimulation and hyperactive lifestyles have impaired our ability to be courteous and friendly with each other. Perpetual tiredness has influenced the frequency of misunderstandings, the length of our meetings and the quality of our human interactions. Most of all, we have collectively conspired to attack the liver, our physical source of regeneration. The environmental and emotional damage can be lasting if we do not wake up to the abiding realities of the language of the body. The liver calls for us to cherish life, its myriad rhythms, and the deepest mysteries that come with rest and contemplation.

KEY WORDS FOR THE LIVER

Heat
Life
Regulating the ebb and flow of energy
Analysis
Irritability, anger, (or brooding) conflict
Getting things done, will power
Planning
Rest and regeneration

8. THE SPLEEN

IN SEVERAL RESPECTS, the spleen can be called the invisible organ, not only because many of the medical texts I consulted give it minimal treatment, but also because of the particular nature of the spleen's task in the human organism. While active in building up the immune system in the early years of childhood, the spleen gradually becomes invisible in adulthood to the point where many people take it for granted. In popular language, one still occasionally hears the phrase "to vent one's spleen" which harkens back to the medieval notions in medicine of the black bile being out of balance with the yellow bile. This idea is similar in Chinese medicine in which the spleen is described as separating the usable from the unusable part of the fluids ingested, with the "clear" part going upward to the lungs and the skin and the "dirty" part going downward to the intestines where it is further separated.[25] Thus we immediately come to one of the essential functions of the spleen, that of separation and redirection.

From an outer or conventional perspective, one can observe that the spleen is inflated for hours at a time after a heavy meal, and then gradually shrinks again. One can also describe the spleen as a plethoric tissue with minute white corpuscles embedded in it, and that as the blood flows through the spleen it is strained as with a sieve. Therefore one can see from the start that the spleen is an intermediary between the digestive and the circulatory systems.

Most people try and eat regular meals—breakfast, lunch and supper. Owing to our modern life style, however, our intentions are not always met in reality. There are those who rush out the door in the morning with just a cup of coffee. Others may skip lunch or just have a container of yogurt. Sometimes there are those unintended snacks between meals, and often the dinner hour is later at night than one might have wished. If one travels across time zones, or simply has to endure airplanes, the intake of nutritious food on a rhythmical basis is further impaired, and our digestion is often forced to work at irregular intervals.

By contrast, the circulatory system is rhythmic and regular. If the flow of blood were to occur in a similar irregular way, we would be very sick, if not dead, within a short time. Everything about the blood depends upon this rhythm and regularity. Blood flows through our entire body, bringing nutrients and oxygen to all parts of a complex system. Despite the vicissitudes of the day—our experiences and the many people we meet—circulation continues uninterrupted until the day we die. The flow of blood is the ultimate paradigm of rhythm.

The spleen is therefore confronted with two very different dynamics: the irregular intake of food and the rhythm of circulation. From this creative tension the spleen rises to the occasion in a remarkable way. With a kind of "backward thrust" the spleen creates a counterbalance to the irregularity of the digestive system and gradually adapts the nutrients to the rhythmic flow of the blood stream.[26] This is seen in the frequent expanding and contracting of the organ. To put it in another way, the spleen is the great "transformer," it equalizes the irregularities of the process of nourishment with the regularity of the circulatory system.

We each have choices in what we eat. Much insight is available to us in terms of basic nutrition and people regularly talk about the Atkins diet, fiber content, saturated fats and other topics. What we eat is very much an expression of our own personal will, or informed choices. In contrast to this individualized nutrition, the laws of blood circulation follow a different form of governance. Just as the Sun and Moon orbit a part of a larger solar system, so the circulation of blood obeys universal laws. With the food we take in we unite ourselves with the outside world, but in digestion and especially in the absorption of nutrients into the blood stream, we have to isolate ourselves from the world. As humans we move back and forth between individualization and unity, separation and harmony. The spleen stands at the crossroads of these dynamics.

This has numerous implications for organizational life. As each person joins an existing group, the outside world enters with fresh energy and new impulses. But if the person remains an individual and unchanged by the group, difficulties will arise. There is a need for a process of acclimation and connection to occur in order for the person to join what is already living in the culture of the group. On the other hand, one who merges too completely experiences a kind of "group speak" that becomes mindless and unconscious, similar to the flow of blood circulation.

This creative tension between individuality and group is fundamental to organizational life. In order to be fully individual human beings, we must separate ourselves from the world. We find our freedom and ourselves. We each become a world unto ourselves, with our own life-styles and rhythms. In a sense we have evolved out of unity into separation to the point that we each stand as a kind of contradiction to the world at large. In the seclusion of our personality, we establish our own inner rhythm. Then something mysterious occurs. Even in our new-found freedom, we long to reunite with the world, with the group. We want to be social, to have friends, to work together with other people. So we enter into groups. But there is an entrance price. In order to join the group, we have to adapt, to give up some of ourselves. Exercising some of our newfound freedom we can choose to give up some of our own inner rhythm and surrender to the larger dynamic of the group or organization. We eliminate part of ourselves in rejoining. That which has become independent now in a sense destroys itself for the larger whole. In Greek myth it was the god Chronos who warned that one of his children would destroy him and proceeded to devour them, thus consuming part of himself to remain whole.

One of the secrets to success in organic organizations is to find the best possible balance point between the dynamics of individuality and the group. When the group stays too far on the side of individuality, organizations tend to be governed by personality. On the other extreme, groups can become so uniform that any dissent is immediately suppressed. We live in a constant state of flux between the laws of group and those set by individuality. Ideally, one can rise above the natural "spleen process" described here and enlist the best of both worlds. This happens when groups recognize the importance of initiative and leadership, and can turn to the individuals within a group to bring their own inner wisdom forward for the good of the whole. This requires that the group give up something, too. When people within an organization can come to agree upon values and goals, they voluntarily give up some of their freedom so as to function successfully in a group. This is the true picture of the spleen, which is able to coexist between the individualized process of digestion and the whole-systems approach of blood circulation.

Using the threefold method to go beyond the physiological, we see that the quiet wisdom of the spleen speaks of another dynamic, that of inflation and depletion. We live in a time when we are compelled to take in huge amounts of information. Our sensory system is often overtaxed and we find ourselves "ingesting" more information that we can possible digest. Like the spleen after a large meal, we become inflated. The opposite polarity is also present. We can become deflated—especially those in the helping professions. Parents and multitasking adults are also in danger of giving too much away. Speaking in the physiological language of this book, one can say that at times people give too much "nutrition" to the world. When this is the case, we can become depleted or chronically tired. To draw upon Chinese medicine again, we can speak of the work of the spleen as that of directing energy to the different parts of the body, especially the muscles. As seen in the following citation from Maciocia, when the *spleen-qi* is weak, *refined qi* cannot be transported to the muscles and the person will feel weary, the muscles will be weak and, in severe cases, may atrophy. The state of the spleen is one of the most important factors determining the amount of physical energy a person has. Tiredness is a common complaint."[27] In terms of dietary indications, it is interesting to note that the spleen likes "dryness" and abhors "dampness" and excessive consumption of cold liquids and icy drinks.

As stated elsewhere, I have seen organizations become dysfunctional simply because those in decision-making roles suffer from chronic exhaustion. Decisions are made and then remade, and productivity declines precipitously when people are tired. Over time, the inner "organs," not just the spleen, become worn out and one becomes susceptible to more serious forms of illness. In organizational terms, this sets the stage for a crisis. Are we compelled to simply lurch from crisis to crisis, or can we develop and listen to the language of the organs that serve as our early warning system?

One way to guard against falling into the same abyss again and again is to gradually develop organizational memory. The ability to remember experiences of the past can help inform the present. The spleen is a vital "filter" or transformer in the human body that redirects and helps keep fluids moving throughout the system. Whether sorting out nutrients or filtering past experiences, the human being is well served in this amazing ability to process and then make sense of past experiences. Ancient Chinese scholars spoke of the spleen as having a strong influence on thinking and memory, especially the recollection of practical work or school related subjects. They saw the heart as also influencing thinking, but in this case more in terms of thinking clearly when faced with life problems and their effect on long-term memory. Finally, the kidneys were seen as nourishing the brain and were especially helpful in terms of short-term memory. Thus in old age, when there is a decline in "kidney essence," short-term memory would suffer while memories of the heart, those of long ago, would still be vivid. People who have worked for years in one field or profession retain this spleen essence while forgetting things that happened yesterday.[28]

The workplace today is poorly served by an educational system that has often stressed memorization over other types of learning. In fact, considering the "organ" language of the previous paragraph, one should say "learning by kidney" instead of "learning by heart." When we stress the memorization of facts that are suitable for the next test and then are promptly forgotten, we are overusing the kidney function in the human being. The inner eye of the kidney becomes burdened with these "stones" of schooling, and then is less able to perform its vital functions in maintaining bodily health. Our schools would do well to look to the heart learning that lasts a lifetime—imaginative pictures embedded in stories and mythology and a sense for truth that is won through the activation of true thinking that is both original and creative. Likewise, our schools need the practical, hands on, experiential learning that speaks the language of the spleen. What is learned by the hands lasts a lifetime. Once taught to knit or play a musical instrument, the hands retain this ability and through it, a true relation to the world.

For an organization to use the wisdom of the spleen and maintain memory tools such as minutes and review, documentation can be helpful if consciously enacted. Regular rituals like retreats assist in using organizational memory to re-enliven the mission of the organization. The farther back you go in the history of the organization to see the original picture or vision, the easier it is to build the future.

KEY WORDS FOR THE SPLEEN

Separation and redirection
Counterbalance
Individual vs. group
Intermediary
Transformer
Equalizes irregularities
Values individual impulses and unity
Separation and harmony
Freedom and conformity
Surrender for the good of the whole
Inflation and depletion
Organizational memory

9. THE LUNGS

"AND THE LORD God formed man of the dust of the ground and breathed into his nostrils the breath of life, and man became a living soul." (Gen. 11:7) Most people quite rightly associate the lungs with the passage of air and forget the "dust of the earth" aspect of Genesis. In fact, the lung does not consist of air but rather holds it. Through the lungs human beings are able to find a connection to earthly life. This will be seen as we examine the lungs not just from the physiology but again using our threefold method in the following pages.

Not only are the lungs an earthly vessel for air, but in many ways they are the coldest, hardest and most strongly formed organs in the human body. There is a great deal of firmness already in the larynx and trachea, but the lungs themselves also have a remarkable firmness yet flexibility in the air passages which serve as the portals between life and death. One of the greatest mysteries in the human body is the remarkable transformation of blue into red blood—of spent blood into refreshed blood. Anatomically, the "blue" blood is oxygen poor and in order to sustain life, we need to replenish the blood through the action of the lungs and the intake of new oxygen. The "old" is released and the "new" is embraced. With each breath, we die and then experience rebirth. Despite many years as a lifeguard during high school and college, I never had to give mouth-to-mouth resuscitation, something we all had to practice on a dummy while in training. What an awesome thing it must be to breathe life back into a victim, perhaps eclipsed only by the miracle of birth. Life comes with the in-breath and death with the last out-breath.

Dr. Holtzapfel tells us, "When a tadpole changes into a frog and moves on to land, it not only changes its gill breathing to lung breathing, but at the same time it develops legs in order to move on land. The legs are an outward picture of what the lung has developed internally in the animal—an earth bound relationship."[29] Considering that statement, it is interesting to compare gill breathing with recoil breathing.

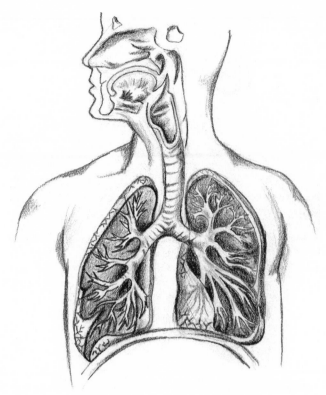

In the former, water streams through the organ in one direction only. In our human "recoil" breathing, inhalation and exhalation alternate. The smooth, fishlike movements of the tadpole changes to the alternating limb-like movements of the frog.

Another earth connection to the lungs is that soil conditions also influence the lungs. People with lung diseases are often sent to the high mountains not only for the purity of the air but because igneous rocks are more beneficial to the lungs than limestone rock. A classic example of this is presented in Thomas Mann's book *The Magic Mountain* in which a patient is sent to a sanatorium and experiences altered states of consciousness while undergoing treatments. Many believe this change was due to the oxygen-poor atmosphere at such high elevations as well as the presence of old volcanic rock formations.

The tendency of the lungs to become too earthly—to harden—can invade the free air space and endanger breathing. For example many people from time to time have phlegm that needs to be coughed up, thus expelling any dirt particles as well. A more serious hardening comes with emphysema in which the phlegm thickens and breathing is labored. Finally, one can have severe hardening as in black lung, or pneumoconiosis, when the lungs become encrusted with earth particles. Later in this chapter we will see how this entire phenomena of the passage of air relates to communication within an organization and the hardening of the lungs to archaic organizational structures.

When we are thirsty, the urge for liquids comes from the voice of the liver but when we are hungry, it is an expression of our desire to link up more strongly with the earth. This comes as a voice, so to speak, from the lungs, according to the homeopathic sources I have consulted. We want to become more grounded, and consuming food is one way to do this. In contrast, fasting leads to an estrangement from the earth. In a modern world in which materialism and a hardening connection to things of the earth can be seen on all sides, we find two opposite tendencies. On the one hand we have rampant obesity and an unbalanced appetite for food, which in recent years has been highlighted in the media. Americans, for example, are growing heavier and even children are subject to being seriously overweight. Then we have the opposite extreme, anorexia nervosa, in which girls in particular are rejecting food altogether. This condition is especially pronounced during the adolescent years, a time when children awaken to earth maturity and to the problems of society. Anorexia becomes a kind of silent protest against modern conditions and the ways of the world.

Homeopathic treatment of anorexia, among other interventions, can consist of iron, which assists in the process of incarnation, or coming into connection with the earth. As will be seen in more detail in the chapter on the metals, iron, like the meteors of late summer, draws in and focuses human attention. As Dr. Holtzapfel says, "Medical iron is also related to the process of respiration and with it to the lung."[30] Iron brings us in contact with the earth so the intake of food binds us more strongly to the earth while fasting serves to disconnect. As a student of history, I have always been fascinated when singular individuals cannot change human laws and ways and that they have often resorted to fasting—Nelson Mandela, Gandhi, or more recently, the prisoners at Guantanamo Bay. In fasting, they appealed to a higher authority, the nontemporal voice of human conscience.

On another level, there is also a close relationship between the lungs and thinking. The lungs cool the blood as it flows through, therefore we are less hotheaded and more reflective as a result of "processing" or breathing. Just taking a deep breath when you are angry can make a big difference. Of course the passage of air through the larynx is crucial for word formation, and we all have experienced how speech and thought are intimately connected. One example of the *dis-ease* that can occur in the connection of thinking and the lungs is tuberculosis or lung decay, which in the past, was a serious concern. Often called the poet's disease, a person starts to live in a fantasy world in an attempt to deny otherwise harsh realities. The physical decay of the lung is accompanied by a loosening of thinking for earthly constraints. Well-known writers who had this condition include the German Romantic poet Novalis, Thoreau, Keats, Morgenstern, and Kafka. Although tuberculosis is thankfully not prevalent anymore, we still need the antidote of firmness of thinking that can strengthen the lungs. This can be fostered through meditation, mathematics or working with a book such as Steiner's *Intuitive Thinking.* As with many lung phenomena, we again have a polarity. In considering the opposite illness of tuberculosis we find lung cancer. With tuberculosis the soul life is full of illusions, or castles in the air. In lung cancer, there is too much solidification and people become bound up with the earth through abnormal cell division and encrustation and solidification.

Because of its prevalence today, we need to consider lung cancer from a spiritual scientific perspective. Rudolf Steiner said that cancer is "a sense organ in the wrong place."[31] This is a riddle if I ever heard one. What meaning can one make out of this provocative statement? Well, in general, we know that our senses have a way of sacrificing themselves to make way for outside influences that can then become perceptions that impress themselves upon the body. Our eyes, for example, selflessly adjust themselves to the light. It is as if the inherent laws of the senses are sacrificed to take in the world. Another example is that optometrists have found that stress reduces the performance of the visual system thus our seeing is easily sacrificed to abnormal inner conditions.[32] But what does it mean to have a sense organ in the "wrong place?"

Smokers feel a new sensation in the air passages where normally no sensation takes place. We know that inhaling smoke is most connected to cancer formation. What is normally an empty spot in the lung passages becomes a sensing organ in the wrong place. The space of the lungs is taken over by a foreign influence and otherwise healthy cell regeneration becomes rampant growth that disregards the wisdom in the structure of the lung. So the cancer becomes a "catastrophe of form."[33]

When I work with organizations, I often find that those in need of help either have experienced too much "hardening" over time or they are lacking in form and structure. Things can become too fixed or too loose. In the hardened organization, people feel trapped and form little "cells" in which they can operate relatively independently of the larger group. People disregard the "wisdom" of the whole—the vision and mission of the organization—and instead create little fiefdoms where they can feel some control. This is the cancer pole, and tends to happen more frequently with old age. The opposite youthful extreme is the fluid organization in which nothing is fixed and policies are crafted in the moment based upon personal self-interests. "We decided that because of so and so..." is a common refrain. Everything swims around in the subjective, and there are no real policies or operating procedures. Even without doing much work with an organization, one can take a quick read of the "temperature" that reveals valid information. Usually the "cancer" extreme feels "cold" while the amorphous organization feels "warm" but undifferentiated. Through interviews with members of the organization and other analysis one can test this initial hypothesis and see if the first impression holds up in structural analysis. If there is an eventual finding of one extreme or another, much of the subsequent intervention can be focused on helping the individuals and the organization as a whole find health through balance.

Similarly in our organizations, we almost always have the polarity of our idealists and our realists. Some people are terrific at picture forming, describing the ideal future and inspiring others to reach beyond themselves. These are our visionaries and artists. In the opposite group, we have those who are bound by the constraints of budget, buildings and scarce resources. These are the practical people who are often the ones who take the actions. Just like healthy breathing that balances inhalation and exhalation, so in our groups we need to find a way to reach for ideals and new possibilities while keeping our feet on the ground. When idealists and realists work together, "blue blood becomes red" and organizations are revitalized.

In a similar way, there is a fascinating correspondence between the lungs and our trees. As we all know, a tree is surrounded by air. The solid trunk grows upward, branches out and twigs and leaves reach upward in hundreds of tiny shapes. Oxygen is released and carbon dioxide is absorbed. The opposite is true of the lungs. The hollow trunk or trachea, reaches down and millions of alveoli form, thus becoming the crown of this inverted tree. And of course, the lungs take in oxygen and release CO_2. Nature and human beings conspire to balance each other in an inextricable web of interconnection. This is health.

LUNG TYPES

In organizations with those people who are lung oriented we often see a soul landscape of loneliness. This type is a mainstay in countless stories of the prince who goes off on his own, traveling many long miles over all sorts of terrain. Loneliness is especially poignant in our time of frenetic haste and apparent connection through the internet and the media. Many people, especially the lung types, feel that they are going through the motions outwardly, but remain deeply isolated within. This sense of loneliness is also related to a sense of being misunderstood, a condition which happens to both the realists and the idealists. It is a big thing in organizations when people are not seen for who they are. We all need recognition and appreciation, and sometimes everyone is just too busy, it seems, to take a few moments to reach out. The frequently heard complaint, "I have not had a raise in years," is a sign of not being seen. There is a need for both social and monetary recognition, without which our organizations wither. Being misunderstood is like having to breathe in and in and in again with no out-breath. The lung hurts and the sorrow can become a physical pain.

A step toward regaining health is to introduce healthy breathing into our organizations. When people speak to me about communication problems, I find they are often talking about what I call organizational breathing. Try to speak without breathing; it is impossible. The passage of air is actually a social event because we are united through our breathing. When we breathe, the air passes between people—as we all know during the flu season. We are part of the same air exchange. In India, wise healers who lived long ago were able to sense how a person felt by experiencing a person's breathing, which forms the basis for most yoga practices. To this day, our emotions affect our breathing even if we are less attentive to it. Our emotions can also affect our relationship to food. When we are enthusiastic about work or a project we often forgo food while depression can lead us to consume comfort food, another kind of "inhaling." The question is how do we work with relationships so that we promote healthy breathing? Communication is more than the sharing of information. I recently attended a meeting in which a group tried initially and unsuccessfully, to clear up communication issues in their organization. As long as they focused merely on the dissemination of information, they were not able to solve the problem. So I asked, "How would the groups in your organization have to work together in order to bring joy and satisfaction to your efforts? Suddenly they all started talking about relationships, and from that we were able to get at the root causes of communication breakdowns. We can overcome misunderstanding and loneliness when we start reconnecting with others.

The chapter in my previous book that receives the most attention is the one on Sun-Moon relationships. In my book *In Search of Ethical Leadership*, I describe a way of navigating the straits between Necessity and Freedom, between working out of the strictures of past dictates and the possibilities of future equality. Creating Sun-Sun relationships is a way out of the labyrinth of misunderstanding. This is evident whenever two or more people are co-creators, working on a project together, for example.

Another thing to note about lung types is that they are known to develop fixed ideas that they share with anyone who is willing to listen. Repeating the same thoughts comes with advancing age; it is a form of crystallization connected to the lung's earth influence. An extreme, found in some at all ages, is obsessive-compulsive behavior. Mental pictures arise repeatedly, defying all efforts at control. The solidifying forces of the lung hold these astral images of the emotional body, the fixed pictures, and these fixations then enter consciousness as obsessions that surge up from the semiconscious emotional life of the lungs into the head, into our thinking. These people long for forgetfulness.

In fact, the lung is a highly sensitive instrument of the soul on which physical and psychological phenomena interact. This indicates a particular kind of vulnerability as Dr. Husemann says, "The astral and physical bodies are more susceptible to external influences in the lung than in any other organ."[34] We know that joy and pain influence respiration; indeed every feeling involves a modulation of respiratory rhythm so that in breathing, our feelings become alive. With pain, our breathing contracts—one can even find it hard to breathe. In joy, we are expansive and we breathe deeply.

Besides the emotional aspects, a lung type experiences the sensation of weight. To understand this you can experiment by exhaling and then refraining from breathing in for a few moments. How does the body feel? We are heavier, more earthbound with the exhalation. For those with a lung orientation, there is a continual oscillation between the experience of the outer world and one's own physical body. The reader need only try breathing out for as long as possible to feel one of these extremes and the deadening sensation of lungs without air. When we see something remarkable, we tend to inhale with the impressions of the outside world. This also gives us the ability to differentiate between experiences. Thus the lung types can offer considerable wisdom and advice to others. Whereas the kidney type responds in a raw, more emotional way, the lung person can be relied upon for a more accurate reflection of outer impressions, sometimes with brutal honesty. Indeed, we all make inner pictures of events in the outer world, and those pictures are influenced by respiration. We "breathe in" the outer world every day, and lung types especially use these phenomena to heighten consciousness. In a way, the lung has a great affinity for the head and differentiated thinking.

This special ability for differentiated thinking also means that lung types react with special sensitivity, and often can balance their reactions to events and experiences because of the way their inner life works rhythmically. Outwardly they can appear somewhat harsh at times, yet when one gets to know a lung type, there is a true vulnerability deep inside. Thus they can also be overly sensitive and easily offended, as described by Dr. Husemann: "Their sensitivity reflects the physical sensitivity of the bronchial mucosae, which can also become oversensitive resulting in either mental or physical allergy."[35]These people also have a tendency to succumb to external influences and to experience their own bodies as something foreign, as something that simply lives out there in the environment. Their inner life can be ruled by external influences, thus many are not only conscientious but also excessively orderly. Their moods can move in and out with frequent depressive episodes; healthy reflection can become a kind of brooding as a strug-

gle to come to terms with what appears to them to be overpowering, inflexible experiences. Dr. Husemann also notes that reflection for lung types can be, "a process that can paralyze their feelings and their will. Thus arises the anxiety characteristic of the pulmonary type, fear of the world, which causes the soul to withdraw into the body."[36]
We have discussed opposites throughout this chapter, and here again we see that the lung type can alternate between two states, just as we have two lungs:

1. A retreat into a fantasy filled inner world that is perceived as safe in the face of the many things that are to be feared in the outer world.

2. This brooding and reflection can then give way to enthusiasm for new projects and wild daydreaming.

Thus we have two polarities: melancholia leads to sanguinity and then back again. Emotional sensitivity in this type of person is combined with a tendency toward abstraction and conceptualizing experiences. For instance, they are good at one-liners that go right to the point. Sometimes they are a bit acerbic and it may take time for listeners to digest what they have heard. The lung type likes to make short, directive statements, and for those that are more open, like the heart type, it can be overwhelming.

In organizations, these characteristics can be observed as part of everyday human interactions. There are many different types of people out there, and one can learn to work with lung types when one recognizes some of the common traits. However, there are situations when the natural tendencies of the lung type start to show themselves as neurotic symptoms that take the underlying psychological polarity to an extreme. As Dr. Husemann states, "their oversensitivity allows even insignificant experiences to traumatize them."[37] This can affect their respiration and even accentuate asthma.

These bronchial spasms indicate a disharmony in the astral body, the emotional life, which has withdrawn into itself due to an upsetting experience. The trouble in dealing with this extreme of the lung type in the group setting is that others in the group may not realize *which* experiences have upset the lung type. The group may continually feel ambushed by highly charged emotional statements based upon trauma that no one else experienced. One then spends an inordinate amount of time managing these brush fires without any assurance that they will not occur again. This really slows down the performance of the group or organization.

Returning to the physiological and psychological conditions, we can compare this type of obsessive-compulsive behavior to a state that is like having food stuck in the small intestine. In a normal human being, the small intestine, shaped like multiples of the letter S, will seek nutrients and pick out the best for the body. Yet if this picking over is too extreme in the soul of the lung type, they are not just "pack rats," but begin to obsess over small things that others want to pass over. Gradually, the person begins to avoid certain actions out of fear or phobias. Compulsive acts, such as hand washing also show themselves. Haptephobia, fear of contact, is at the root of this obsessive hand washing. The repetitive motions are indicative of fixed ideas, a strong antipathy to certain things and people. In an abbreviated form, one can say that with the obsessive-compulsive person, there is too little exhalation because of a psychological "blockage."

As parents, we need to be careful not to be too rigid in our child rearing practices, as this can accentuate obsessive-compulsive tendencies later on for some children. They need form, but rather than strict, arbitrary discipline, children need management that is based upon rhythm, not beat, to use a musical analogy. Rhythmically performing daily tasks—brushing one's teeth, washing, changing clothes, and listening to a story or a song each night at bedtime—can build strength for later life. A warm, playful manner can enliven even the most ordinary tasks. The heart can become the counterweight to the lung.

In fact, at the very beginning of his first course for Waldorf teachers, Rudolf Steiner stated that, "the task of education, understood in a spiritual sense, is to bring the soul-spirit into harmony with the temporal body...of all the relationships humans have to the physical world, the most important is breathing...education consists in teaching proper breathing."[38] Indeed, some children are quite naturally more earthbound because they are quickly pulled in by their physical organizations. Others, by contrast, do not unite enough with the physical organism and this condition can turn them into "vain enthusiasts and visionary dreamers."[39] Here again we have our realists and idealists.

The consciousness mood of the heart is one that casts no shadow.
Here we stand in highest connection with ourselves and can
enter the realm of being able to bless. The harmony of the
whole body is carried by the consciousness of the heart.

The journey woman is devoted to her task. The work is being done.
The soft, lush, watery realm of the liver is balanced by
inner fire and love for the deed.

Far distances must be travelled to connect the inner and outer
dimensions of experience. Grace can unite polarities.
Loneliness finds comfort in the end.

A cave filled with bright crystals mirrors the insight that can be gleaned from the world above. Likewise, the calm waters of the underground cavern support enlightenment that rays into the darkest corners of consiousness.

In human biography, it is interesting to observe that the lungs' capacity increases until midlife and then gradually decreases again. This illustrates the path of the soul as it is gradually integrated into the body and then slowly released again. With greater lung capacity, more oxygen can stream into the organism. Later on, there is less available as the life forces diminish.

An example of this type of function in an organization is the life cycle of employees. Is turnover good? Is it better to promote longevity? As with many management issues, there are no true absolutes. One can work with the interplay of the two possibilities. Longevity brings with it not only stability, but also an experience base that cannot be fully measured. Many things can be decided based upon the expertise of those who have simply done it for years. There is a fairly predictable "face" to the community. People know how to interact. The downside is rigidity. Those that do not fit in do not last long. "Our way or the highway" can be the implicit rule. In contrast, new employees bring new "oxygen," vitality, fresh perspective and unimagined possibilities. Unfortunately, an organization with many new people each year can lurch like a ship without a rudder, moving first one way and then the other. I suggest looking at the groups and organizations you are part of and asking whether you have the benefits of both. Is there a need to rebalance and have more of one or the other?"

Another result of lung imbalance in groups is the "asthmatic organization," leading to difficulty breathing out. In fact, there is too much in-breath; too much is taken in and not enough released. I have seen committees that continually gather information but seem unable to digest the material sufficiently, and certainly cannot share what they've gathered with the larger group. One often hears "send it to committee," which perpetuates the phenomenon. Likewise, some organizations do one study after another, continually assembling groups of "experts" to study a problem, yet the fundamental realities remain the same. Margaret Wheately describes this eloquently:

> We often tend to limit our explorations of what's possible by surrounding ourselves with large amounts of information that tell us nothing new. We collect information from measures that tell us how we are doing—whether we're up to standard, whether we're meeting our goals. But these measures lock us into learning only

about a predetermined world. They keep us distracted from questioning our experience in a way that could create greater possibilities.... they don't ask us to notice what learning is available from all those things we decided not to measure...; whatever we decide to notice blinds us to other possibilities.[40]

Increasingly, the consciousness surrounding a topic does not itself move anything forward. When a report is released and opened up to a larger group, the possibility of "unknowing" trust is demonstrated. A larger perspective and a larger world exist beyond our own small space. Letting go can be an act of trust.

This gesture is contrary to those who cannot easily take in an in-breath. Asthma is closely related to the psychological condition of fear, the absence of trust. When there is fear, people are divided from one another. As Margaret Wheately says, "The forms of the organization bear witness to how people experience one another."[41] Trusting systems tend to be more open; fear filled ones are more closed. An asthmatic organization creates more fear with each in-breath, with each new issue or task because the basic relationship between self and world is not in harmony. Pages upon pages could be filled with examples of this.

Many social problems arise out of fear, leading to an inability to breathe in and out in human interactions. One can be very intelligent but also secluded, even isolated in one's own castle. People such as this may be very clear about things in their own minds but can have erratic ways of relating to others. In the effort to find a balance between pulling in and letting go they experience confrontations in the workplace. This usually manifests itself socially or in statements that have an "edge" or it can be experienced as erratic behavior. Asthmatic people can also suffer from nightmares in which they are confronted with things beyond their control. There is a "coldness" that can make daily living challenging. The boundaries are hard, and more warmth is needed to counteract this effect.

How can organizations foster the needed warmth to bring healing to an asthmatic group? One way is to get the blood circulating. Set up retreats, do projects together, bring groups into dialogue, and circulate new ideas; such interest will generate energy and increase the level of warmth. Above all, I believe in using the arts as a pathway to "warming" an organization. While working creatively, people get out of the head and into the limbs so that all sorts of new possibilities can arise. Breathing and circulation combine to bring new life and vitality to our common work.

In summary, lung types in organizations are great at perceiving, seeing through issues and people and can bring a lot of acute knowledge to problem solving. But because of the many polarities described above, they can be socially difficult and hard to work with in a team. It is often "my way or no way" with lung types and they do indeed tend to change jobs more frequently than others do. They bring many gifts, but one must also learn to work around their prickly manner. Those who are insecure or in subservient roles can suffer at the hands of a lung-type supervisor. One has to be inwardly strong to meet their controlling manner, and self-deprecating humor goes a long way in getting something done in a group setting. In short, one is well advised to limit the number of lung types one engages in an organization, but to take advantage of their insights when offered.

In a lung organization, one often finds power and trust issues rising to the surface between groups and individuals. It takes a great deal of common work to resolve these issues. For example, the power, influence, and control that reside in a school board can create real problems if it dictates policy to the faculty. Such issues require that the lung influence be balanced with the other organs—for example, by promoting greater circulation or conversation through the heart impulse. In other words, the group contending with issues of power and influence must use heart wisdom to balance the one-sided lung tendencies.

KEY WORDS FOR THE LUNG

Cold, hard, earth
Blue becomes red, old becomes new
Thinking as inhalation, speech as exhalation
Misplaced sensing, cancer cells
Loneliness
Organizational breathing, communication
Fixed ideas, recurring mental pictures
Ability to accurately portray outer impressions
Brutal honesty
Differentiated thinking
Obsessive-compulsive
Asthmatic organizations
Fear vs. trust

10. DUAL ORGANS

IN HUMAN ANATOMY, several organs have dual structures or special relationships with other organs. Examples of this include the kidneys and the adrenal glands, the liver and gall bladder, the exocrine and endocrine pancreas—the part associated with digestion and the internal secretions of insulin—and the inner ear and the function of equilibrium. One common trait of these dual organs is that usually one is more externally oriented while the other has an internal focus. A good example of this is in the cardiopulmonary system.

INNER ORIENTATION	OUTER ORIENTATION
heart	lungs
adrenal gland	kidneys
liver	gall bladder
insulin cells	exocrine pancreas
parathyroid glands	thyroid glands[42]

PARATHYROID GLANDS AND THYROID GLANDS

Concerning the latter pair, the parathyroid and thyroid glands, it is interesting to characterize the degenerative processes of either extreme. On the one hand one can have hypothyroidism that entails subnormal activity, and in the other extreme there are symptoms of hyperthyroidism that characterize overactivity. Overactivity of the thyroid gland indicates that too much vitality flows to the periphery of the body. One may experience sweaty skin, protruding eyes, quick, excited speech, tachycardia (an increased heart rate), or nervousness and trembling of the fingers. When the activity of the thyroid gland is below normal, too little blood flows to the periphery, one's skin becomes coarse, thick, and dry, the eyes grow smaller, speech is slowed, and one may experiences constipation, bradycardia (slowed heart rate), tiredness, and general apathy. On the one hand, therefore, fluids have too much influence, and on the other, a kind of mineralization occurs. In the former situation, calcium and phosphate are removed from the bones and excreted through the kidneys and there is a kind of bone disintegration. When the parathyroid or thyroid glands are overly active, a person "looses" skeletal material through the kidneys. By contrast, subnormal activity leads to calcification and a kind of tetany and a slow death through dryness; one becomes as the bark of old trees.[43] When we consider these glands in light of groups and organizations several questions come to mind. Have we ever experienced groups that are dry, boring, and bark-like in their adherence to form at the expense of content? Or can we remember situations that were "juicy" in content but lacking in form and structure? In the human body, the thyroid and parathyroid glands work to find equilibrium between the two extremes. They can inform us as to how organizations can do the same. One litmus test is in the realm of activity. Is there too much going on? Do people move from one stimulus to another? Is there a kind of nervous energy in the organization? On the other hand, does the activity of the place feel like the activity in a funeral home—structured, measured and weighed, ritualistic but without much vitality? Is the organization more like the dry bark of old age or the slender shoot of springtime plants?

In order to achieve organic organizations we need to train our eyes to view our work in groups from a new perspective. It is too simplistic to just render an opinion as "good" or "bad," or "I feel comfortable," or not. In fact, in terms of working with groups, opinions on comfort level can be more self-revelatory than anything else divulged. We tend to seek our natural habitats, and old trees tend to be found in groves. Yet, as humans, we can work with the natural processes of the human body in a more enlightened way. It is possible to understand the work of the glands, for example, and use their teaching to inform and redirect our work? Even in an old grove, one can seek out new life. Precisely in the counterpart one can find the most astonishing remedies. Once the need for a counterbalancing activity is identified, one can do innumerable things to effect change. An old, tired group can get up and move for a few minutes. A hyperactive group can be asked to reflect for a while. The basic assignment for understanding organizational health from the perspective of the glands is to look for the balance of moisture/vitality/activity versus dryness/slowness/rigidity. We need the help of both the thyroid and the parathyroid glands in our organizations.

THYMUS GLAND

One of the most fascinating glands I have encountered is the thymus. An elongated, bilobed organ located above the heart, it rests on the pericardium behind the breastbone. Each lobe of the thymus has two main regions, cortical and medullary. The cortex, however, makes up eighty-five to ninety percent of the thymus and has most of the lymphoid cells. There is also another division within this organ, as the cortex itself is divided into the subcapsular outer cortex and the deep cortex, which contains more differentiated, mature thymocytes. Some of these differentiated cells migrate to the thymic medulla where they develop further before they are released into the blood. Remarkably, only about two percent of all thymic cells leave the thymus to move into the periphery, to the lymph nodes, the tonsils, the spleen and other organs. There they function as mature immunocompetent T cells, which provide many, many essential roles in the survival of the individual.[44]

This means that the thymus plays a crucial role in the immune system of the human being. In fact, the thymus actually "educates" immature thymocytes to become immuneocompetent T cells. This "education" involves the selection of "mature thymocytes that express cell surface receptors to react against non-self antigens rather than against the host-self antigens. The reaction of immune T cells against host antigens is what occurs in autoimmune conditions such as lupus, rheumatoid arthritis, and Sjogren's syndrome.[45]

Before going on to discuss this remarkable gland in relation to organizations, I would like to mention just one more aspect. The thymus is a unique organ in the overall working of the immune system in that it has an age-related decrease or involution in its overall function. In terms of its activity and volume (thymocytes, epithelium and dendritic cells) there is a marked decrease in activity as a person ages. In fact, the thymus reaches its maximum size during the first twelve months of life, after which there is a decrease as thymic tissue is replaced by adipose or fatty tissue. The rate of decrease is about three percent per year until middle age—forty to fifty years—after which the decrease slows down to less than one percent per year. Thus the removal of the thymus at birth can have devastating, life threatening immune deficiencies, but if this occurs later in life it is not as severe a loss of immune function.[46]

Earlier in this book we looked at the etheric, or life body of the human being. Here we have, in the form of the thymus, a key physiological manifestation of this life force, only in this case referred to as immune function. This offers the possibility that the thymus is a physical contact point for the working of the etheric body, especially in fetal life and early childhood. Moreover, we can say that it is also possible that through the thymus the etheric body becomes functional within the immune system. I added this for two reasons: First, he talked about "possibility," above; and second, he does not cite any other research. How does this happen? In the chapter on evolution, we looked at the role of warmth in creation. During the involution process of the thymus, there is a progressive decrease of warmth ether permeating the thymus; its creative, health-giving work decreases as we age. It is consistent with other statements made in this book to say that warmth is generally creative and builds, while the cooling process is part of the aging process and degeneration. This applies, of course, to the human life cycle, but not as much attention has been given to the evolution and involution of organizations.

In my experience working with schools, there is a robust, even palpable life force of energy in the first few years. People come together and do much work, more than any could have imagined possible such as constructing buildings, fundraising, establishing financial systems, hiring, and much else. Even when setbacks occur, the "immune system" is so strong that entrepreneurial organizations tend to bounce back quickly. It often seems that in the early years, a new organization has a wellspring of human resources, a thymus of opportunity. As the years go by, similar to the decrease in function of the thymus, less happens spontaneously and more needs to be done out of conscious intent. Nature does not provide as abundantly in a maturing organization, and the differentiation of function tends to compartmentalize people. An aging process sets in with organizations and "the bark" aspect mentioned above can make the outer shell of the organization at times impervious to new influences. The antidote to involution is hiring of new employees and the new families that can bring a "youthful" impulse to an aging school or company.

What, in fact, is an organization's immune system? In human beings, the life-giving processes support and nourish the individual.

This is the central subject of this book, and at this point I would like to highlight three processes in particular:

1. Formative processes are those that work through the nerve-sense system into shaping and forming the organs in the embryo, for example. These are the life processes that enthusiastic people bring to their work—people who sweep us off our feet with their captivating presentations.

2. Rhythmical processes work through the breathing of humans and have to do with the alternation of activities in groups, rites of passage, celebration of festivals and community events at particular times of the year. Living organizations need to work with "seasonality," not just the annual meeting, but also celebrations, birthdays and special occasions that come regularly each year. Organizations that embrace seasonality and rhythm tend to have a stronger immune system.

3. Finally, there are the processes of consolidation in which projects are brought to completion and things are made visible to the surrounding community. Consolidation is a metabolic process, one that is akin to digestion in that it takes time and will force us to move forward. Groups and organizations that cannot complete things gradually loose their strength and vitality, whereas even a small project, when finished, can give a boost to everyone. It may be as simple as putting up a garden shed for a school's sports equipment or it may be a new logo to use on letterhead. For the purposes of consolidation, it is not so much the item that matters as the sense of "rounding off" and completion.

The fascinating thing about the three steps outlined here is that they closely mirror the development of organs during embryology. In most cases, physiological development includes formation, rhythm (or secretion), and consolidation. Thus these three processes are true, life processes that occur in the development of organs and when sustained over time within group situations, enhance the immune system of organizations.

A very simple technique available to those who wish to promote organizational health is to ask which of the three processes are stronger or weaker in an organization. Even when it is not possible to do a quick diagnosis, just asking the question opens issues for discussion, and good things happen when people attend to life processes. Too often people are simply task-oriented, trying to get things done rather than tending and caring for the whole system. This has been exacerbated by downsizing and the pressure to become ever more productive. In pushing people to do more, we have lost some of the very things that can sustain us over time, as exampled by the person who works too hard and becomes ill. Organic organizations need maintenance and nourishment to be truly supportive of the people who circulate within them.

To summarize, we have looked not only at the dual organs but also at the bifurcation within organs, as with the thymus. This differentiation, when it occurs in organizations, can enhance specialization and focus. We also discussed the thymus in relation to the immune system and self-sustaining systems in organizations. Finally, we mentioned the contrast of evolution and involution as dynamic processes that build or break down organ-izational processes. All these considerations play a vital role in promoting and sustaining organizational healing. By looking specifically at the glandular organs, we see once again a recurring theme of the etheric, or life, forces as an aspect of the basic human constitution as presented in Part I of this book. The glands are, in fact, part of our recurring theme that the life forces can make a huge difference in the vitality of organizations.

11. Corpus Callosum and Other Matters

T HERE HAS BEEN a great deal of research into the brain in recent years, and I have chosen to consider just a few aspects as it relates to organizational dynamics. As we know, the cerebrum contains two hemispheres, which develop and process information in very different ways. To state it simplistically, the left, or logic hemisphere deals with details, linear patterns and the parts of language and the right hemisphere is more global and deals with images, rhythm, emotion and intuition. Let us compare the various functions:

Logic or left hemisphere	Gestalt or right hemisphere
starts with the pieces first	sees whole picture first
parts of language	language comprehension
syntax, semantics	image, emotion, meaning
letters, sentences	rhythm, flow, dialect
numbers	image, intuition
analysis – linear	intuition – estimates
looks at differences	looks at similarities
controls feelings	free with feelings
planned – structured	spontaneous – fluid
sequential thinking	simultaneous thinking
language-oriented	feelings/experience-oriented
future-oriented	now-oriented
technique	flow and movement
sports (hand/eye/foot placement)	sports (flow and rhythm)
art (media, tool use, how to)	art (image, emotion, flow)
music (notes, beat, tempo)	music (passion, rhythm, image)[47]

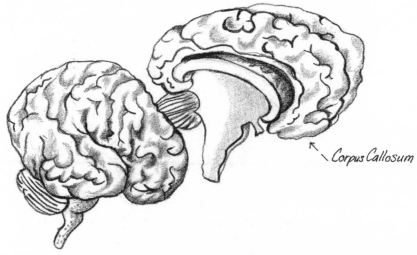

Corpus Callosum

The various functions of the two hemispheres shown here is current knowledge, and people today tend to identify themselves or others as right or left brained. Indeed, hemisphere dominance exists and becomes even more pronounced during times of stress. However, in normal life, we use both hemispheres daily because we need both to do anything well. How are the two connected? White matter, connective motor and sensory axons, form the "bridge" between the two hemispheres in what is called the *corpus callosum.*

This very special part of the human brain allows for crossover patterns that help the two sides of the brain communicate with each other. So for example, information that comes in through the left ear goes to the right temporal lobe of the cerebral cortex. The left hemisphere controls all sensory motor functions on the right side of the body. Left and right hemispheres work in concert, and the connections take place thanks to the corpus callosum. As Carla Hannaford notes, some researchers have estimated that "when fully developed, the corpus callosum carries four billion messages per second across the 200 million or more mostly myelinated nerve fibers connecting the two hemispheres of the brain. This integration and quick access leads to full operational thinking so that ideas and concepts can be manipulated, resulting in formal reasoning."[48]

The corpus callosum is so important because much of our higher functioning depends on the full cooperation of both hemispheres. Even things like painting a picture or other creative pursuits require not just the gestalt or right brain, but also the technique and detail that comes from the left hemisphere. The integration of the two sides is needed for reading, writing and any comprehension. As an educator, I was particularly interested to learn that the two regions at the front of the corpus callosum are significantly smaller with those who have ADHD (Attention Deficit Hyperactive Disorder) and that women have ten percent more fibers across the corpus callosum than men have. Activities such as learning math through motion (using a jump rope for multiplication tables) involve both hemispheres, for example, and can strengthen the connections for everyone, not just those with ADHD.

Now let's look at this organ in the context of organizations. Imagine that there is a plan to build a new wing or addition and and the leadership has the option of assigning the work to one of two groups. Group A will immediately grasp the bigger picture of how the addition will help meet many of the present needs of the organization. They will engage in animated discussion, have spontaneous inspirations, share their different perceptions freely, and come up with a host of color drawings showing not only the design, but also the traffic flow and social mixing areas in the new design.

Group B will work more deliberately, spending time to understand first the assignment and the specifics of how much money with which they have to work. They will begin by looking at the future needs of the organization and project the specific needs of each unit and the exact space requirements. In a well-managed and orderly process, they will design the wing with appropriate attention to the heating and ventilation systems as well as wiring to support technology. Their written descriptions will be precise and factual, with everything completed on schedule.

The reader may remember encountering some of the above differences at work. It is not unusual for organizations to have left and right brain functions under the same roof. In extreme situations, there might be a dominance of one sphere throughout the organization. We tend to attract people with many different tendencies, and I have found that the more frequent scenario is to find right-brain qualities versus left-brain qualities within subgroups in organizations. Compare the folks in the tech-support department with those in marketing, for example. The crucial decision for those in leadership roles is to assign tasks as shown in our example of the new building addition. One can be simplistic and just give the design portion of the project to the right-brain group and its implementation to the left-brain logical folks, but that scenario would not really work. As mentioned, we really need an integrated approach at all stages of development. This is where the corpus callosum makes a huge difference.

How do organizations integrate these kinds of functions? Are there certain crossover people as ambassadors between the right and left? Are there ways to design the process itself so that both hemispheres are valued from the beginning and the corpus callosum has a place at the table? The answers to these questions should be positive in a high performing organization. Like the myelinated nerve fibers that play a crucial role in the brain, so the connective tissue in organizations can make or break a project. Just as crawling can help infants develop coordinated movements, so cross-lateral movement in organizations is supported through attention to process. Two questions can help us connect these two groups in an organization: When do we need to have joint meetings? When does the work of this department affect those working elsewhere? Too often we tend to focus on outcomes and products, while groups are left to sort matters out on their own and somehow get the job done. The stress level can become unnecessarily high for all concerned, as dysfunction in organizational process affects the corresponding human physiological process. Poor communication affects breathing. Just plowing ahead with a task can lead to human casualties in an organization. The ends do not always justify the means.

How can the *corpus callosum* be valued and strengthened within group work? Here are a few key points to remember before and during a project like the one mentioned above in designing a new addition:

- Whom do we need at these meetings? Do we have people who will bring different perspectives, talents, and skills?
- Can we balance our natural orientation to finishing tasks with attention to process? What sort of process do we imagine?
- When at work, let's remember to draw forth the best of both gestalt and logic thinking.
- We aim to finish our work, but it is also all right to enjoy the company and make some discoveries along the way.

Perhaps the most important aspect of the corpus callosum in organizations is the notion of versatility. The ability to move back and forth between right and left brain work is crucial in the workplace, as more and more people are asked to do multitasking in a downsized environment. The manager of our local coffee shop is no longer there just to hire and supervise employees. He has to jump in and out of activities such as working the cash register, making lattes, and resupplying napkins at the table dispenser. A productive person is able to do many things in the course of a day, and the corpus callosum is all about versatility. The modern workplace with its emphasis on multitasking is asking more and more of what the *corpus callosum* can provide.

Just as the corpus callosum grows with time, particularly between the ages of nine and twelve, so also organizations can expand the connective fibers in the workplace by holding inter and intradepartmental meetings on a rhythmic basis. When divisions or groups are brought together the corpus callosum of their work expands through shared insights, joint problem solving and face to face dialogue. Many organizational "knots" would be avoided if this middle ground were cultivated with greater regularity.

Dr. Paul MacLean, Chief of the Laboratory of Brain Evolution and Behavior at the National Institute of Mental Health in Washington, D.C., described three distinct areas of the human brain in his Triune Brain Theory: the reptilian brain, the early mammalian brain, and the neo-mammalian brain.

The Reptilian Brain, or Brain Stem

This is the oldest evolutionary part of the brain and the first to develop in humans—between conception and fifteen months—and its main job is self-preservation. Through the senses, it monitors the world and activates the body to ensure physical survival. When a company is struggling to meet payroll, or there is a personnel crisis of some sort or another, the reptilian brain of the organization takes over. Survival mode thinking means that many things are neglected in favor of a "first responder" mentality. Interpersonal relationships, group process, entrepreneurship, and innovation fall by the wayside as everyone tries simply to remain solvent. An external consultant in such a situation is challenged with the narrow focus of the leaders and a natural reluctance to expand the field of vision.

THE LIMBIC, OR EARLY MAMMALIAN, BRAIN

This portion lies between the reptilian brain and the cerebral cortex. Through its links to the neocortex, the limbic system allows for emotional and cognitive processing. Working in concert with the body, it helps to coordinate things such as the flush of embarrassment or the smile of joy. As Hannaford notes: "Limbic system emotions also determine the release of neurotransmitters that either strengthen or weaken our immune system."[49] We remember something best when it is associated with a feeling or an experience. There is an emotional filter in the limbic brain that helps us evaluate the meaning and social context of things. Emotions interpret our experiences and help us place ourselves in groups and organizations that fit us.

If the limbic system of the brain is all that is present in an organization, participants may find themselves lurching from one emotional encounter to another. These organizations have a high level of conflict, and productivity grinds down, as people have to continually deal with interpersonal issues. A process coach in this situation needs to ask thought-provoking questions that promote self-reflection and an impulse to break out of the emotional stupor to a higher level of human interaction.

THE NEUROCORTEX, OR NEO-MAMMALIAN BRAIN

This crucial part of the human brain represents the ability of all higher human functioning. In a lecture at Antioch University in Keene, New Hampshire, some years ago, Joseph Chilton Pierce stated that ninety percent of the cortex is unused. That can mean it is still waiting to be developed, and this has enormous implications for human growth and self-development. If the human being is an unfinished work in progress, then self-development becomes a crucial consideration for those who care about organizational health. Indeed, there are many spiritual pathways on the road to self-knowledge and inner growth. For the purposes of this book I would like simply to outline the eightfold path originally taught by the Buddha, and recapitulated by Rudolf

Steiner many years later. If we were to take up the words of Joseph Chilton Pierce and expand the potential of the neurocortex as a physical manifestation of human capacities, our organizations would benefit from some of these individual practices:

1. Each thought must be a true mirror of the outer world.
2. Every deed must be preceded by good reasoning.
3. Every word should have substance and meaning.
4. Our actions should fit in with others and with events around us.
5. We should strive to live in harmony with nature and with spirit—neither to be too fast, nor too slow; neither too active nor too lazy.
6. To make every effort to respond to what life calls forth from us.
7. To learn as much as possible from life, especially from our mistakes.
8. To ponder repeatedly our life's purpose.[50]

Imagine what the work place would be like if everyone, to the best of their abilities, took up the practice of the eightfold path. It would not be that everyone would be walking around with halos over their heads, but rather, following a practice such as the eightfold path, would provide for the quickening of each person's inner life, and the social benefits of self-awareness would make a difference in human interaction. Instead of performance driven organizations we have the possibility for true learning organizations.

Finally, I would like to add just one more aspect to this brief look at self-development. In many spiritual practices, reference is made to developing the chakras or lotus blossoms, which can unfold at various places of the body when one engages in exercises such as the one described above. In view of section two of this book and our extensive examination of the organs, I find it interesting that these also provide very special locations for spiritual development. For instance, the twelve-petalled lotus blossom develops at the heart chakra, the ten-petalled lotus blossom at the solar plexus, and the two-petalled lotus blossom in the region between the eyes. This seems to indicate that spiritual organs can be developed to serve our life intentions.

In chapter 1, I described a threefold methodology involving fact, feeling and essence. This approach is used in viewing each of the organs described in part two. For instance, we have just looked at the logic (fact), gestalt (feeling) and corpus callosum (essence) of the brain. In a later chapter we will see this threefolding in the structure of the bones as well. In synthesizing all the systems of the body, the organs can be seen in this threefold way as well—with the brain and lung more of the earth pole of *fact*, the kidney, liver and spleen in the middle realm of *feeling*, and the heart as the embodiment of *essence*. Indeed, threefolding is a fundamental characteristic of organic organizations. Monistic, single directive, hierarchical structures, going as far back as the pharaohs of Egypt, are indeed outdated. Polarity is part of the struggle we have experienced in the last century such as communism versus capitalism and east versus west. Threefolding is a direction for the future because it consists of collaborative, mutually supportive systems of interdependence. We will discuss this third way in more detail in the next part of this book.

PART III

OTHER ASPECTS OF
HUMAN PHYSIOLOGY

12. Is there a Skeleton in Your Closet?

IN PART TWO, we looked at specific organs that are the limbs of our tree representing organic organizations. In this section we will focus on the leaves of our tree—the senses, patterns and pigments. We will begin by looking at some of the archetypal forms found in our bones to see how they can inform us about organizational structure. Along the way we will also consider metamorphosis, inversion, threefolding and other secrets from the wisdom of the human body.

THE THREE ASPECTS REVEALED AGAIN

As a classroom teacher in middle school, bringing in a real human skeleton was always a sensational event. After the initial unveiling and some time for class commentary, we simply observed what we saw. We began with the head and found it remarkably small, round and concentrated. Except for the jaw, we could not find any moveable parts. The bones of the skull were, so to speak, fused together with sutures and we traced these ragged "seams." The top of the head was compared to a dome, and the front and sides had gaping holes where the sense organs had been. In fact, as we looked at the front of the skull we saw three parts, the forehead, the nasal region and the jaws. Next we examined the thorax. We counted the ribs and observed which ones were "floating" i.e., not attached to the sternum. I pointed out the rhythmic pattern of the ribs and how, with the cartilage, they must have been able to move in and out with each breath. Indeed, we once again saw three regions—those ribs attached at the top without cartilage, those in the middle with cartilage and the floating ribs at the bottom. Finally we looked at the limbs. We observed the upper arms and legs, the lower arms and legs with two bones each, and the hands and feet. Threes again! We marveled at the ball and socket joints of the shoulders and hips. Then we started to do some serious comparative anatomy, of which just a few aspects can be mentioned here.

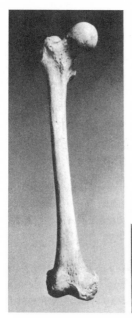

A thighbone and Kneeling Boys *by George Minne (Ghent, Belgium, 1898)*

For instance, we found some similarity between the ball of the femur and humerus—the rounded shapes at end of arm and leg bones—and the rounded shape of the skull. We also discussed how the limbs were the most mobile, thus giving humans the possibility for creative work. Within the skull there was a small part that echoed the thorax, namely in the nasal region that also involved the passage of air. Likewise in the skull there was a part that somewhat resembled the action of the limbs in that the jaw could move with chewing and with speech. Then, thanks to a tip from L. F. C. Mees, one of the authors consulted for this section, we all knelt with arms crossed and head slightly to one side. I asked them what part of human anatomy we were imitating. They responded immediately—the thighbone. I then showed the students a picture of the sculptures of the artist George Minne, and the resemblance was even more evident.[1]

We also did many drawings, such as of the lower jawbone and the upper thighbone. Repeatedly, we found similarities, correspondences, and examples of metamorphosis, or gradual changes and permutations of generic forms. This approach to teaching—making the students aware of the process of metamorphosis—awakens and develops imaginative perception. Much of what happened in our Waldorf middle school we left at the level of the phenomena, but for the purposes of this chapter I can draw a few more conceptual aspects.

The three aspects revealed once again in our study of the skeleton is an example of the notion of threefolding that has intrigued me for years. This has been referred to many times in this book, including the last chapter on the dual organs in which I mentioned the nerve/sense system, the metabolic system, and the rhythmic system. A simpler realization, used elsewhere, is the fundamental notions of thinking, willing, and feeling. This is one of the essential core principles behind organic organizations, as the threefold view of the human being allows for a more holistic approach, one that values not only cognition, but also emotional development and motive energy or will power.

Many of our contemporary issues are placed in a dual context: input–output, male–female, communist–capitalist, big oil–consumer. In my work with organizations I have found that when things exist in a state of polarization there is usually a problem. My task is often to help people create a third way, a bridging alternative that can unite opposites. We can see this concept revealed in human anatomy through our study of the skeleton. The head exemplifies rest and contemplation (thinking), while the limbs are all movement (will). There are those in groups who want to talk about things, to do analysis and study. Then there are those who want to move into action planning right away. Of course there is value in both approaches, yet they seem to fall into a kind of stalemate when left as dueling poles. The thorax is the third element; it can release the organization from the enchantment of stalemate and get things going again—not in the blind rush to action of the limbs or the frozen conceptualization of the head, but through rhythmic breathing, which serves both. This third aspect is the breathing, the part of the human being that unites sensory experiences with inner processes. We can also make the case that having just feeling and willing without thinking is unbalanced as well, all movement, action and experience but no order or reason given. The point is that we need all three aspects of this threefolding to function as humans and for organizations to be effective.

For this to happen one needs to develop an eye for how the whole resides in each part. Just as the complete human form can be seen in a simple thighbone, so also we need to look for the "genius" of the entire organization, the vision, in each committee, leader or working group. Rather than the duality of policy vs. task, we need to see how each step along the way can either manifest the destiny of the whole or detract from it. To work with the whole in each part one needs to practice attunement, the ability to resonate with the mission and vision of the whole even while performing a small task in one part of the organization. If the human being is indeed a complex matrix that exists on several levels—biological, emotional, environmental, spiritual to name just a few—then each action, even each utterance can set into motion a complex web of interactions that can bring about health and organic growth.

Before all this can come together, we need a degree of simultaneity. Each person needs to do their own rebalancing, groups need to attend to threefolding, and leaders need to value the language of head, heart and hand in planning meetings and strategy. No longer can we afford inattention to the "organs" of organizations. As with the liver that can quietly suffer for years with the intake of toxins or alcohol only to finally rebel, so too, our organizations have reached the breaking point of tolerance. Absenteeism, declining health of workers, dysfunctional meetings, and financial costs have increased. Too often we are not even asking the right questions. As stated throughout this book, the starting place has to be a whole-systems approach. Comparative anatomy or the examination of human organs presents an opportunity to start looking at our organizational phenomena with different eyes. Just as the bones give structure and form to the human body, so our organizations need to look at "framing" issues and tasks in a morphological manner, an approach that can be stimulated through comparative anatomy.[2]

13. Salt, Mercury, and Sulfur

In the pale light filtered between the slats of a dusty old railway car, three unsavory characters found themselves debating the next steps on their journey. Their clothing was eclectic. *S* wore the remains of a tattered brown suit and a stained bow tie, *Oh* wore the cheerful yellows and oranges of a clown costume of bygone days, and *M* was continually changing his attire based upon the fluctuating temperature and his passing fancy. Seldom had three such unusual figures gathered in one place. No wonder they had a hard time reaching agreement on anything.

Oh: Soon we will pull into Townsville! We'll need to hop out before the train stops and run for the side streets. Let's hope the bars are nearby, and perhaps we'll see the fairgrounds, there will be music and so many pockets to explore!

S: Forget about bars, fairs and music. We don't have any more money.

M: We can do what *Oh* said, relieve a few fairgoers of their unnecessary funds and then get something to eat and drink.

S: It looks like it will rain.

Oh: Then we can sneak under the flap of the circus tent and watch the clowns and tigers!

S: If we're caught, we'll spend the night you-know-where.

M: That would be unfortunate, but if we're careful we could catch the circus and even some discarded food.

Oh: Oh what fun!

S: While you blokes were chattering we missed our stop.

These three bumpkins were not always so eccentric, and if one knows something of their background it helps explain their responses. They had once been upright, taxpaying citizens with different approaches to life. *S* was a banker, *Oh* (you guessed it) a party entertainer and *M* had played a variety of prominent roles on stage. What had been "tendencies" over time became eccentricities, and thus the railway car. What were their tendencies?

In this chapter we will look at three substances or trace elements found in the human body and in nature—salt, mercury and sulfur. Unlike the comparative anatomy just covered, in which we saw three-folding in terms of form, here we will look at three substances that, when considered individually are one-sided, but taken together can collaborate to promote healthy group functioning. Each of these elements presents a type of person many of us may have encountered while working in groups.

SALT

These folks tend to focus on practical matters, everything that can be associated with the earth. Their tone and attitude speaks of gravity and limitations. Here we have the sediment that settles out of water. They are people who are grounded and wise in the ways of the world. Every situation is seen as an opportunity for practical problem solving and the application of experience. As seen in the above skit, the salt person is worried about the rain, going to jail, and notices that they have missed their stop—all practical matters. Though not exactly inspirational, these salt folks can be relied upon in group interactions for seeing the facts and using common sense.

SULFUR (OTHERWISE KNOWN AS OH)

Here we have just the opposite tendency of salt—a release from the constraints of gravity. Sulfur folks are full of light, imaginative suggestions and colorful possibilities. Like the air, they can disperse and move on with a moment's notice. They are oriented toward the periphery and always see others and the wider horizon of possibilities. Their enthusiasm can be quickly consumed and without regret, they move on to the next opportunity. In the story, the sulfur influence was seen in playful suggestions such as going to the fair and sneaking under the tent flaps. These people live on the periphery, always seeing possibilities around the next corner. They can also see the big picture and love to imagine new and exciting changes in an organization.

MERCURY

People who typify mercury live in the alternation between light and gravity, moving up and down, in and out in a continual search for balance. Mercury types work with rhythm and can negotiate between extremes. They are good interpreters and can smooth out differences between friends as seen in our brief dialogue when M bridges the worry of going to jail (S) and the possibility of finding discarded food (an appeal to OH). Mercury types make good mediators in group interactions as they love to move back and forth between different perspectives.

An inexpensive form of entertainment is to sit in a meeting and listen for *salt*, *sulfur*, and *mercury*. They will certainly pose with different names and most likely will be better dressed than our three railcar travelers, yet their voices can be discerned if we listen for them. When the stakes are high, the three approaches can escalate to arguments in which each one seems to say, "See it my way!" Solutions to a problem also tend to be proffered in one of the three styles. Do you want to put up a new building? The *Oh* people will get very excited about all the designs, the new spaces, the meetings, and the functions now possible. The salt folks will focus on the capital campaign and the financial realities. Mercury folks will move between the two groups and mediate possible solutions. If the three work constructively together, there will be a good chance the building will happen.

On another level, we each have the three substances within us. We can select to look at an issue through the eyes of salt, mercury or sulfur if we so choose. Some situations require more of one substance and less of another. Rather than be tossed about in the chemical meeting of group work, we can clear our lens, see what is at work, and calibrate the response that would be most helpful. It really helps to step back and ask ourselves what we are observing. Are we experiencing too much salt or sulfur? Do we need more mercury? One practical tool in meetings is to take advantage of the "help" each of our three friends can give. For example, I favor using a healthy dose of "salt" in reports, as the group needs clarity, dispassion, and a straightforward style in gleaning the facts from the person sharing a report. There is nothing worse, in my view, than a report that is full of flights of fancy, subjective opinions and entertaining tangents. Reports can use a healthy dose of salt. In contrast, a discussion by its very nature has a strong element of mercury, as people go back and forth, looking at one scenario or another, and weighing the possibilities. So where is sulfur in our meetings? There are many aspects, one of which has to do with the inner imagining of those who are listening, the quality of letting ideas light up and stir the imagination. Also, when leaving a meeting is it good to "let go" of what has happened so as to move on, and this is a sulfur contribution. Nevertheless, the best use of these three friends is to remind yourself they will be present in organizations and let them work for you in meetings. Consciously look for and observe their behavior and then let these observations become tools for healthy human interactions. This cast of characters can provide another lens through which to view group dynamics.

14. Sense Perception: Eye and Ear

W E HAVE LOOKED mainly at the internal aspects of the human being—the organs, the skeleton and substances such as salt, mercury and sulfur. Now we will turn our exploration outward to the world of sense perception.

One way to ascertain the vibrancy of an organization is to look at how it interfaces with its clients and the wider community. When that relationship is strong, many successes are possible. But when there is a gap—a disconnect—then the core mission of the organization is quickly compromised. This can be seen in examples like a car company that loses touch with the tastes and needs of buyers and incentives and thus fails to lure more customers into the showroom. A bank that writes too many questionable mortgages starts to lose money and a private school that loses touch with the parent body will have enrollment drops. There are few things as fundamental to success as the relationship of an organization to its community.

The success stories of organizations that interface positively can be found, for example, in some of our more innovative technology companies. When Steve Jobs or Bill Gates introduces a new product, it is fascinating to watch. Rather than a one-dimensional, "talking" presentation, they put on a show, complete with visuals, demonstrations, sounds, and experiences that capture the attention of the audience. They are very good at using a multisensory approach to new product introductions. Of course the products have to match the hype in terms of quality, otherwise they would not be commercially successful, but the launching is often indicative of leadership that is in tune with the public, with their wishes and tastes. This multisensory approach to community development leads me to a more detailed examination of the importance of human senses as windows between internal organizational dynamics and what happens in the surrounding world. We all know that seeing is better than just telling, and that experiencing is better for retention than just seeing. However, are there other senses beyond seeing, hearing and touching that can open up new pathways between organizations and their community? Are we using all the sense organs of our body, and if not, how can we activate them?

> The range of what we think and do
> Is limited by what we fail to notice,
> And because we fail to notice
> That we fail to notice
> There is little we can do
> To change
> Until we notice
> How failing to notice
> Shapes our thoughts and deeds.
> — R.D. LAING[3]

As beautifully described in this poem by the noted psychiatrist, Laing, we often fail to notice because we have not used our senses. We listen to the weather report and forget to look outside, we read long reports rather than observe firsthand what is going on in a meeting, we often talk more than we listen. Thus the range of experience is narrowed and we cut ourselves off from the world.

This can change when we begin to reactivate our senses, for our sense organs are portals to the environment. We open ourselves through our senses and take in valuable information, process it, and then use our senses again to share with others what we have worked with. We have to want to reach out and experience, to want to open the portals, in order for the world to find us. We especially need to cultivate attentiveness. The more intense our attention, the more easily the soul can continue to carry the sense experiences later as memory pictures. The crucial first step is attentiveness. One of the most interesting phenomena in organic organizations is when we start to attend to something it begins to change, grow, and improve. So, for example, if we listen and observe the use of air time in a meeting—who speaks when and how much—often the situation begins to improve right under our noses, so to speak, and people start to share air time with more consideration of others. That which receives our attention becomes more important.

When we perceive something directly, as objective perception, there is at first nothing of ourselves in it. The percept can and should stand

alone. Too often we jump to conclusions based upon very little information. I urge more of a holding of attentiveness—a space in which the
phenomena are allowed to speak their own language. Listen, observe,
taste, touch, and smell with inner quiet and an openness of soul to the
external impressions. For indeed a sense impression is characterized
by the very fact that attention is concentrated to the point of eliminating judgment. As soon as we jump into saying "that is sweet," or "that
is blue" we have a judgment. One of the central goals I want to articu-
late for organic organ-izations is that we try and hold a judgment-free
state of full attention open as long as possible so that we can expand
the range of perceptions. For example, as an exercise, read the poem
by Laing cited above, listen with full attention without any interpretation, liking or disliking. Let the sounds speak. Let his voice be heard
without your own coloration. In our path to self-awareness, exercises
such as this can help us to hold attentiveness in our organizations.

This kind of attentiveness can help us to fully perceive and better understand situations. Granny D, the elderly woman who walked
across the United States to call for campaign finance reform, said
during a talk at High Mowing School on October 1, 2006, that if we
strive to understand, we are less likely to apply simplistic solutions to
geopolitical situations. Do we really see the people involved in these
situations? For example, if 600,000 Iraqis have died since the start of
the war intended to "save" them from Saddam Hussein, what have we
accomplished? Moreover, is 600,000 just a number? To understand in
these circumstances, we need to clear our lenses and perceive without so much filtering by the media, thereby gaining a chance to better
understand what is happening in our world.

One thing that can help those working in organizations to expand
the range of perception is to activate more than the traditional five
senses. The senses can be increased to the twelve detailed below as
described by Rudolf Steiner in his lectures now called "Foundations of
Human Experience" and expanded by others like Albert Soesman.

Senses directed especially at our own physical body:

> Touch
> Life sense
> Self-movement sense
> Balance

Senses that help the individual human soul relate to the world:
Smell
Taste
Vision
Temperature or Warmth Sense
Senses directed inwardly help the human spirit develop
    socially:
Hearing
Language or word sense
Conceptual or thought sense
Sense of the other person's "I"[4]

We will look at each of these twelve briefly, particularly in relation to organizational perception.

TOUCH

We "wake up" when we touch something because we become conscious of our boundaries. We are in fact separated from things around us, and the resistance we experience in touch reminds us of this bounded existence. With touch we also give certainty to something, and we use touch to express intimacy. Touch, also, has wider implications as noted by Dr. John Ratey: "A famous study by Tiffany Field at TRI showed that premature human babies who were massaged for fifteen minutes, three times a day, for ten days gained forty-seven percent more weight than similar 'preemies' who were given the same diet but not massaged" [5] In addition, there was also an economic side effect in that those infants that had experienced extensive touch through massage could be released from the hospital earlier.

The writer Novalis once said, "Touching is separation and connection both at once."[6] And this wonderful expression shows how touch is really an unsolved riddle, for no matter how hard we try, we can never really get inside the things we touch. I can touch the arm of this chair in which I sit, but although I am thereby more connected to it, I immediately become aware of how separate it is from me. The chair will always be outside of me.

This issue of boundaries is prevalent in many organizations today. Where does my space end and yours begin? Many people today simply accept the prevailing notion that a person's importance is indicated by the size of the office and the amount of space afforded to that person's work. Answering service cubicles provide us with another aspect of the artificial allocation of space and the illusion of boundaries, for the sound travels over those dividers. In addition to physical boundaries, many others come up in my conversations with teachers and parents. People are searching for the boundaries between work and home, between personal and professional demands. Some people have fallen into difficulties because they have confided too much in another person, and unspoken boundaries are then broken, like the new teacher who shares too much personal information with a parent only to have it come back to haunt her. There is a greater need than ever to give careful attention to one's own boundaries.

LIFE SENSE

This is one of the hardest senses to describe, as many of us are only vaguely aware of it. Rather than having a location in one particular spot, as with eyes and ears, we experience our life sense generally in the well-being of our physical constitution. If we are hungry, thirsty, sick, or well, we have an overall feeling of ease or discomfort. In addition, this is related to the fact that the parasympathetic nervous system helps regulate the internal organs such as heart and lungs so that the cortex is free to work with sight, speech, hearing, movement, and so on.[7] The sympathetic and parasympathetic nervous system spread out over the entire body, thus serving our general well-being and sense of life.

Pain is an extreme manifestation of the life sense, and one of the most important. In fact, pain helps us get at the real problem because it can educate us, so it is not good to suppress pain routinely by taking aspirin, for instance. The life sense is an early warning system that keeps the body under constant surveillance. When we are tired, for example, it is often due to sensory overload and the life sense tells us to slow down. There is a body of literature now praising slowness and challenging the pace of life that many people are forced to perpetuate.[8] In *The Sabbath* by Wayne Muller, a doctor recounts that when he is tired and too busy, he routinely prescribes a lot of tests for his patients. However, when he has had time for a walk, a nap or some down time, his intuition is able to give him a pretty good sense of what is needed and he can prescribe just one test to confirm his diagnosis.[9] Imagine what we would save in health care dollars if we could just get the medical establishment to support doctors in slowing down.

In terms of organic organ-izations, one test question would be— if working within it enhanced our personal and professional growth or inhibited it? Healthy organizations support the development of those working together, find ways to remove hindrances and allow for new opportunities. Our life sense can tell us, on an instinctive level, if we feel this environmental support in the workplace as well as other situations.

SELF-MOVEMENT

This can also be called the "muscle sense," since we feel our movements mainly through the action of our muscles, whether chewing or running. These movements are also very much connected to our intentions. For example, if I want to reach out for another sip from my cup of coffee, I inwardly move toward it before my hand actually moves. Our sense of self-movement is an awareness of our plan of action, our intention to realize certain goals.

Many schools call upon me for advice on strategic planning, and when I am able to conduct direct facilitation, what has impressed me— when this work has been done well—is that so much more than a document is created. When a group takes on strategic planning, the entire community begins to move, change, and open up. Like the life plan of an individual, the planning process for an organization reveals the vast network of encounters that have made the institution possible. After some strategic planning, a school can have a new sense of self-movement that truly propels it to the next level of its development. Time is activated to serve organic growth.

BALANCE

Thanks to the semicircular canals, at ninety degrees to each other in the human ear, we are able to achieve balance, thus freeing human beings to do much productive work with their hands. When our state of equilibrium is disturbed we feel the need to recover something of ourselves that has been lost in the world. Balance is a spatial sense that puts us together in a common space with others. We are able to stand upright so that we can determine our standpoint, meet other people and take initiative. This is possible because when we are in balance we experience our "I," our own particular point of view.

Organic organ-izations are able to rebalance and regain equilibrium when external challenges occur. Non-organic organizations are brittle, and crack when challenged. An evident example of this is that in the days after hurricane Katrina, some organizations, such as churches and many of the not-for-profit service organizations were able to deliver help relatively quickly, while FEMA and other governmental agencies were not. One cannot explain these Katrina-related responses just due to size. To take initiative requires not just focus and hard work, but also balance in weighing up the needs and responding appropriately.

SMELL

If one walks into a house after a family has had a meal, one can sometimes smell what has been cooked. Our sense of smell is extremely discerning, and often we know within moments if something smells good or bad, rotten, aromatic or disgusting. We can call smell a hygiene sense and one that also points to issues of morality. In the Parcival legend, the knight Amfortas receives a wound because of his sin—his seduction away from his duties. Creatures such as the evil Orcs in Tolkein's *Return of the King* are often described as foul smelling, whereas cleanliness is associated with smelling good. The nose discerns.

In ancient Egyptian times, the physician would give the patient a general examination "in which the physician's sense of smell was as much a guide as palpation, percussion, and pulse taking."[10] Why would a doctor use the sense of smell for diagnosis? Use of the senses as a diagnostic tool is a natural development of survival skills. To this day, unlike other senses, smell has a hotline to the emotional brain and does not have to pass through the thalamus first. This is a carryover from ancient times when smell was used for hunting, mating, and a warning system for danger.[11]

The nose is also one of our most human facial characteristics. Actors know that, to alter their faces drastically, all they need to do is to wear a false nose, and thus the entire persona undergoes a change. There are also people who have "a nose" for what is going on in a group. They can sniff out all sorts of intrigue and follow up on stray bits of information. Like a dog on a trail, the sense of smell can lead to all sorts of discoveries that can either be shared or buried for future times. There is an old saying that captures the organizational implications of the sense of smell: "Noses in, fingers out." A good leader has a "nose" for what is going on throughout the organization but delegates much of the day-to-day work to others. Oversight without interference is a worthy goal for productive work.

TASTE

Whereas smell just enters the body, taste is subject to the voluntary opening or closing of the mouth. As such, the mouth is more private and tasting takes place inside. In earlier times medicine men had a refined sense for judging. As Albert Soesman notes, "The taste of each plant told them whether it would have an effect on the liver, on the kidneys, or on the eyes."[12] If we can begin to reclaim some of this refined power of judgment through taste we can make progress in nutritional choices that would support bodily health. Often however, we are just content to determine if something is salty, bitter, sour, or sweet. Of the four, the prevalence of sweet things has dulled the other aspects of taste. Wet foods give us a sense of well being, while sour things refresh and activate. Bitterness gives us the experience of resistance for the will—it grounds us, while salt adds more to the conceptual life and human thinking.[13] Physiologically, taste receptors near the tip of the tongue are especially sensitive to sweetness, while salty and sour tastes are noticed mostly on the sides of the tongue. Bitter foods are most noticed by the back of the tongue and the soft palate. Dr. John Ratey mentions, "Recently, Japanese researchers have identified a fifth primary taste category, called *iumami,* which is Japanese for delicious or yummy. This proposed fifth receptor may be a taste enhancer—a receptor that makes food taste delicious."[14]

What are the taste buds of an organization? As with wine tasting, one has to learn to take samples and then let them speak. Before launching a new product or program, it is helpful to try the taste test first. This could be in the form of a trial run, a report, or a simulation.

Just as our taste buds can tell us if something is sweet or sour, so a sample can help us get a foretaste of what is to come. A focus group could then help test the new program or product and reflect back what they experienced. We need the sensory perceptions of those around us to make good decisions.

TEMPERATURE

It is interesting that we truly experience our warmth sense only when there is a difference between our own temperature and that of the world around us. If I go outside on a cold, snowy day, I feel the bite in the air in relation to the warmth under my down parka. There is always some sort of flow between the environment and me when the temperature sense is activated. Cold makes us contract, heat makes us want more room. Yet the temperature sense is also very much related to how we attend to things. For example, Soesman indicates that: "When we are interested, when we open ourselves, we either get something back, or we get nothing back. When we get nothing back we are cold, but when we do receive something we experience a sense of warmth."[15] Thus even a tired guest lecturer can feel energized and warm after a successful talk. The audience gives back warmth in the form of interest, attention, and stimulating questions.

Organic organ-izations would do well to value the warmth factor, not only as a crucial element in evolution as described earlier, but also as a generative capacity in drawing people together. When we capture the attention and interest of coworkers in a worthwhile project, this absorption brings warmth and inclusion. I often advise groups that are having difficulties, such as low-level conflict, to stop talking and get out there and do a project. Real tasks that generate enthusiasm activate the temperature sense and help people feel part of the community.

LANGUAGE, CONCEPT, AND "I" SENSES

In the Monday, October 2, 2006 edition of *USA Today*, Bill Gates is quoted as saying, "As you get high up in the organization, the jobs really demand great individual thinking skills, being great with people, and great with strategy. However, when you want that combination, it's rare. And I don't know why it is." Moreover, he is right; this particular combination is crucial and yet not often found in people. Some tend to be better at thinking, sensing ideas and working with concepts and strategy, and others seem to be more people oriented, able to communicate and sense the intentions or "I" of others. Putting them together really involves all three of the higher senses described here.

The language sense encompasses being able to listen to what is behind a person's words, to penetrate through everyday speech to understand what is trying to express itself though the spirit of the other individuality. This is a huge challenge at a time when language in general has been devalued, when responses are often monosyllabic, and the media in an attempt to conserve space, "dumbs down" the use of the word. For many there is not a large vocabulary base to begin with, but this loss of the language sense means that people are far less attuned to the subtleties of speech. I feel there is a correspondence between loss of language skill and the rising need for conflict resolution in our organizations. It is not just about listening, but rather the ability to perceive the intentions of others through language.

This rises to a higher level still when we talk about the "I" sense, or the ability to sense the individuality of the other person. Earlier we spoke of touch as the sense that helps us experience boundaries. With the "I" sense, we are again dealing with boundaries, but now with the ability to break through and truly see the other person. Again, it is a great need of our time. So often I hear people saying, "I am not seen, am not appreciated, not recognized." This is often interpreted in an outer sense as the need for more airtime, a promotion, or new role. Yet many times when I investigate further, those making these remarks are really asking for something more fundamental. They want to be seen as people, recognized as an individual. This requires a particular sense activity, and when it is active, contributes to the kind of people skills referred to by Bill Gates.

Finally, I want give a sense of concept. In this realm, we are dealing purely with spirit and nonmaterial reality. A person with this sense can sit in a meeting and visualize the ideas being presented by someone else and can see them as vividly as if the new product were already on the table. Seeing the ideas of others is also very much related to building strategy and connecting these ideas. Innovation, as discussed elsewhere in this book, arises first in the mind and then starts to take form in reality. Experimentation with the idea helps it find form, and new inspirations may gather around the first one. It is fascinating to observe the evolution of the cell phone for example, as more and more thought power is devoted to the development of this practical device. Those who work in technology are in fact working with one of the highest spirit senses, the sense of thought that brings innovation into reality.

I will mention at this point, and before moving on to a more in-depth examination of the eye and ear, that nowhere have I found the twelve senses more active in an educational setting than in a Waldorf school. Starting with kindergarten and moving right through the younger grades, children are given many opportunities to develop their body oriented senses of touch, movement, life and balance through crafts, spatial exercises, eurythmy, knitting, house building, circle activities and much more. In working with curriculum throughout the grades, Waldorf students experience the teaching material in multi-modal ways. Rather than emphasizing just the visual sense, they prepare the foods to taste and smell, they develop their hearing through music instruction from an early age, and the social senses are cultivated in a wide array of special subjects. Finally, the pictures and experiences are allowed to ripen in time to become articulation in language, original thinking, and a sense for the unique contribution of others. I urge the reader to visit a nearby Waldorf school and walk through the building with the twelve senses in mind. You will see them all at work.

Now, because they are so important for our participation as adults in the workplace, I would like to develop the senses of seeing and hearing further through a somewhat more detailed examination of the eye and ear.

Eyes

How is it possible for the whole organism to live in the part, and for the part to be integral to the "whole?" To examine this riddle more closely, let us look at the development of the human eye as an example of inversion.

Beginning with the brain vesicle, the illustrations below show a process of invagination in stages until the other side of the "cup" is reached. As if in response to this contact, Dr. Husemann indicates that the enfolded tissue begins a further differentiation process to transform itself into the retina. This inner imaginative action is answered by a similar movement from the outside, in which a piece of skin (ectoderm) is brought to the inside, which then forms the lens. At the point where the lens becomes transparent the whole process has reached the stage of inversion: what began as a separate movement inward in the form of the eye vesicle has broken through to the light on the opposite side.[16]

If you gaze at these forms for a while, you begin to understand their revealed mystery. That which is open, unformed, common, begins to change with an impulse that comes from the environment. The movement gathers momentum and a second opening or opportunity is carved out. Finally, in the last two drawings we see a third imagination: a cup within the cup. That which was outside is now inside, an organ has been formed. This organ, the eye. contains the light that surrounded it from the beginning. The outer light has become inner light. This organ formation through inversion is a Grail process—the cup is formed to hold a drop of the divine.

In this organ formation there is a conversation between the impulse of the cosmic light and matter. its receptacle. These two converse, and the lower matter forms itself into a cup to serve the higher purpose. In the process one becomes free, and the eye can now see. Goethe said, "If the sun were not in me how could I see the light?" If one simply walks along the road of life, one can see things. However, stopping to talk with someone, one begins to *see* the personality. the spark that lives in that individuality. One can see the surface or one can see the light within the cup. How far are we willing to look?

What are the implications of eye development on organizations? One can relate the above process to the founding of a nonprofit, for example. Usually there is an impulse in the community that creates a stir; people begin to talk with one another and an initiative is taken. Parents gather in living rooms to

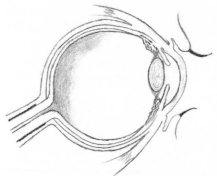

discuss a possible charter school, and as they work together greater differentiation occurs, plans become clearer, the form takes shape. Eventually, if the initiative is successful, a new entity finds itself in the community, something that is of the community but now also distinct from the environment. Then the process continues, as the impulses go through an inversion process and the individuals are hired and programs are developed internally. One hopes that at least a drop of the originating impulse/vision resides in the individual teachers and staff members as they now work from inside the organ. A school, company, business, or museum are in their highest aspect "organs" of community.

When groups forget their community roots then aspects of the organization such as profits, gross margins and mergers take over. When this process goes too far, the entity becomes cut off from the community or shareholders and there is an inner implosion just like the experience that occurred with the corporation Enron. Invagination goes too far and the walls between the organ and the environment are too numerous or too thick. People forget that we are all born from the light (eye) or that we are all part of a community we call humanity. The bankruptcy of a company or the closing of a museum is a "return" to the early stage of undifferentiated stage of oneness with the environment.

One way to help organizations avoid "bankruptcy" is to maintain the health of the organization along the way. The eye can help us with this as well. We have not yet spoken of the lens, that part that helps the eye focus and yet also serves as protection for the cornea. Similar to contact lenses that need to be cleaned periodically, individuals in organizations need to "clear" their lenses as well. This clearing can occur through a crisis or natural catastrophe, but is better served as a way of life rather than a traumatic event. As a consistent practice in an organization, the clearing of lenses involves wiping away preconceived notions, examining assumptions and learning to "see again." In one example of this need for clearing, I have found that when an internal candidate applies for a new leadership role in an organization, it is especially important that those involved in the process clear their "lenses." There is a natural tendency to remember some incident, recall a situation even from years ago that influences the decision of whether to hire. Neither the candidate nor the organization is well-served when dirt on the lenses impairs our vision. Let the internal candidate go through the same process as the others, ask the same questions, but above all, see the person as if for the first time. After all, our cells are continually being replaced, we have new experiences, and we are continually growing and learning. We should ask the question, who is this person really? Can I set aside my assumptions and experiences from the past and see this person in this new context? Many a school or organization has deprived itself of good people due to a failure to clear the lenses of perception.

EARS

When Ray Charles (Robinson) was seven years old, he began to lose his eyesight. With the limitations of medicines in 1937, his mother could do little as the world gradually faded from his vision. However, she knew that unless he learned self-sufficiency early on, he would be condemned to life a life as a "cripple" as dramatically depicted in the movie *Ray*. In the movie, we see him one day as he stumbles over a rocking chair and bursts out crying for his mother's help. Instead of responding, even though she is nearby in the kitchen, she silently waits. Ray picks himself up and tilts his head as he hears the kettle whistling on the stove. Then he hears the sound of a horse and carriage passing the open window. With a new sense of discovery, Ray listens more acutely and hears a cricket that he follows on all fours until he catches it. In a moving scene portrayed in the film, he stands there in the kitchen, looking up to his silently sobbing mother and says, "I can hear you too, Mom." From that day on, he used his ears not just for his amazing music, but for navigating through life as well. Ray Charles lived to raise children, overcome a heroin addiction, perform on road tours and cut many records all thanks to that moment when his mother gave him the gift of using his ears.

The other day I spent a few minutes observing the ears of my students in class; suddenly a completely new perspective opened up. I

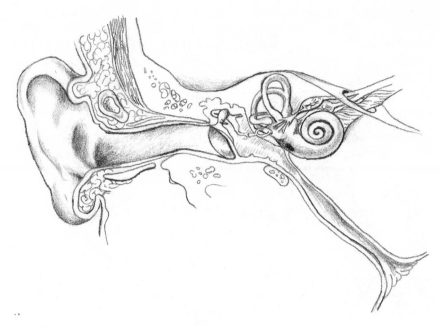

saw all sorts of ears in one room. I saw petite and gently sculpted ears; I saw ears with long lobes and some with barely any; I saw ears that curved in so much they began to resemble snail shells and ears that were open and almost flat; some ears were rounded and others almost pointed—although there were none that came close to the alien Spock's ears from *Star Trek*. Dividing the ear into proportions of upper, middle and lower ear, I found great variety as well. Especially notice-able were the ones with a large upper region, which belonged to the profound thinkers in the group. Finally, some had their ears conve-niently covered, leaving me with no choice but to speculate if this was intentional or not.

This observational exercise led me to look for some detailed descriptions of what ears are all about. We know that the ear is a very delicate structure that lies in a cave-like shell filled with liquid. Like the patterns on a snail's shell, a spiral form leads gradually toward the inner ear. The passage to the eardrum is like a vortex in its funnel. The ossicles of the middle ear are like a minute limb system that passes on the rhythms they receive to the membrane of the inner ear, only to be taken still deeper into the inner regions of the cochlea.

This amazing inner ear combines the spiraling surface with spi-ral twisting of the vortex, a microcosm of the oceans' movements left visible on sandy beaches. Sensitive to the smallest imaginable movements through its fluid content, the vortex is molded into the most delicate, differentiated of all sense organs. Theodore Schwenk describes this further:

> As the sounds of the external world enter, whole vortex trains pass through the fluid of the inner ear. In connection with this a sorting out of the rhythms takes place, by which the long wave trains of the low frequency notes reach the end of the basilar membrane, while the short, quick rhythms of the high notes fade away right at the start.... The sorting that takes place in the inner ear can thus be compared to an analysis, a splitting up the constituent components, followed, however, by a synthesis, in which the human being reassembles what has been separated, piecing the sound images together again in a body of sound. This process is analogous to that of metabolism, where all food is at first broken down before being built up again and integrated into the organism in a composition fitting to the nature of each human being. This is a creative activity in the realm of number ratios, on the one hand in the realm of sound or music, on the other in the process of breaking down and building up of substances, where whole-number proportions prevail.[17]

Thus we can say that the process of hearing echoes the digestive processes, or that hearing is a metabolism of sound. When we listen, sounds are broken down and then built up again according to musical number ratios. The fluid elements in waves and vortices play rhythmically on the sensitive boundary surfaces of the ear, making it an invisible sense organ in the human being. These rhythmic movements reveal what we experience in sound, welling up to fill the human soul with content. Our inner life is nourished by what we hear. Flowing liquids in the inner ear provide an opening for us to experience the most sensitive sounds that have the lawfulness of musical rhythms and numerical proportions. The soul is refined as the sounds move through us. We become inwardly alive when we truly listen.

Because of the emphasis on physiology in this book, it is interesting to notice how the body is affected by different sounds. We all know how upsetting the fingernail on the blackboard can be. We feel deep discomfort right through the body when someone makes that unpleasant sound. Likewise, if you have a neighbor in the next apartment that plays the violin off-key, it can drive you crazy. But more specifically, those who have worked with music and physiology have said that singing, especially one's own, positively affects the kidneys; that the striking of wood instruments affects the bones; and the silver flute enhances healthy breathing. Furthermore, I found references in Albert Soesman's book on the senses that the violin, when played beautifully, can be felt all over on the skin, whereas the horn or trumpet penetrates right through to the blood. Throughout history the lyre or harp has been used to soothe, as in bedtime lullabies, since it affects the nerves.[18] These observations cannot be proven in the context of this brief description, but you can try them out the next time you listen to music and see if they have any validity.

Where is the ear of an organization? Are we frequently so busy that we hear just sound bites and not full sentences? Have we not all experienced instances of "selective hearing"? Most organizations are so task oriented that the people within them seem satisfied with constructing outward leaning structures. By this I mean boards that respond to shareholders, committees that are given specific mandates, and public relations departments that put a good "spin" on whatever happens. Indeed, if one stops to look at the structures within organizations, one finds that most are geared to the outer world. I propose that organizations that are future oriented will need to develop more fully the functions of the inner ear.

The organizations of today need the inner chamber, the space apart, that allows for work that may at first appear totally unrelated to the stated mission, but may have a great deal to do with ultimate sustainability, or even success. What would such an inner chamber look like? It would need to be formed by eliminating most of what occupies us on a daily basis. Take away the agendas, the reports, the management issues and the rest, and begin with an empty space. Find a few people who are willing to think out of the box, willing to suspend assumptions, and willing to live with ambiguity. Take them away from the usual scene of work, and begin by asking questions that "no one has dared to ask." Collect those questions that usually lie below the surface, and bring them back repeatedly each time the group meets. Let the questions do the "talking." Push aside all urges to find answers. Live in the questioning mode. Like the sounds that enter the inner ear, let them be disassembled. Then gradually listen for patterns, like the rhythms of the ear, and through the grouping and sensing of the "fundamental" questions; let some rise to the surface. Only after weeks of this echoing process can one then try to rebuild. Let the insights and inspirations find you when they are ready to. In the inner ear, the meaning rises to meet us, we cannot seek it out. Deciding what we hear, or seeking meaning too early, kills it. In the inner chamber of an organization, we need the reverse dynamic; we are nothing until the sounds find us. We can provide space and gradually over time develop the inner "limbs" that can become ever more sensitive. However, the most important thing is to remain for a while within the "shell" of protection from the outer world. In short, I suggest that just as a city has its parks, each organization needs a sanctuary, a place apart. This could be something as simple as a small meditation room or a more expansive greenhouse area with lots of plants, running water, some interesting sculptures and quiet places to sit and reflect.

On a lighter note, I have always carried images of not-yet famous entrepreneurs holed up in a garage working on a software program, in a dark attic experimenting with light bulbs or bent over a small desk working on a new formula. Images of Ray Charles all alone after hours at his keyboard also haunt me. What is it about genius? Whence comes our creativity? When do inspirations find us? Those fleeting moments are often when we are in our inner sanctuary, away from the noise of the world.

Just as our peripheral vision seems to have narrowed over time, we are gradually losing the ability to hear. Several people have told me over the years that they have read studies attesting to hearing loss, often caused by exposure to loud noises. No longer just a phenomenon of old age, hearing is less differentiated, and people are less attentive to the nuances of sound. When we cannot hear the inflections and subtleties of speech we have more struggles in working together. Organizations need both listening/speaking participants and the sanctuary of the inner ear for spiritual renewal.

In the cerebellum (Latin for "little brain"), the motor and sensory systems roughly parallel each other; much cortical space is devoted to the work of hands, arms, lips, mouth, feet, and so on.[19] This means that the work of the senses are coordinated and integrated in the human brain in a way that allows millions of interactions within seconds. The work of the eyes and ears and indeed all the senses depends upon a high level of sophisticated integration. Likewise, in an organization one cannot plan and design every step of the way, in fact, that slows things down and hinders creativity. As with the sensory system and the cerebellum, one has to clear the "pathways" and trust in the positive work that organic systems perform when the human conditions are healthy. Organic organ-izations stress the unconscious yet valuable web of sensory integration.

PART IV

LEADERSHIP

15. Testing our Metal as Leaders

W HEN RESEARCHING HUMAN physiology, in particular the organs, I frequently encountered references to various metals in our bodies. For instance, I found that the brain, pancreas, heart, muscles, and bones contain three parts per million of copper, while the liver contains seven and a half parts copper.[1] This led me to ask what role metals play in human physiology. Again, using our threefold method to look at the trace minerals from the point of view of facts, feeling and essence, we will gain a deeper understanding of their role. Furthermore, if there is a story line here, I would like to discover whether there is a correlation between the metals and leadership. For instance, former Prime Minister of England Margaret Thatcher is often called "The Iron Lady." I question, for instance, what it means to lead with iron as opposed to copper. (The metals covered here will be grouped as opposites or related geographically.) Why has gold been so often associated with kings and queens throughout history? Moreover, why are there references to planets, such as "the sun king?" I took up the hypothesis that there could be a connection between the metals and leadership and thus began another journey of exploration.

Iron and Copper

Iron permeates the earth everywhere and is one of the world's most abundant metals. It gives pigment and rich color to rocks, plants and even human skin. It is mined in about fifty countries, but Australia and Brazil are the chief iron ore exporters. Almost all—ninety-eight percent—of iron ore is used in steel making.[2] Thus, much of our industrial world is an iron enterprise, from cars to appliances to ordinary tools. Iron is still used extensively in construction and weaponry. The adjectives that come to mind in describing iron are strength, energy and courage.

Spiritual initiatives need to find a "home" on the earth because they need to incarnate. Ideas have to become action for change to happen. Great personalities in human history were able to assist these initiatives and ideas to do just that. For example, many wrote about slavery, but it took people like Harriet Tubman and Abraham Lincoln to change the reality of the situation with their leadership skills of strength, energy and courage. Determination is a force of iron in the world.

Rather than conforming to existing realities, an iron leader follows the guidance of an inner compass. This compass, instead of floating off in esoteric theory, is based upon geographical reality; the initiative is thus grounded. Just as a meteor (cosmic iron) seeks earth, so determination has practical outcomes. Iron gives us the presence of mind, the capacity to do things in a practical way. Like the popular products of iron, tools and utensils, we say that a determined person has "steel in his blood," or one has to "steel oneself" for an important event.

On the one hand, iron likes to retain its form once cast into an implement, yet at the same time it "breathes" in that it gives and takes in oxygen easily. This is mirrored in the human body as noted by Wilhelm Pelikan, "Through iron, the breathing process is closely bound up with that of the blood formation.... In the hemoglobin iron confronts protein, taking hold of it as the latter decomposes and incorporating it healingly into the organism."[3]

In ancient mythology and folklore the figure of the blacksmith stands at his forge of fire with hammer and sweat forming, shaping tools for work. With the help of his iron efforts, work could now be done that elevated humans above nature. Cooking implements and tools for farming and hunting became extensions of human limbs. With our implements we were able to care for ourselves more efficiently, produce things, and exercise our freedom of action. No longer bound by mere survival, humans could aspire to do things creatively, such as draw or weave.

We can compare the blacksmith and his forge to the inner battles of contemporary leaders who seek to transform dead laws of the past through entrepreneurship and innovation. Gutenberg's invention of moveable type made reading possible for the masses, which affected the control previously held by the church. Erricson's invention of the ironclad submarine changed the course of the Civil War. The iron leader needs awakened consciousness and inner fortitude.

Unless it is transformed, iron can bring with it the forces of death. This is outwardly evident in our long history of iron weaponry, from swords to cannon to modern jet fighters. How can we overcome the death forces in iron in our world? Looking to our physiology for an answer we have a good example in human blood, especially in the way hemoglobin/iron content of the blood is overcome by the "I," our inner resolve. This means that something that could become death is transformed into service as described by Pelikan in his book on metals: "Iron in the blood no longer obeys the laws of nature, but the will impulses of the 'I.'"[4] When we decide to do something, our resolve (iron) can overcome our environmental or natural influences, as in a heroic determination to climb Mount Everest. Every movement we make can become a free deed rather than a reflex. In our conscious movements we are creative; sickness and death are transformed into service for human evolution. Young children who are given opportunities to move, act out a story or do a dramatization are bringing will impulses and creativity into their futures far beyond their immediate situations.

Iron's essence provides a leader with assertiveness. An anemic person, who lacks sufficient iron, is unable to bring warmth and energy to a task and suffers from a lack of resolution; one is poor in blood, weak in "I," and unequal to earthly tasks. Our organizations have many directionless people who cannot carry things through, who don't have enough iron in the blood. Thus, an anemic organization has trouble getting things done. Like a hamster in a cage, discussions go round and round due to the lack of any real progress. Things are said but not acted upon, and follow-through is weak. The same topics tend to come up repeatedly, and people gradually disengage.

In my consulting work, I have seen both anemic and iron organizations in a variety of forms. What does an iron organization look like? The iron organization takes risks and supports strong leadership that serves. Often, especially in the early phases of an organization's biography, the iron element is present in the construction and forming process. Individuals take initiative; people rally around, and entrepreneurship is valued and supported.

Let's now look at copper. It is indeed one of the most colorful of metals, with all sorts of variations including rose-red, sunrise-red, reddish-yellow, and brown-red. When used in transparencies or chemical solutions, copper reveals many other colors as well. It is found in significant quantities in the western states of the United States—Montana, Arizona, Utah, New Mexico, and Nevada. Copper is also found in Chile, Indonesia, and Peru. Copper and copper alloy products are used in plumbing, electrical products, transportation and industrial machinery.[5] Copper is one of the best heat and electrical conductors and has a wonderful relationship to sound, a true euphonious metal. Many wind and percussion instruments are made with copper, such as the trombone, horn, and timpani.

When one travels through cities, one can see the copper roofs of churches and state buildings. Indeed, the qualities of copper are enveloping, linking, and adapting. For example, when two copper objects are pressed together they give a little; they adapt to each other. This makes copper ideal for taps and other connections in plumbing. Because of its conductivity, copper is of course also ideal for telecommunications.

Unlike some metals, handling copper does not produce any diseases. On the contrary, copper is health giving and miners, for example, have shown greater resistance to cholera epidemics.[6] Wilhelm Pelikan states, "We also know that treating cut flowers with copper keeps them fresh longer."[7] Further, copper maintains and even stimulates a lively circulation of fluids, as circulation is enhanced with warmth. Pelikan tells us that, physiologically, copper "helps the ego organization generate warmth in the digestive tract whenever this warmth has become deficient."[8] Thus some homeopathic doctors suggest copper ointment for stomach cramps.

The lower region of circulation (the veins) tends to contain more copper while the upper region (the arteries) contains more iron. In embryology, the fetus tends to gain gradually in iron while the womb has more copper. Iron has the quality of individualization, while copper holds and supports. As an educator I also find it interesting that whereas the amount of iron in the human being remains relatively constant during childhood, there are two periods when iron in the blood serum spikes upward. That occurs at age three and age nine, times when the "I," or individuality, of the child becomes more evident.[9]

When I was an elementary classroom teacher, I used to play circle games with the younger children. Much to my initial surprise, I found a rich treasure trove of ring games and circle songs for all occasions. In the first grade class, we did one called "Round and Round the Village" in which the children held hands and moved left around the circle. As the verses unfolded, one child would step out and weave in and out "the windows" between the circling children. Eventually the circle stopped, there was a kind of tag game, and a new child would be selected. This memory came back to me in considering copper and iron. Copper is about circling, meeting and group work. Even shaking hands is a copper activity because of its linking quality. In contrast, the child who steps out, the one who is "it" manifests iron. This takes courage, initiative, individualization, and separation from the group.

Looking at organizations from a copper perspective, group dynamics, meeting conduct, and connecting all involve copper qualities. Some questions to ask from this copper perspective are: What observable data can one find in attending meetings and watching what happens between people? How is the warmth in the "digestion" of reports or presentations? How are people connecting, listening, building upon each other's ideas? From the iron perspective, the questions become about the leadership. Are there leaders willing to step out and do what is needed to get the work done? Is there risk taking? How is the follow-through? Are leaders supported or cut down? Is there a connection between responsibility and authority?

In my experience, organizations tend to lean either toward the copper or toward the iron pole. Attaining the right balance, as in embryology, is a matter of organizational development and the confluence of external and internal demands, the value placed in meetings versus. individual leadership, for example.

Lead and Silver

Found today mostly in the Western Hemisphere (Alaska, Idaho, Montana, Australia, and Peru), lead is used mostly in lead acid batteries, but also in pipes, construction, solder, ceramics, pigments, and chemicals. Historically, it has been used in printing, ballast and counter weights, wire, and stained-glass windows. Anyone who has sat in a dentist's chair has experienced the protective shield used when taking X-rays.[10] As seen with many of the above uses, lead has a "locking function" in which things are held, protected, sealed, and bound. With the old-fashioned printing presses, lead literally "bound" thoughts in the printed word, holding them for posterity.

As we found with its presence in paint, lead is highly poisonous. It can penetrate the body through the skin and respiration. People become pale, and there is a general loss of vitality and premature aging. Lead enhances the death process. Everything that is *finis* or ending, even in our thinking, is connected with the lead process. A person who speaks with aplomb exemplifies this characteristic; indeed, *plumbum* is Latin for lead.

Dense and sluggish, soft and pliable, melted by a mere candle flame, lead is the heaviest metal. Pelikan further elaborates this in the following statement: "The ways of the earth grip and affect this metal with ease; it can hardly defend itself."[11] Lead is an exceptionally bad heat conductor. One can heat one end of a bar to the melting point and still not feel any heat at the other end. Likewise, lead offers great resistance to electricity. Lead salts and lead glasses (lead silicate) refract light, sometimes with a brilliant play of light rays. Lead is not a sounding metal. It would be inconceivable to use lead strings on a violin or cast a lead flute or bell. With lead, the tone is smothered in dullness. Even if one touches a sounding instrument with lead, the vibrations cease and the sound immediately congeals or stops entirely.

Rudolf Steiner commented, "In lead the cosmos prepares a substance for itself in which to concentrate its most powerful splitting forces. By bringing lead into the human body you place the body directly amid the processes of world disintegration."[12] Three key words for lead are *splitting, disintegration,* and *decomposition.* "Splitting" can be understood by noting that the Romans were the first civilization to use lead extensively. They made plumb bobs, catapults, pipes, barrel staves, hairpins, and tokens for admission into the arena—all involving lead. Indeed, water flowed into their homes in lead pipes. Consequently, they absorbed traces of lead through drinking water. Today, we know that small doses of lead, while poisonous, can strengthen consciousness in the short term. Therefore, lead "splits" awake what is naturally asleep in the human organism.

When lead is introduced into plants we find that it has an inhibiting effect, even causing dwarfing in them. In humans, one finds lead in higher proportions in the bones, gallstones, and kidney stones. Speaking of the bones, I find it interesting that lead deposits in the earth are frequently embedded in limestone—the same calcite of carbonic minerals mirrored in the human skeleton. As Dr. Hauschka says, "Bone-building is the final stage of the lead process in the human organism. Human beings incorporate death into themselves with the bony structure. But at the heart of this mineralized precipitate of our physical selves, at the core of what is most dead in us, we find the scene of life's creation: the red marrow, where new blood, new red blood corpuscles are made."[13] Thus we have both death and resurrection within our organism, mineralization, and renewal. By the time we reach adulthood, bones are not growing; they capture the forensic evidence and hold it throughout time. However it is in the bone marrow that the red blood cells are formed. Because we are always experiencing partial death, we can be conscious beings, coordinate our sense perceptions, and relate them to our "I," our inner core existence. This can be likened to an essential function of the brain as a coordinator and processor of a multitude of sense perceptions. The lead process can give us firm footing for functioning in the world, or it can make us captives of our physical bodies.

If given small amounts of lead over time a person develops melancholia, dizziness, and severe headaches. Gradually, the optic nerve degenerates, muscles become sluggish, and cells atrophy. A person with lead poisoning then becomes spastic, cramped, the joints ache, the pulse weakens, limbs become cold, and a chronic cough develops. Finally, intestinal problems develop; there is retention of gases, urine, and chronic constipation. In short, with lead, the body contracts and suffers a slow death. Fortunately, cases of lead poisoning are decreasing and only trace amounts of lead are found in most people.

However buried in the heaviness of lead, it is possible to find an inner fire that should not be overlooked. This secret quality is best illustrated by describing an experiment that is not generally well known. Dr. Hauschka explains:

> Lead citrate is put in a glass tube sealed at one end and gently shaken till it settles at the bottom. The open end of the tube is attached to a vacuum pump. The citrate is slowly broken down with the heat of a small flame, while the vapor and carbon monoxide thus generated are drawn off by the vacuum. The end product is a metallic lead in the form of a fine powder. When the tube is sealed with a glass cock, taken off the flame and the pump disconnected, the lead can be kept for weeks or months, provided the seal is tight enough. But the moment air gets in, the lead bursts into flame and is gradually consumed.[14]

In groups, we find that the most lethargic (lead) person can suddenly burst into "flame" when filled with enthusiasm. Like the air in the above experiment, enthusiasm can literally lift people off their feet.

Curiously, lead veins in the earth are often intertwined with silver, our contrasting metal. Silver is also found mostly in the West—in Alaska, Peru, Mexico, and Chile. Unlike lead, silver is a great conductor of heat as it retains little for itself. Of the seven metals to be considered here, it is also the best conductor for electricity. Silver is soft, ductile and flexible; it does not assert its own form. When you hear silver bells or a silver flute played, you can realize the inner nobility and purity in silver's nature.

Because silver declines to absorb any light for itself, silver's mirroring power makes it ideal for photography. It is extraordinarily sensitive to light. It also has a peculiar relationship to air. When gradually melted, silver greedily sucks in oxygen up to twenty times its own volume. But when it solidifies again, it suddenly releases the oxygen with an explosive force called spattering or splashing.

When we view silver through our threefold method we see that unlike lead, silver supports the building processes in the human being. The essence of silver is that it supports growth. Instead of decomposition, silver tends to support an opening up toward the world, creativity, and the rhythms of life. Dr. Hauschka refers to silver as "a dense form of moonlight. It is a substance very much like the moon in brilliance and reflecting power."[15] In Greek mythology the goddess Diana, or Artemis, ruled the cycle of the moon and the various vegetative and reproductive processes in humans and in nature. Celebrating their rites by the silver light of the full moon, the followers of Diana experienced creative powers streaming down, bestowing new powers of soul and spirit. Silver was also seen as the earthly counterpart to the reflective powers of the moon. Mirrors likewise reflect what is placed in front of them. The images are always moving, changing, and inconstant. As Dr. Pelikan notes, "When one looks at a reflective surface one does not see a mirror, one sees oneself."[16] Silver leaders have this reflective quality. They can tell you what everyone said, but one is left wondering "where did that thought really come from?"

In contrast, "leading out of lead: means to plunge to the depths with unalterable facts: "We have $x left in the budget." Facts and images can perform a kind of dance together, each eluding the grasp of the other.

To understand this in medical terms if arteriosclerosis is a lead-like illness, then a fever is a silver one. In extreme cases, delirium induces fantasies, ever flowing, changing images provoked by high temperatures. Lead and silver are counterparts, much like darkness and light. Lead fixes, creating charts and tables. Silver releases, creating images.

An organization burdened by lead is intent on form and structure, impervious to the light and sound of the people around it. Like old age, those in such an organization are acutely aware of their limitations. They want to do things in a well-defined, predictable way. Each meeting and event is shaped and formed until there is no chance of spontaneity. Silver organizations are all about the flow, the movement of ideas. They are quite susceptible to outside influences and incorporate them readily in decision-making. Resolutions are made and then changed with the ebb and flow of events. Transformation is valued; definition (lead) is boring. In the extreme, a silver organization performs a feverish dance or dervish in which things spin out of control in a wild swirl of competing images and impulses.

Just as a ring game can illustrate the balance of copper and iron, so a riddle can contain both lead and silver. If one tells a riddle to a group of young children, they will jump from one possible answer to another, building up each other, increasing their responses with joyful enthusiasm (silver). All the while, the adult has to hold to the answer like an anchor at rest in the swirling sea (lead). In such circumstances I have often felt how inadequate my preconceived "answer" was and how interesting the children's responses were. For a riddle to be satisfying one has to have the solidity of an answer; both lead and silver are needed on the path of inquiry. Thus for leaders in organizations, it is helpful to let go of the "script" at times and let the group do brainstorming. The balance of holding and releasing is an essential leadership function.

MERCURY AND TIN

Twice as dense as iron, fourteen times heavier than water, having one of the highest atomic weights, mercury is nevertheless liquid. At the slightest nudge, it disperses into drops and droplets, only to come back together again just as easily. It has great powers of cohesion. The mercury enigma continues when one considers that it does not easily adhere to its surroundings, does not moisten what it touches, but immediately returns to itself. Other metals age, but mercury tends to remain "young." The Greek god with winged sandals, Hermes, is associated with this metal. Later on, it became the metal of merchants. Mercury has been depicted as the god of trade and of thieves—an interesting combination, for the latter spreads out again what the former has accumulated.

Medieval alchemists sought to transmute matter and saw in mercury something capable of this changeability. In modern usage, mercury is contained in our thermometers and barometers, tools that help us measure the changeability in our weather. Since mercury remains liquid even in cold weather, in a sense it contains a hidden flame.[17]

This characteristic of changeability contains both separation and concentration. For example, human cells tend to want to separate but too much separation of the cells can create illness. The essence of mercury is that it wants to bring detached forces back into resorption and bring the parts back to the whole when separate processes have taken over. In group work a mercurial leader has the ability to move between small groups and connect the pieces. The leader as messenger is very much the mercury type.

Whereas iron supports individualization and consolidation, mercury or quicksilver, forms many tiny globules and has tremendous mobility. Carried too far, the iron tendency can lead to a kind of mummification or egoism almost like being trapped in oneself. With mercury, the tendency toward amalgamation when carried too far leads to an erasing of identity. Besides delivering the message, one wonders, what does the mercury person really think? Is there anything one can hold on to? Yes, you told me what so and so said, but what do you think?

In contrast to mercury, tin likes to maintain its own form. It defends itself against heating as well as cooling, wanting at all costs to remain in equilibrium between melting and congealing. In fact, tin has a most peculiar way of dealing with heating. First it grows softer, and then, at 160° centigrade, it gets quite brittle. When subsequently cooled, it disintegrates. Indeed, tin is reluctant to surrender its shape.

Found in Indonesia, Peru, Bolivia and Nigeria, we can say that tin is a tropical metal. Twenty-five firms use about eighty-one percent of the primary tin consumed in 2005. The major uses are cans and containers, twenty-seven percent; electrical, twenty-three percent;

construction, ten percent; transportation, ten percent; and other, thirty percent.[18] The prevalence of use in tin cans and other containers accentuates the theme of shape and form. In earlier times it was also used as a component in bronze to make church bells and statues. Tin jewelry found in old Persian tombs shows how well known tin was in ancient times. The Greeks and Romans traded tin, which was also used in the Middle Ages in making pewter utensils. These practical implements seem to last forever and are examples of the nature of tin to provide outline and shape.

Often found on islands, tin withdraws from water and seems to conjure plastic, material forms out of the fluids that surround it. In fact we could say that tin dislikes water and as Dr. Hauschka notes, "[tin] condenses fluids into solid forms and has a drying action on them"[19] In the human body one finds a high level of tin in the mucous membrane of the tongue, as well as in the skin.[20] Here we have an organ of the periphery, as the skin forms the boundary between the inner and the outer world for humans. The internal organs also have protective shields, which also contain tin. Thus we can conclude that tin assists in maintaining and forming boundaries, something that requires both plasticity and rigidity. With the tongue in mind, there is also the ability to discern and analyze through taste, a function that is then carried further by the liver, the major internal organ with the highest amount of tin.

When joining two pieces of metal together through soldering, one uses tin. This points to another aspect of tin in the human organism. Dr. Hauschka states, "Tin links bone with bone through the agency of the cartilage in our joints, and on a higher level is active in the capacity of the mind to link thought with thought in logical sequence."[21] Likewise, the chemistry of tin is simple and logical compared to some of the other metals. Therefore in terms of leadership capacity, those who have strong organizing skills, those who think logically and sequence their actions deliberately can be seen as working under the guidance of tin.

Youth is to old age as mercury is to tin or laughing is to crying. The one is flexible and the other fights to retain its form. Mercury is like the smooth skin of a child, while tin represents our wrinkles. For example, with each set of metals I have indicated a childhood activity that contains some of each quality. For mercury and tin consider the bedtime story. Sitting down, a tin gesture, is the posture of old age. Yet the inner content of the story, if age appropriate, will move like the Greek messenger, Hermes.

Together, they form a balance and can help a child find peace in sleep. In organizations, the balance of mercury and tin can reconnect individuals through leadership and finding common ground.

GOLD

Much in the news of late due to its increase in value, gold is currently mined in South Africa (twelve percent of world production), Australia and the U.S. (ten percent each), China (nine percent), Peru (eight percent) and Russia and Indonesia (seven percent each) according to the London based researchers GFMS, Ltd.[22] Most gold today is used for jewelry and arts (eighty-five percent), electrical and electronics (six percent) dental and other (nine percent).[23] These numbers reveal some of the main qualities of gold. The majority of its use is in jewelry and the arts thus its reason for existence is to be looked at, to be valued.

Since earliest times, gold has been the metal of kings and queens. One has only to experience the tomb of the Egyptian Pharaoh Tutankhamen to see the majesty and complete splendor of gold as a royal prerogative. There are indications in ancient teachings that the priest kings surrounded themselves with gold not only as a sign of power and wealth, but also as a spiritual instrument of their authority. The ideal for their meditations on the metal gold was to develop receptivity and wisdom. Thus gold may be said to serve as a schooling of consciousness for early leaders. And we can see many examples throughout history of the influence of gold on rulers and leaders. We trace the rise and fall of entire civilizations as gold passed from one to the other—Egypt, Persia, Greece and Rome. During his extensive military campaigns throughout most of the world known to the Greeks in the fourth century BC, Alexander the Great gathered much gold. During the Middle Ages, the Knights Templar derived much of their authority as early bankers by virtue of their vast hordes of gold and other valuables. Gold has also brought out the worst traits in human nature as "gold fever" gripped the soul. One has examples in the building of Aztec temples with the enforced help of slaves, the greed of the American and Australian gold rush, and the slave labor of South African mines.

Most other metals are gradually destroyed over time by earth processes such as rust, weathering, oxidation, and calcification, but not so with gold. In many ways it is the prototype of the precious metals.[24] To describe gold as yellow is too simplistic. There is an "inner heaviness" in the yellow of gold and this satiated yellow radiates with a dignified permanence.[25] Gold, in dilutions and as an additive, produces a wide array of other colors. We know for example that the red stained glass of great cathedrals is due in part to the addition of gold. Gold is also ductile and malleable, as seen in the ultra thin gold leaf ornaments. One ounce of gold can be stretched into a super thin wire thirty-five miles long. Gold is an excellent conductor of heat and electricity. So in the characteristics of this metal we have light and gravity, elastic fluidity and weight.

In literature and medical references, one frequently finds that gold is related to blood circulation and the human heart as evidenced in the following quote from Pelikan: "From external analogies it is assumed that the ancients saw in gold a representative of the sun. When they looked at gold, with its self-possessed radiantly yellow color and its modesty and dignity, they actually felt something related to man's entire blood circulation. Confronted with the quality of gold, they felt 'you are within this, here you can feel yourself.'"[26] It is possible to say that in gold, humans can feel the sun working—even in their own blood. We know that blood is a very special fluid. Here is where we experience our sense of "I," our individuality that finds its expression in the flow of blood. In the same way that the central meeting place of blood is found in the heart, gold holds a central place in the family of metals. A gold leader is someone who works out of this radiant center, the source of all true authority. Gold radiates life and strength like the sun.

It should also be pointed out that the essence of gold is that it likes to harmonize, to bring into relationship that which would otherwise be separate. Moreover, when you consider the mixed history of gold, you see that below the surface of this search for harmony is a struggle that is related to human conscience. When Goethe's Faust paces up and down, tormented by conflicting emotions and impulses, the torment of conscience is a battle for his inner gold. Through our struggles we have a chance to get to the heart of the matter, our most precious gold.

Certainly a leader working out of gold has many of the attributes one can admire—wisdom, equanimity, the capacity to mediate differences, confidence and joy. It is the royal flush of the metals, the noble high road. Most people feel comfortable around the golden leader; things seem to turn out right under this beneficent guidance. When standing directly in the light there is no shadow, and so with gold it is hard to find any negatives. Yet I have found that gold leaders are sometimes quite passive, even inactive. When they are personally at peace with an issue they tend to hold back, refrain from action. Much destruction can occur in the environment and the gold leader remains impervious to it all. No rust or outer damage accrues, and with some polishing or even recasting, gold continues to shine forth.

In short, we need all the metal attributes in leadership. There is a place for the image making of silver, for the strength of iron, the social skills of mercury, the formative ability of tin, the radiance of gold, the connecting possible with copper and yes, even the clarity and definition of lead. When we find ourselves in groups, can we develop the perception to see which metals are strongest in our decision-making patterns and our ways of interacting? If there is a preponderance of one, can we call forth the balancing qualities of another? The question is whether we can we truly perceive which metals are at work most strongly in our organization? This is not easy, as we often see attributes of all the metals in the people with whom we work. One place to begin is with self-assessment. To this end I have formulated a leadership inventory of the metals (see Appendix A) in which individuals can respond to key descriptors and then rate themselves on a score sheet. The groupings end up in the seven basic metals. Then the implications for leadership and group rebalancing can be discussed. At the least, consciousness around leadership styles can be enhanced and taboo subjects around expectations can be placed on the table for conversation. Iron needs copper and vice versa, tin and mercury are partners, as are lead and silver. Gold alone stands in radiant self-sufficiency.

16. PLANETARY INFLUENCES

THE METALS THAT reside in the earth have a connection to their surroundings, not only in terms of geography but also to the greater cosmos. The wise teachers of olden times knew of the connections between the metals and the planets, and it is part of our quest for organizational health to reawaken the living relationships that exist between the earth, the planets and the human body. In this chapter we will look at the Greek gods, their Roman counterparts, and their connections to the metals and aspects of human physiology described in earlier sections of this book.

Chronos was a Titan, or an elder god, who ruled for untold ages. The Titans had great strength and were of an enormous size. Chronos ruled over the other Titans until his son Zeus dethroned him and seized power. In her book *Mythology,* Edith Hamilton writes, "The Romans said that when Jupiter, their name for Zeus, ascended the throne, Saturn [Chronos] fled to Italy and brought in the Golden Age, a time of perfect peace and happiness, which lasted as long as he reigned."[27]

In Greek mythology, when the sons of Chronos drew lots for their share of the universe, the sea fell to Poseidon, Hades ruled the underworld, and **Zeus** became the supreme ruler of all, lord of the sky, the rain god, the cloud gatherer, and the one who could wield the awful thunderbolt. Greater than all the other divinities, Zeus was nevertheless fallible and could be duped by Poseidon or his wife Hera.

Zeus and Hera had a son called **Ares** (Mars), who became the God of War. Even his parents detested him. "Homer calls him murderous, bloodstained, the incarnate curse of mortals; and, strangely, a coward, too, who bellows with pain and runs away when he is wounded."[28] The Romans liked their Mars better than the Greeks liked Ares. Phoebus **Apollo**, the son of Zeus and Leto, was born on the island of Delos. He delighted the Olympians as he played on his golden lyre; he is featured in poetry and known for having taught human mortals the healing arts.

Above all, Apollo is the God of Light "in whom is no darkness at all and so he is the God of Truth."[29]

Some years ago I had the pleasure of visiting Apollo's oracle at Delphi. Despite the passage of many years, I was able to experience the clarity and vision of the place—the clear air, the sharp outline of stone against blue sky, and the sacred ground that had been the meeting place for people with urgent questions they wished to ask. In ancient times, people from all over the world came to the sacred springs of wisdom for answers to their questions. Seekers for truth listened in rapt attention as the priestess of the oracle went into a trance before speaking. With vapor rising, the words would pour forth, at times incoherently. The word Phoebus means "brilliant" or "shining." Indeed, Apollo was viewed as the Sun god of ancient Greece.

His twin sister **Artemis** was the lady of wild things, a hunter, and protector of youth. When a woman died a swift and painless death, she, too, was slain by the silver arrows of Artemis. If Apollo was the Sun, Artemis was the Moon. One can picture the lovely hunter flashing through the forest by the silvery light of the moon. The cypress was her sacred tree, and she loved all wild animals, especially the deer.

Aphrodite was celebrated as the goddess of Love and Beauty. She beguiled both gods and mortals and laughed sweetly, yet would mock those whom she had conquered. She was the irresistible goddess who stole the wits even of the wise. Some say she sprang from the foam of the sea (*aphros* is the Greek word for "foam") and that she had a special connection to the islands of Cyprus and Cythera:

> The breath of the west wind bore her
> Over the sounding sea,
> Up from the delicate foam,
> To wave-ringed Cyprus, her isle,
> And the Hours golden-wreathed
> Welcomed her joyously.[30]

> Homer

Finally we introduce the winged **Hermes**, messenger of the gods. Graceful and swift of motion, his feet were winged sandals; wings were on his low-crowned hat as well. Most cunning of all the gods, he was also the master thief who began his first day of life by stealing

Apollo's herds. When forced to give them back, Hermes made amends with Apollo by presenting him with a lyre that he had just made out of a tortoise's shell. Hermes later became the solemn guide of the dead, the divine herald who accompanied souls to their last home. As messenger on all sorts of errands for the gods, Hermes appears more frequently in Greek tales than any other god.

To summarize, we can list the Greek gods with their Roman counterparts:

Chronos	Saturn
Zeus	Jupiter
Ares	Mars
Apollo	Apollo
Aphrodite	Venus
Hermes	Mercury
Artemis	Diana

It is fascinating to note that the Roman designations begin to veer more in the direction of the planets known to this day. If one substitutes "Sun' for Apollo, and "Moon" for Diana, we have the planets with their corresponding metals:

Saturn	lead
Jupiter	tin
Mars	iron
Sun	gold
Venus	copper
Mercury	mercury
Moon	silver[31]

In working with these connections, in his medical lectures Rudolf Steiner showed how we may consider lead the result of certain "undisturbed effects" of Saturn; tin the "undisturbed effects" of Jupiter; iron that of Mars; and so on.[32] Spirit and matter correspond to each other; for everything on Earth, there is a spiritual counterpart. (Undisturbed effects are the direct influences between the planets and the metals.) In the old manuscripts of Paracelsus, one of the first physicians, one finds that the word "planet" did not simply describe the shining globe we know in the night sky or through our telescope. Rather, he viewed the orbits of the planets as spheres of motion around the earth. Thus one had a "moon sphere" which was close to the earth and a "Saturn sphere" which was furthest away. The planets were not simply things, but points of orientation. In Greek mythology these spheres of motion were divine beings, or "gods." Today, we can speak of leaders who are echoes of the greater cosmic picture. Instead of planets orbiting the universe or metals trapped in the earth, leaders have organizations in which they try and activate spheres of motion. For wherever there is movement, there is the possibility of creativity and initiative.

Now we can look more closely at what I call the "planetary types" and how they can help us achieve collaborative leadership when taken to a new level of consciousness.

THE SATURN TYPE

This person cultivates his or her inner world with great energy but generally has a poor relationship with the outside world. They do not relate to the moment, to the present, but rather tend to see everything in the context of the past. So when an issue comes up for consideration, the Saturn type tends to say, "Five years ago when we faced this situation...." or "last time we did this we found that...." Saturn types are so focused on the past that they find it hard to make decisions. They need much time to assimilate events and facts. It is hard for them to spring into action, for they would rather take the time to consider precedents and examples from the past. Although they appear outwardly inactive, they have lots of thoughts, even profound ones. I have found that a Saturn type will often wait to speak until the end of a meeting and say something that not only summarizes, but also goes further than an hour of talking. However, Saturn types can be awkward in practical matters (they are typically not good car mechanics), and they can be easily offended. Life is generally seen as a burden. Their virtue is loyalty; their vice is spite. Saturn types can often be overlooked because many of their talents are hidden.

How can one work with a Saturn type? You need to take a deep interest in the Saturn type, prepare inwardly for your conversation, and give advance notice of things that will happen so they can make impressions into a memory, their favored way of processing information.[33] Rather than spring a conversation on a Saturn colleague at work, you can say, "Could we get together tomorrow to talk about ... ?" This helps the person create a memory picture of the introduction, inwardly reference the topic, and come to the meeting prepared.

THE MERCURY TYPE

The Mercury type is much more common than the Saturn type. In the life of Mercury types, as Max Stibbe says in his *Seven Soul Types:* "Chaos is generally the rule. They jump from one thing to another, and undertake a million and one different tasks that seem to happen their way by chance. They know all kinds of people, make friends with everyone, and are exceedingly adept at dealing with people."[34] The Mercury type can observe things and people with great acuteness and have the capacity for corrective thought and change of thinking. They always seem to be in motion, dancing through life as it were, but they are inwardly quite passive because they are led by outer impressions. They live in the details and are reactive, both to things around them and to their own feelings. Whatever is happening in the moment is of utmost importance.

The virtue of the Mercury type is their light-footed cleverness; their vice can be a kind of superficiality that can border on dishonesty. Remember the previous reference to Mercury and thieves. If one is in a workplace situation with Mercury types, encourage them to do even more detailed observations and elicit comparisons and reflections so they are stimulated inwardly and bring more thoughtfulness to their actions.

THE MARS TYPE

In many ways this is the direct opposite of the self-conscious type. Here the outer world is paramount, and action is preferred over reflection. Instead of the past, the Mars type looks continually to the future. Action is a means of establishing a relationship to the outside world, and the Mars type feels that it is better to "do something" than nothing at all. These people are goal oriented, they push obstacles aside, and they can be quite rude at times, even forceful. The Romans were known as Mars people but other strong personalities in history belong to this group as well, including Napoleon, Voltaire, and Elizabeth I.

When attacked from the outside, as England was during the time of Elizabeth I with the invasion of the Spanish Armada, the Mars type can rise up and achieve greatness.

In working with the Mars type, it is important to maintain a certain inner composure in the face of their forceful outbursts. Indeed, their virtue is courage, but their vices are anger, excessive zeal and the tendency to give free rein to their passions. Much of our modern world caters to the Mars types; "Just send in the military" is seen as the answer to most problems. The transformation needed here is for more and more people to fight their inner battles rather than to externalize them. This can mean taking a walk to overcome feelings of anger before letting it out in a meeting. If we can learn from our inner battles, then Mars types can bring that wisdom to our future efforts.

THE MOON TYPE

These people are wonderful mirrors of their environment. This is possible because they are inwardly passive and have few defenses against the outside world. You can notice this mirroring even in their language, as they soon start to use the words and expressions of people around them. They are artistically inclined and can absorb a lot of intellectual content while not necessarily doing any original thinking. Moon types often have a poetic inclination yet can give in to unconscious instincts. Historical examples from the eighteenth century include Louis XV and Louis XVI of France, both of whom were considered indecisive and were unable to reform the monarchy. They illustrate this point by Max Stibbe: "The passive element in the soul of this type can give rise to excesses which are best counteracted by artistic creativity."[35] Indeed, the virtue of the Moon type is their artistic inclination and circumspection, while their vice is passivity, even licentiousness.

When in the workplace with Moon types, try to get behind their mirrors and the images they portray by asking probing questions and requesting them to give amplification. As with all the other types, it is important to build upon their virtue. Artistic work for the Moon type is an ideal way to stimulate connection with the outer world and stimulate activity that goes beyond imaging. The arts also help us observe more accurately, something the Moon types need to develop.

The Venus Type

These folks are often closely related to the Moon types and, of course, are often women. The Venus type has an intimate, though passive, relationship to the outer world. They react to everything out of sympathy or antipathy, liking or disliking, or at least responding with personal opinion. They form judgments of all that happens around them. Thus the vice of the Venus type can be a kind of one-sidedness that restricts things to the life of feeling. The extreme can be greed. Their virtue is a disposition that always seeks to have an object or person for their love and affection.

In the workplace it is helpful to encourage Venus types to modify and amend their initial instinctive judgments. Rather than just let them respond out of love or dislike for people or proposals, try and get them to get engaged, to do work that brings a broader perspective. Activity in the will and in thinking can balance the preference for feeling responses. An example would be to ask: Have you read any books recently that illustrate this situation? This promotes reflection that is lifted to a more objective plane.

The Jupiter Type

To the relief of many, this type is not so common because this regal soul can create all sorts of problems in the workplace when allowed to rule unchecked. They are so intent on achieving a balance between the inner and outer world that chaos is seen as an abomination. The Jupiter type tries at all costs to create order. These folks can assess all problems in an instant and want to solve them right away. Their goal is to end up with complete, all encompassing solutions and grand designs. They act with calm assurance and are willing to go all the way in grand style. Remember our reference to Zeus. The poet Goethe with his far-reaching abilities as poet, writer, scientist and artist, was a Jupiter type, for example.

The virtue of these folks is that they have great capacity for hope; they always strive for the big picture: While we are at it, let's build the gym as well." Their vice can be arrogance and a feeling that those who do not live on Olympus are inferior. In the workplace, it is important to meet the Jupiter types by having entertained their ideas oneself and thought about their images of greatness. Try and see their widely ranging concepts and the perspective from the top of the mountain. This will help you gain entrance to their shining castles.

THE SUN TYPE

Just as gold can be placed in the center of all the metals, it is possible to strive toward a state of harmonious integration of all the planetary types. We can take all the positive attributes of the above types and reach an active balance between the inner and the outer, the willing, feeling and thinking, the reactive and the proactive. This last type, the Sun folks, work out of the heart. They are seen as being kind and considerate and their goodness endears them to others. This final stage, the Sun type, can be achieved by individuals, or can result from the intense collaboration of many "planets" working together in our organizations.

In youth, human beings are most influenced by Saturn, Jupiter, and Mars, those planets that are beyond the Sun. In the later years of life, human beings are influenced more by the so-called inner planets— those within the Sun's orbit, including Venus, Mercury, and the Moon. Therefore, we can ask whether there is such a thing as youth and old age in organizations. One might assign observation tasks based on the planets and metals discussed in this text. For example, if we have a clear picture of the quality of Mars and its earthly counterpart of iron, can we see a preponderance of energy, strength, youthful enthusiasm, and courage in the organization?

It's important to keep an open mind to the possibilities of these types and suspend previously held assumptions that interfere with clear perceptions of folks around us in the workplace. It is part of human nature to draw conclusions based upon a sliver of information, and this clouds our perception. In my consulting work, for instance, I often receive an initial inquiry on the phone that "presents" a need or request. I have learned to be especially careful not to take the "presenting issue or question" at face value, but rather to see it as an invitation to explore further and with more people involved in my first site visit. The "planet" of the person calling me should not be allowed to prevail as the signature of the whole organization.

In addition to the individual planetary qualities, when looking at leadership traits in an organization it is sometimes helpful to keep in mind typical "pairs" that pop up in teams. There is a tendency to match the more active type of one planetary leader with the passive qualities of another. So for example, Saturn is often paired with Venus (in relationships, too), Jupiter with Mercury, and Mars with Moon. It is natural to have one leader more oriented to internal matters (like Steve Ballmer, CEO of Microsoft), and one geared more toward the public (Bill Gates, for example, the founder of Microsoft, who seems to enjoy introducing product and meeting the public). This planetary pairing can help maximize each person's potential while serving to balance the competing needs of the organization. It sometimes happens instinctively or spontaneously, but I am suggesting a more deliberate approach based upon the increased understanding of human beings that can come with planetary types and other considerations in this book.

So what does a healthy organization look like? We are so used to describing dysfunction that less attention has been placed on organizational health. Just as we need heart, lung and liver to be functioning properly for physical health, so too we need to see the correspondences between humans and larger influences in order to achieve organizational health. I would like to draw one more connection; this time between the metals described earlier, the planets of this chapter, and the human organs:

Saturn	lead	spleen
Jupiter	tin	liver
Mars	iron	gall
Sun	gold	heart
Venus	copper	kidneys
Mercury	mercury	lungs
Moon	silver	reproductive organs and glands

Medicine must not act without the participation of heaven; it must act together with it. Therefore, you must separate the medicine from the earth so it will obey the will of the stars and be guided by them.

PARACELSUS

As we consider the marvelous completeness of the starry heavens, let us contemplate several questions. Can we imagine an organizational structure in which all the planets revolve in harmony? Can our leadership needs be met by different metals at different times, depending on the immediate tasks? Can we use the language of the heart, lung, kidneys, and other organs to speak of whole-systems work that promotes health and regeneration?

Having now looked at several aspects of leadership, the next chapter will return to the theme of group dynamics and reveal ways that leaders can use group geometry to achieve greater success.

17. The Geometry of Groups

A WELL-KNOWN DRAWING BY Leonardo da Vinci portrays the human being with legs and arms outstretched over a circle and a square, clearly showing the fivefold nature of the human form: two legs, two arms, and the head. The drawing addresses the geometry in human beings and the wisdom of form. What does this mean? Is there a relationship between "forms" in nature, human physiology, geometry, and organizations? Fat cells, for example, are three-dimensional shapes packed together. They have faces just like other geometrical solids, only in the case of fat cells, approximately seventy-five percent of the time their faces are in the shape of a pentagon, twenty percent of the time they are hexagons, and for five percent they are quadrilaterals.[36] In light of these observations, I felt encouraged to pursue further the notion of geometry in the human body and *organ*-izational forms.

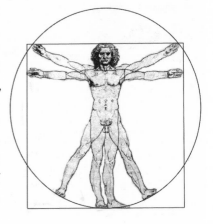

I looked up lectures I had read a long time ago in which Rudolf Steiner described the four kingdoms of nature. In the first, he portrays the physical aspect of humans as essentially polyhedral. In other words, if we did not have other aspects to our essential nature we could be walking around as cubes, octahedrons, tetrahedrons or icosahedrons— subject matter for a new, extraterrestrial movie, perhaps. However, as we all know, we are not just physical in nature; we have life (etheric) forces, akin to the plant world, as described in chapter 1. These life forces are essentially spherical in nature. The plant world is full of rounded forms, whether we look at trees, sunflowers, stems, or lily pads. The vibrancy of nature fills out the forms of the material world. Living things are full, even succulent. Dead things tend to shrivel.

The next kingdom of nature features the animal world, which is characterized by a dawning level of consciousness, or astral body. Here, according to Steiner, the spherical forms become indented (see diagrams.) "Pockets" form, especially around the senses such as eyes and ears, for instance. Finally, the human being has an aspect that the others do not, namely the individuality, that which lives within the form. Here (see diagram) we have the "pocket" with a filling.[37]

If these four aspects (physical, etheric, astral and "I" as discussed in part one) are archetypes of deeper truths, can we find them in organizations? I suggest that the polyhedral, crystalline form is the one that lives most in leadership teams, committees, and work groups (which will be developed further). The spherical and spiral forms are more akin to large-group staff meetings. The pocket form with its curious indentation lies in the realm of counseling and human resource work,

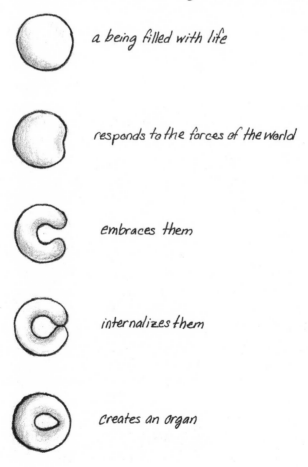

a being filled with life

responds to the forces of the world

embraces them

internalizes them

creates an organ

where one has to create a space for new kinds of perception. Finally, the "pocket with filling" stands, in my view, for the individual who takes initiative, a person who fills the vessel of his consciousness with intent to act. A balance of all four aspects helps create healthy organizations.

Now let's look more closely at the polyhedral forms in organizations, those having an orientation toward committees and leadership teams. The different solids are *prisms, bipyramids, antiprisms,* and *trapezohedra,* all solids bounded by four or more faces of flat polygons.[38] When people get together and sit around a table, not only is a geometrical shape formed by the arrangement of their bodies, but also the shape of their conversation creates geometry in the space between them. These three-dimensional, geometrical forms happen when people gather and create content through conversation and mutual effort. The substance of each group will differ, but here we are interested in the configuration of the group. For the sake of simplicity, we consider these in terms of the more common two-dimensional figures: triangles, squares, and pentagons.

As we know, there are a variety of types of triangles: acute, equilateral, and so on. Observing architecture, we see the acute triangle in church steeples, obtuse triangles in the roofs of federal and municipal buildings and equilateral triangles in the ancient architecture of Egypt or Greece. Speaking qualitatively, acute triangles speak to human striving to connect to the heavens, obtuse triangles are more earth bound, and equilateral triangles attempt to capture the essential balance in humans as a reflection of cosmic laws. There are of course many additional variations on the theme, such as the one-sided weak triangle we call the pointed isosceles or the "unbalanced" scalene.

So what happens when three people come together in a group? Rarely are they of equal standing, seniority, or experience. In most cases one person takes a more active role, as either chair or defacto by virtue of experience of expertise. This is not a bad thing as long as it is visible and discussible when needed. Sometimes the environment around the group assumes an equilateral shape when in fact the group functions more like an acute triangle. An example of the latter is when the chair of the group has special expertise or experience on the subject being discussed.

Then there are the obtuse, earthbound triangles, in which the immediate task predominates, and leadership is less distinct. Here we have the danger that the group follows its nose, moving from job to job without exploring new territory or communicating much with the outside world. Many of our organizations are filled with the obtuse triangles we call work groups. They are practical but can become impervious to outside influences. Sometimes it takes a revolution to crack open a power group in the shape of an obtuse triangle. I once knew a business manager, bookkeeper, and treasurer in a non-profit organization that had worked together for years and everyone learned "not to mess with them." As an obtuse triangle of three, they were unassailable and succeeded in getting their way for a long time before new management arrived to upset the apple cart.

Of course, if one has three in a group, the ideal would be to have equal sharing of responsibilities, rotational leadership and complementary talents and expertise. A three-person team can have the virtue of getting a lot done in a short amount of time, meeting on short notice, and doing regular follow-ups. This is often the shape of an organization design when it is in transition or when a more traditional, hierarchical structure gives way due to the retirement of a strong founder or CEO. When there are reluctant successors, often a three-person team is the way to go. Likewise, it is a good way to test new leadership, as it requires a high degree of collaboration.

A square is more of a human creation. Rarely do we find perfect squares in nature, yet many of our buildings and rooms seem to aspire toward "squareness." Native American cultures valued the four directional points of view, the seasons, the winds, types of corn, the sacred colors (red, yellow, black or blue depending on the tribe, and white). Four also represents the main representative human faces of child, youth, adult, and elder. The square is a great shape to represent "what is"—the reality of a situation. It is also quite static, a portrayal of the status quo in contrast to new leadership. In organizational work I call groups of four our "safety modality." This is when you want all your bases covered with someone on "home plate" as well. Generally, I try and avoid forming groups of four other than on a short-term basis, as they tend to resist change. Why is this a problem? In my experience, an organization is either growing or dying; rarely do things stay the same for more than a few moments. Anything alive is dynamic, and groups of four tend to squash or at least undervalue innovation.

Then we have the pentagon, of which it is possible to write an entire book regarding its organizational properties. Plato referred to the dodecahedron (the only solid made up entirely of regular penta-gons) as the quintessence, the essence of life, and the most special of all the geometrical forms. For example, if one draws a pentagon and then a pentagram within it, followed by a pentagon within that and so on, one can find a "golden ratio" by measuring the length of the line segments and comparing them to each other. This ratio, 1:618, can be found in many other proportions, such as the proportions of the finger bones in the human hand. Finally, the pentagon has just two different shaped triangles within it, and they exude symmetry.[39]

In many ways the pentagon stands alone. Other shapes, such as squares and triangles, can be close packed—placed next to one another so that they form equal tiles, as in a floor. If one tries this with a pen-tagon, however, gaps appear, while in a three-dimensional solid such as a dodecahedron, several pentagons can come neatly together. This so-called Platonic solid is the hardest to construct, whether with clay or cardboard, yet it has amazing properties.

Now, what happens when we bring five people together in a group? As in Leonardo's drawing, we have the potential for the most human of all relationships. Within this configuration there is the possibil-ity of the virtue of the triangle as a "working group" with the most cosmic aspect of the five-pointed star. The pentagon of the big pic-ture can reside in the earth form of the pentagram and the vision can inform each agenda item. There is a wonderful balance in a true pentagon, with the possibility for delegation so that each part carries tasks outside the meeting yet finds a part in the whole. Leadership is cultivated through the fact that the pentagon forms a true learn-ing organization; when five perspectives can inform decisions, it is less likely that any constituent group is left out in the cold. A school for instance can have the points of view of faculty, staff, board, par-ents, and community. Finally, there is the issue of the gap referred to above, the space that is created when one attempts to place pentagons together in close packing. What is this gap? Geometricians may have their own answers, but I would like to postulate that close packing is the relationship of one meeting to the next. In the case of triangles and squares, one meeting can soon resemble the last in a lonely dirge as the weeks pass by. No such chance with the pentagon. When you work in groups of five, something remarkable happens in between meetings. In the spaces between, something else is able to enter the dialogue, and members come back with insights that are often greater than the sum of the ideas shared in the previous meetings. I will go as far as to say that the pentagon, as a leadership form, is an invocation. I believe it is the leadership form of our time because the pentagon is human and cosmic, living and yet precise in its nature. Organic organizations would be well-advised to use this constellation for an executive leadership team.

Sometimes organizations form six-person groups, which include qualities of the square, with the addition of the two directions of above and below. Native Americans had the six Grandfathers, the spirits that presided over the directions with the sixth being the highest. Black Elk, the Lakota holy man, had an incredible vision of these six that concluded with the sixth Grandfather growing backward into a youth. When Black Elk could finally see the face, he saw it was his own face.[40] Therefore, in the six-person group we find the element of time introduced.

Although groups of seven are less frequent, we can once again draw meaning from our Native American ancestors who say seven is the number of completion. Many tribal governments used the seven chief systems that were equal, though with different responsibilities (spiritual life, government, hunting, ceremonial, and so on). They sat in council and heard each voice. Traditionally, they met during the winter. Many tribes had seven clans, and many were headed by a woman. The Cherokee nation is an example of this. In my work with organizations, I have found that to exercise the way of taking council one must have at least seven members. In the group of seven, wisdom can flow forth. It is not so much an action group as a means of collecting wise guidance and advice.[41]

If groups and organizations took some time to consider the geometrical and numerical implications in forming groups, we would see greater clarity in purpose, a closer alignment of expectations and a higher level of productivity and satisfaction. This is a low-cost way to improve the efficiency of our organizations. Leonardo da Vinci's drawing of the geometry of the human body provides us with the inspiration to continue to look to the body for tools to create organic organ-izations. The basic philosophy underlying the organic organ-ization—and indeed all the previous chapters—is that of whole-systems thinking, the topic of the next chapter.

18. Systems Thinking

IN HIS BEST-SELLING book, *The Fifth Discipline*, Peter Senge elaborates a variety of ways that systems thinking can be seen as an antidote to the helplessness many feel in this age of interdependence, "Systems thinking is a discipline for seeing the "structures" that underlie complex situations, and for discerning high from low leverage change. That is, by seeing wholes we learn how to foster health. Systems thinking offers a language that begins by restructuring how we think."[42] He notes that the words "whole" and "health" come from the same root, the old English *hal*, as in hale and hearty. Thus the lack of health in our world today is due in great measure to our failure to see things as a "whole."

For example, in his various books on nutrition and health Andrew Weil, M.D., states that when illness persists "the healing system is blocked, stalled, or overwhelmed and needs help. The true purpose of medicine is to facilitate healing: The aim of treatment should be to unblock the healing system and allow it to do its work."[43] Weil makes a big distinction between treatment and healing. Medical treatment, including drugs and surgery, can facilitate healing by removing obstacles, but in the end true recovery occurs when the healing mechanisms of the human body are able to take over. Healing, according to Weil and many others, is a whole-systems endeavor.

However, even within a whole-systems approach, one can differentiate between what Senge calls detail complexity and dynamic complexity. In the former, the weather forecaster gathers all the bits of information available from satellites, complex instruments and computer generated patterns of past storms and makes a forecast. Even in reams of information, the accuracy of most weather forecasts diminishes after about two and a half days. Most of our conventional systems thinking is of this type. As we have seen in terms of hurricane forecasting or military planning for an invasion of Iraq, there are serious limitations when the dynamics of the situation are not given full consideration.

Dynamic complexity is evident when there are dramatically different effects in the short run and in the long. As Senge states, "When an action has one set of consequences locally and a very different set of consequences in another part of the system, there is dynamic complexity.... The real leverage in most management situations lies in understanding dynamic complexity, not detail complexity."[44] Unfortunately, most "systems analyses" focuses on detail complexity at the expense of the other, and thus we see so many strategic planning failures in government and elsewhere. Just consider our examples of weather forecasting and assumptions about Iraq.

In short, systems thinking calls for a shift in mind set, away from the information processing to seeing the interrelationships rather than linear cause and effect, to seeing processes of change rather than snapshots.[45] To train ourselves in this direction for building organic organizations we need to begin to look for types of structures that occur again and again, the interrelationships and patterns that surface when a change is introduced, much as the ripples on a pond when a stone is cast. We need to look beyond the two-dimensional, the actual ripples, to see things in three dimensions. We need to consider what is happening above and below the surface as described in various ways in this book. Ultimately, if we do this, we emerge from the complexity of detail and through the patterns of systems work, the simplicity, and the inherent wisdom of life emerge.

One significant example of systems thinking is the way Rudolf Steiner described the major systems in the human body. For the purposes of this illustration, I would like to focus on four basic physiological systems in relation to human temperaments, which form another way of viewing the ways that different personality types influence our joint efforts in organizations. In an earlier chapter on vocation, I described how we all have a heritage, a connection through DNA to family and ancestors going back through the generations. One of my mentors, Francis Edmunds, used to line children up one after the other and say, "Here is Jenny, then her mother, grandmother, great-grandmother and so on." This gave us all a real sense for time, grounded in people as opposed to abstract facts and dates. The row of generations also illustrated the importance of honoring ancestors. Likewise, we are connected to a particular nation or ethnic group. Together we can refer to these as the "hereditary stream" of influence. Much of what we get from heredity influences our life and bodily processes. There is another significant factor as well, and this has to do with the soul-spiritual heritage that is unique for each individual. Thus we see that siblings, for example, may have the same parents, ethnicity, and birthplace, yet each will emerge quite differently as they age. The stream of individuality meets and interacts with the stream of heredity. How they meet and interact goes a long way toward determining a person's temperament.

The first type of human temperament occurs when the force of a particular individuality penetrates deeply into the human organization. When the "presence" of this person is felt in dramatic and forceful ways, we experience the choleric temperament. Such a person likes to take charge, enjoys impossible assignments, and forces a path through difficulties. This strength in overcoming obstacles can have a downside in anger, which can be furious at times. When a person is in such a state one can see the veins protruding as the blood gushes through the angry choleric. Indeed, this temperament is most closely connected to the circulatory system in the human body.

In contrast, the melancholic person often feels trapped in his or her physical body. The weight of the world rests upon the shoulders of the melancholic. Life is full of struggles, challenges, and grief. This type of person can spend hours telling you all the things that are difficult, elaborating in detail on physical ailments and perceived injustices. A. A. Milne's character of Eeyore is a classic example of a melancholic.

A third type, the sanguine person, is more connected to the nervous system, flitting in and out of experiences, meeting people and engaging in new interests. The nerve ends in our body are constantly dying; likewise, the sanguine type finds it hard to sustain interest for long before moving on to the next encounter. These people are good social mixers, help smooth over interpersonal problems, and can change their perspective on a dime.

Finally, the phlegmatic person lives in the watery element of the glandular system. Comfort and ease are of paramount importance. Food is very popular with phlegmatic types; indeed, they can spend much time digesting the last meal and joyfully anticipating the next. Winnie the Pooh is a great example of a phlegmatic temperament; if it's ten o'clock, it must be time for a "smackerel" of something.

Of course these are extreme examples and most of us, or so we like to believe, have developed some balancing tendencies. For example, shades of the melancholic and choleric are often found together in one person. Alternatively, you will find the sanguine person revealed as outer clothing and the melancholic in the inner recesses of a personality. The point of considering these types for the purposes of whole-systems thinking is that if we can become aware of these characteristics in people, we are more likely to navigate our way through groups successfully.

There are ways to deal with the extremes of each temperament in children. In response to the single-mindedness and the temper of a choleric type, one can nurture respect for authority and personal accomplishment. The choleric likes nothing more than working with people who have achieved things in life. When a melancholic type complains constantly of grief and "woes," we can relate our own struggles. "You would never believe what happened to me today" is a great opening when working with a melancholic. Likewise, when confronted by the apathy, even dullness, of a phlegmatic, try to awaken the individual's interest in other people. Like a sleeping bear, once awakened they can lumber forward with consistency and excellent organizational skills. Finally, in extreme cases, the flightiness of the sanguine person can border on mania. Sanguine types can progress when allowed to develop love for particular individuals. Sanguine children who love their teachers will do anything, even overcome some of their sanguinity.

To summarize, we can correlate the temperaments as follows, including their connection to the essential sheaths described in chapter 1:

Temperament	Physiological Connection	Sheath	Extreme Cases
choleric	blood	ego	anger
sanguine	nervous system	astral	mania
phlegmatic	glands	etheric	apathy
melancholic	bones	physical	insanity[46]

Let us consider an example of how these temperaments might be revealed in a meeting or organization. The owners of a successful local café are considering expansion, adding a new store in the neighboring town. The four owners have gathered to discuss the idea, and because they are busy people, they decide to begin with each person sharing a brief reaction to the idea:

CINDY: Great idea! I love it. Just think of all the people that we will meet, I mean serve! We can have joint events, sponsor a band, and hire students form the local high school. (Sanguine)

ELLEN: Yes, of course, Cindy, but do you know how hard some of us work already. My children barely ever see me anymore. Making all those lattes is killing my back, and my feet always ache. (Melancholic)

JOHN: Although there are obvious advantages to increasing our sales volume, I feel we should study this proposal for a while and bring it up again at a later meeting. (Phlegmatic)

ERIC: While all of you have been talking, I drew up plans for the new site. Based on my estimate of square footage, we can do it. John, why don't you come with me to the lumberyard—they have a sale on two-by-fours. Furthermore, we can install sprung wood floors for sore feet. Let's go! (Choleric)

Which of the above viewpoints was appropriate to the situation? The response may reveal one's own temperament as well. The point is that we can either work against one another through opposing temperaments or consciously choose to work with one another through insight into these differences. Collaboration is a key ingredient of organic organizations.

This idea of human temperaments is not new. The Greek physician, Hippocrates, born 460 BC on the island of Kos, held the view that the origin of all illness lies in the wrong mix of the "humors," the result of lifestyle and diet. Characteristic temperaments of people are connected with a preponderance of certain fluids in the organism. Hippocrates directed attention to the correspondence of the fundamental elements (air, water, earth, and fire) to the humors (blood, phlegm, yellow bile, and black bile) and their related organs (heart, liver, spleen, and brain).[47] Because of the strong connection to diet, ancient wisdom also prescribed certain foods that would help each temperament overcome their one-sidedness, listed here:

choleric	bitter almond
sanguine	sweet fruit
phlegmatic	salt
melancholic	sour

Examining oneself in light of these four basic human tempera-ments and then taking oneself in hand and rebalancing through diet and lifestyle changes, one could gradually work toward the ideal "fifth temperament." The fifth temperament combines the strength of each temperament and mitigates the weaknesses. If each person in a clan, family, group, or organization takes on their own conscious self-heal-ing, forces that would otherwise be trapped in internal dynamics are released for the good of the whole. We then become more productive and joyful and our groups and organizations reflect those qualities.

The interactions revealed by the different types seen in the above example of the café, offer many practical applications to using the temperaments in working with groups. However, the issue of temper-aments was raised mainly to illustrate a whole-systems approach to group work. First, leaders need to be self-aware; in this case, of their own temperament, and to remember that the Greek adage "know thy-self" speaks to more than just temperaments. Second, groups need to work from the whole to the parts by seeing the full array of human possibilities, working with them rather than against them, and harness-ing the "genius" that resides in every person. Third, a whole-systems approach requires that organizations be flexible enough to adapt to the changing dynamics of both the external environment and the internal conditions of employees. By this I mean rather than just being task ori-ented: "here do this job," we need to also ask: "who is the right person for this job?" Finding the right people to draw into the organization and making assignments based upon human capacities is crucial to sustaining organic organizations. Advertisers speak of things being "user friendly." I urge leaders to consider the term "people friendly." Specifically, this means considering, whenever possible, if a task or assignment is good for the person doing it, if she or he is happy, ful-filled, growing professionally in carrying out the task in question. Traditional organizations use people to get things done and increase profits. Organic organizations grow human capacities as well as the bottom line.

There is inherent wisdom in the human body that can be used for organizational work. This is particularly true when one uses a whole-systems approach. Just as the circulatory system knows how to interact with the digestive system, so also we need to see the organic processes in groups. Just as digestion goes through numerous phases, so also do groups. In my book *School Renewal*, I describe in detail how groups tend to want to find themselves in orientation, and then go through dissatisfaction, only to emerge gradually in resolution and finally achieve high "production" of high performance. When a change is introduced in any system, it affects all the parts. We need to develop the perceptive capacities to see the "ripples" through the whole system and work with them as creative agents rather than hindrances.

For example, if a new person is hired in an organization, everything changes. Even those not directly associated with the new person will be affected, though indirectly at first. A new person alters the chemistry of the whole system, not just the particular unit. A new pitcher on a baseball team might give them more wins, but the team will also be an entirely new group as a result of the addition of one new member. Everything changes with the addition of one new person. So what do we do to integrate a new person into the entire organization, not just their specific sub group? Does the orientation happen concerning the whole system or just their particular tasks? When we treat new people as cogs in the wheel, then that is just what we get—pieces of metal. But when we have an organic approach and see the new hire as an agent of change and new vitality, then their talents can be used from the first day and the whole system can take a fresh breath of air.

Finally, there is great value in whole-systems meetings. These occur at regular times during the year (or weekly in the case of a small organization), when all employees gather to discuss issues and reignite common vision. Just as the body houses all the organs, so a living organization needs to gather to itself all parts, divisions, and committees and integrate their work. The body does this instinctively; organizations need to do this consciously. When we restrict the circulation, respiration or digestion we no longer have a whole system. Fragmentation hinders life. At the very least our meetings need to have concise reporting, focused discussion on topics that affect everyone, and support for the work of leaders carrying tasks on behalf of the whole. Teleconferencing is fine, e-mails help communicate information, but organic organizations need some face-to-face time to sustain living systems. When this happens, as noted by the Senge quote at the start of the chapter, it starts to change how we think. It is wonderful when people leave a meeting saying, "This has changed how I see things. Because of these meetings, I am a different person. I can return to my job with a new perspective. Because of this contact with others, a picture of the whole lives in the little part that I carry, yet my work is a vital part of sustaining the whole."

CONNECTING THE DOTS

HUMAN	ELEMENT	PHYSIOLOGY	SENSES	GEOMETRY	TEMPERA-MENT
ego	fire	blood	balance	tetrahedron	choleric
astral	air/light	nerves	movement	octahedron	sanguine
etheric	water	lymph/glands	life sense	isosehedron	phlegmatic
physical	earth	bones	touch	cube	melancholic

PART V

HEALTHY
ORGAN-IZATIONS

19. What Is a Healthy Organ-ization?

Freeing Initiative

NATURAL PROCESSES IN the world tend to block or at least resist human initiative. Clearing trees in a New England forest is not only hard work, especially when it comes time to remove the stumps, but if left alone for a few years the acreage will soon return to a natural state. A house, no matter how well designed, begins to age as soon as it is built. If left untreated, the wood will begin to rot, water will enter in the most unlikely ways, and over many years, a house will be overtaken totally by nature. Likewise in the human body, without some constant application of consciousness, bodily functions can take over and humans can return to a vegetative state—otherwise known as couch potatoes.

In particular, the absorption of proteins and digestion tend to occur in the unconscious world of natural processes. The four organ systems, heart, lung, liver, and kidneys described earlier in this book, work with their own set of rules and are worlds unto themselves. Natural processes take place continually within our organism, and we are not very aware of what is happening.

Using the threefold method, we can see that a counteracting force in the human body is the result of trace amounts of metals in the body and, with increasing frequency, in nutrition and the immediate environment. Imagine the influence of iron, for example, working against protein formation and the vegetative processes just described. Iron radiates, bringing wakefulness and energy. To varying degrees, as described earlier, the metals bring different states of consciousness to the human organization. The metallic influence radiates and brings change in consciousness, while the protein and vegetative processes resist and block the change directed from the human "I." An illustration of this is trying to write an important report on a full stomach. It is much more difficult to get the thoughts flowing during the subterranean activity of digestion.

Similarly, left to their own devices, organizations tend to sink into the vegetative world of mere functioning. Things take their course under the heading of "organizational procedures," and humans can easily become automatons, functioning and yes, surviving. Traditional factory settings promoted this sort of semicomatose human functioning until it was discovered that one paid a heavy price in terms of both profits and human health. Changing tasks (mercury), empowering workers to take initiative (iron), and holding regular focus group meetings (copper) all tend to activate people.

Like the metals, leadership is a counter force that can wake us up from what the poet Christopher Frye referred to as our "sleep of prisoners." Like iron in the bloodstream, leadership can radiate out and influence every cell, every department of the organization. It can be simply the kind of leadership that holds up a mirror (silver) to promote self-reflection, or it can be leadership that facilitates and connects people (copper). In one form or another, however, leadership tends to bring movement and change to organizations. Good leadership energizes.

Iron is a key ingredient, as it is found in the earth, the blood and in all human initiative. A central task of our modern world is to make the workplace human again, to place human beings, in every sense and need, at the center of our consciousness—to have organic organizations as opposed to profits and exploitation of natural resources and human beings. One way to work with the iron principle is to do everything possible to support initiative. This may be in the simplest form of a "mere" suggestion, or it might be a proposal, a new idea, a task performed voluntarily—initiatives take on many shapes and forms.

The key is to understand that, when a person steps out with an initiative, one is placing the "gold" of one's own heart at the disposal of the organization. Great things happen when people are recognized, validated, and appreciated. But it is not just a matter of making people feel good, it is about the health of our organizations. Unless we learn to value initiative more, especially from those who are not part of the inner circle, we will continue merely on a survival basis. We need to become more adept at tapping into the inner gold of human initiative. Even a small suggestion is an initiative on the pathway to leadership. Groups need to recognize and value these glimpses of human gold. Specifically, we need to do much more in appreciating and celebrating human achievement, even for the smaller things in life.

Biodynamic agriculture aims to use only what can be sustained without depleting natural resources. What is sustainability in organizations? In a very basic sense, as in nature, sustainability has to do with the ability to replenish in proportion to what is consumed. Some people are starting to get the message in terms of our ecosystem, but I have found that this is rarely a topic of discussion in business and organizations. There is still a mentality of using people and their ideas, rather than working with sustainability and health as a goal. How many meetings and conferences are arranged around the physical, emotional and intellectual health considerations of the participants? We would never sit for hours at a time under florescent lighting if we fully valued human health. How many people feel wrung out at the end of the day? How many people feel that work is a matter of endurance rather than joy? I have spoken with far too many who are living for the day of retirement. After a lifetime in unhealthy working environments, too many people experience heart attacks or other debilitating illnesses soon after their release from work. Does it have to be this way? If we can begin to study human health as considered in this book, can we apply these principles to organizations? As with any really important matter, no recipe will do, but to stimulate further discussion and change in practices, I will describe a few essential practices that can promote organizational health.

Independent, Yet Integrated

In his booklet "Forming School Communities," Mattias Karutz observes that the human social organism is arranged according to its functions just as the natural human organism is arranged. "The human organism deals with thinking through the head, not through the lung [and breathing not through the head or the nervous system. Health is present where] the nerve-sense system and the rhythmical system of blood and breathing coexist independently and work together in a living way."[1] This idea of "separate but interdependent" is not new. It exists, for example, in the tripartite system of the Constitution of the United States with the separate but equal branches of government. Thus the relationship of the social structure to the human body is a further aspect worth pursuing. Is there a relationship between the human organism and the social organism? As I understand it, the different "systems" such as respiration, circulation and digestion, for example, each have their own laws, their patterns, and functions. You cannot make the lungs do what the kidneys do, for instance. The genius of the human organs and their related systems is that they are different and perform different functions.

The importance of "separate but independent" is often not grasped or properly valued these days. One sees this in the overextension of the executive branch of the United States government in recent years with FBI searches of congressional offices and wiretapping. Moreover, one sees this in organizations where some people feel they should be involved in everything that goes on. Under the banner of democracy, everything is placed in the same bowl of soup with results that are often chaotic. Our New England town meetings can sometimes be chaotic, mixing teachers, administrators, parents and single-issue voters all in one Saturday meeting. Often those with the most influence are those who can pass the endurance test of sitting through six to eight hours of talking before votes are taken. I feel for the teachers in these meetings who have to listen to all the criticism of the school budget while earning relatively low salaries and trying to do their very best on a daily basis. Perhaps they should be given more authority in school governance. And perhaps we should consider taking the politics out of education by effecting the same separation between the state and education that we have between church and state.

A healthy organization values the distinct functions of the parts while making sure that they are integrated. Just as the circulatory system and respiration relate in the heart, so the parts of an organization need to find their relational work. The methodology I recommend is to continually move from differentiation to integration and back again. Practically speaking, this means looking at the vision and mission of the organization, then breaking down into functional groups to clarify, then reconvening to integrate, then breaking apart again into task groups and regrouping again to report. As with systole and diastole, this expansion and contraction in organizations promotes life. Our intellectual thinking wants to place everything in a box and have it "settled," while in fact the demands of life are that there be constant movement that values both separation and integration.

In our department at Antioch University, program directors meet separately every two weeks between the full department meetings. When things work well, the smaller group can do things such as review the budget that then allows time for larger issues in the department meeting.

Know Thyself

From earliest times, wise elders have sounded this exhortation. They have urged human beings to see themselves truly, to become self-aware. In my experience of developing organizations, one of the more significant contributors to overall health relates to the degree of self-awareness of the people in the organization.

Let us examine this in more detail. I once worked with a group that consisted of hard-working, intelligent people who were individually quite successful. Yet when they came together in meetings or to do projects, they had serious problems. They had tried all sorts of meeting "techniques": restructuring, communication exercises, and facilitation, all to no avail. In fact, some of the aforementioned work forced the real issues underground as people learned to go through the motions in "learned communication skills" that masked the real issues that rested, indeed smoldered, beneath the surface. When I conducted one-on-one interviews as part of my assessment, these interpersonal issues burst forth, frequently accompanied by tears, anger, threats, and abiding resentments. They had a real problem, but all the interventions thus far had failed to address what was really going on. My assessment ended up showing that it was not primarily an organizational problem but personal and interpersonal issues that were untransformed and holding everyone hostage. This can be seen in a group by convoluted attempts to work around the problem of conflict between two or more people.

The individuals in this group needed to start by seeing themselves more clearly. For reasons of client confidentiality, I cannot go into the details of what transpired in the following months, but we essentially took the road less traveled, namely working on personal change as a catalyst for organizational transformation. Working as much with one-on-one sessions as well as with groups and encouraging individuals to do the things they knew were needed, the work of the entire group began to lift gradually. Only when a measure of personal change had occurred were they able to do some meaningful organizational restructuring.

To illustrate the "know thyself" theme more concretely, I would like to use four examples out of this field of organizational therapy. The four areas of emotional life discussed below are classic in terms of unprocessed material that I frequently find hindering organizational health.

GRIEVING

At our most recent Memorial Day event in Milford, New Hampshire, the local pastor spoke the well-known lines, "Blessed are they that grieve, for they shall be comforted." To mourn the loss of those who have departed, those killed in war, or family or friends who have crossed over is a healthy process, one that should happen as a normal part of life. Mourning is good for the soul; it feeds the inner life and helps us be mindful of those who have departed. Grieving can help us along the road of self-awareness. However there are those who long to grieve and have not yet been able to do so. They sense within themselves an abyss and do not wish to look in for fear of falling over the edge. Within the human psyche is a deep, dark place that one does not want to enter, for it can take a long time to reemerge. It takes great strength to look into the abyss without falling in. Our organizations have members who carry deep sorrows, contracted and held for a long time and never released through healthy grieving. The pain can actually be physical at times. These people carry their unprocessed sorrows into their organizations, and their condition affects all around them.

This condition reveals itself in different ways. Some feel persecuted and consequently attack others for often-unimportant reasons, including outbursts or outrageous statements with no apparent cause. For these folks live in their own bubble of untransformed grief. At other times their attention can appear dispersed, even shattered, as they go through the motions of work and living while all the time holding the inner grief. Some even get upset if one is too nice, as they see it as a preamble to something more sinister. Like a crystal caught in a rocky cavern, these suffering colleagues are longing for release and anything else that transpires on an organizational level is mere *maya*, or illusion.

Anger

Anger manifests in many ways. The expression of anger is not always bad, as is commonly believed. For example, there is the justifiable but moderate anger of the parent who is firm with the child who has "crossed the line" and needs to know it. In this case the "I" is present—the parent is still in charge, and the anger is contained. In contrast there is irrational, uncontrollable anger that lashes out destructively. Such anger seeks to destroy the opponent by any means. Another form is "white" anger, the cold, cutting remark that is short and chills to the bone. It is helpful to know the many faces of anger, because we can recognize them better in ourselves and in the workplace.

In terms of organizational health, we are concerned here with the general phenomena of suppressed anger. There are a great many angry people walking around, few of whom know it. This has an influence on groups and human relationships in all forms. For instance, the suppressed anger can be like a volcano bubbling under the surface, ready to explode. Others resort to tiptoeing around the person, communication is stilted, and the flow of feelings becomes constricted. I have found it is not just the occasional outburst that can be destructive, but also the trepidation of others that live in fear of the potential for another outburst. The group finds itself in an enabling role.

Part of self-knowledge involves knowing the faces of anger and which aspects each of us tends to experience. Sometimes it is as simple as recognizing one's "trigger points," those things that are like red buttons that, if pressed, tend to provoke anger. Then when a person makes a certain comment, you can tell yourself, "Oh yes, this is my trigger point. I can see it for what it is and step over it." Instead of reacting with anger, you can speak your truth: "By the way, these kinds of comments are challenging for me. I used to respond to them with anger." This sort of comment also serves to bring in or educate the other person so that there might be fewer of these kinds of offensive comments in the future. Just as anger can destroy the environment, when it is overcome it can inspire closer working relationships. I urge groups to be alert to the influence of suppressed anger in their midst. So often the responses of individuals have less to do with the surface disagreement on a particular issue and more with the inner weather individuals carry into the meeting.

Fear

This one is subtler yet can be equally influential. Fear tends to lie below anger, a subterranean emotional region that lurks in the dark shadows below observable behaviors. Fear is a contraction, a cold light that shines out of the depths. The use of the word "cold" is intentional, as known to all who have had cold shivers down their back, or who have felt a coldness grip their gut. Fear is realized in the mind, and the thoughts associated with fear can take over. In this state of coldness, warmth flees and the human organism becomes more susceptible to disease and illness. In a fairly tale called *Iron Hans,* the central figure had to wear an iron brace around his chest until he was released. This constriction vividly portrays the grip of fear, which in fact affects the breathing and, in extreme cases, can stop the flow of blood, causing a heart attack.

As the writer and thinker Georg Kühlewind described, "Fear is the feeling of 'I am not': denied, lacking, and reduced growth. In this sense, fear is mutilation."[2] By contrast, in creating love one needs to practice surrender, dedication and receptive attention that receives and transforms. The path from fear to spiritual vitalization is one of transmutation, of consciously finding the "I am" in thinking and in daily tasks. Over time, it is possible to develop our capacities by reaching into the dark corners of our being and letting the soul embrace the fullness of life.

When people come together, they bring their hopes, wishes, intentions and their fears. We often verbalize our hopes and wishes for a meeting, as expressed in the agenda and the stated purpose of a gathering, but groups are less likely to surface the fears of the individuals present. This needs to be handled carefully and with skillful facilitation, yet it is sometimes helpful to name some of the fears or at least the concerns that arise concerning an impending decision. When fears are lifted into the light of daytime consciousness, they are disarmed and become less dangerous. Mostly, each individual needs to become aware of personal fears and face them. The alternative is to end up creating circumstances that manifest our fears and force us to confront them anyway.

LOVE

What can one say about love that does not diminish its breadth and scope? When truly present it is so vast and immeasurable that words cannot do justice in any descriptive form. As one get older, it becomes more and more evident that in fact, love carries all; its embrace is limitless. Love endures all things—it is timeless. When we are able to step from self-interest to love, we find a kind of objectivity that connects all. It is like the extended family—there are many combinations and permutations, yet somehow the whole is connected. When achieved, this objective love is such that one can do the difficult things, say the difficult words, and still know the ground upon which one stands is solid. A parent or grandparent can say things to a child that no one else can when the foundation of love is deep and abiding.

As with the other topics covered in the last pages, love too has different faces. The Greek names for love are *eros, phileo, charitas,* and *agape.*[3] Eros, known so well to our present culture, exemplifies strong feelings of physical attraction. The body culture we know so well in fashion shows, advertising and cosmetics is all an appeal to *eros:* love of everything physical. The Romans referred to him as incarnated in the god Cupid, the lusty offspring of the voluptuous goddess Venus, while the ancient Greeks saw Eros as the central driving force or motivation of all human ambition and action. Their worship of Eros also brought music into Greek culture, especially as a stimulant of sensual ecstasy. With a quickening tempo and incessant drumming, *eros* can lead to a feeling of being overwhelmed by physical longing and desire, sex without love. Billboards and advertisements know the appeal of *eros;* it sells things of this world. Indeed, the desire for something or someone specific is *eros,* which involves a self-centered quality akin to lust.

Phileo loves only when loved in turn and is more like affection. Indeed, when the object of *phileo* becomes displeasing, *phileo* disappears in proportion to the displeasure. This mutuality is the cornerstone to friendship, another word for *phileo.* In the early stages of relationships, *phileo* works with *eros* to provide "allure," but when one person moves to another level of affection, it can lead to a painful break in the relationship. It takes two to be friends.

There are those in this world who have a natural ability to care for others, to give charity, or *charitas*, which shows itself as strong empathy and compassion. What must it take to work daily with the homeless, or to serve with doctors in a refugee camp? This community service is indeed a higher form of love.

Finally, we have *agape*, or spiritual love. Such affection remains, regardless of attractiveness, desirability, or even value. The film *The Mirror has two Faces* tells of this attempt to love without *eros*. The two protagonists try to get past appearances to see inside the mind and heart with different eyes. The hope in this film was to create a less complicated relationship, without the highs and lows of emotional infatuation. *Agape* is a love that does not wait to be acted upon because it is spiritually active. However as revealed in the aforementioned film, it is not easy to achieve.

One of the oldest laws of humanity is to love your neighbor as you love yourself (Lev. 19:18). Less well understood, perhaps, is the following transformation of that sentence: "Love one another even as I have loved you" (John, 13:34, 15:12).[4] The former implies "give and take"; love the other as you love yourself becomes a kind of spiritual equality. It assumes that we love ourselves very much; otherwise, how would it benefit one's "neighbor?" In the second citation, we are asked to reach for the ultimate love, one beyond the ordinary and full of expectant potential. We are asked to stretch beyond loving ourselves and our neighbors and embrace a social leaven that can lift all of humanity to new heights.

In daily life, we constantly move between all four types of love, which is natural in human biography and the passage of life. A healthy marriage or partnership can include all four kinds of love, each speaking a language of the soul that can bring intimacy.

In organizations, many bring *charitas* in terms of community spirit and in service to the ideals or mission of the organization. In most workplaces we are also fortunate to find people who can be counted on for *phileo* and for supporting colleagues in good times and bad. Only occasionally do we glimpse *agape* in the unconditional, selfless service of the one for the other. An example is the continued service of former parents on the school board long after their children have left school. They serve the destiny of the organization selflessly and without prejudice. However, things get complicated when *eros* shows its face. Shifting personal relationships, especially those of a romantic nature, often cause seismic shifts in organizational alignments.

I have known groups that were split right down the middle when couples broke up and new romantic relationships were formed. This may sound old-fashioned, but I believe we each carry considerable personal responsibility for how we live out the various expressions of love when we work as a team. Too often the health of the organization is sacrificed by the personal desires of its members.

These themes of grieving, anger, fear, and love have been addressed from antiquity. Chinese medicine and other ancient practices have spoken these truths and even related them to the organs of the body. So I mention them again here as echoes of the earlier chapter in this book: grieving is connected to the language of the lungs, anger to the liver, fear to the kidneys, and of course, love is always associated with the heart. Our strengths and our challenges concerning these different emotional regions often have a correspondence in the state of wellness of the associated organ. Holistic medical practices tend to treat both the physical and the emotional/psychological symptoms. Using the information given in this book can aid organizations in recognizing that the emotional well-being of a single individual influences the health of the whole organization. When we are alone in our homes, we are private within the realm of family and friends. However, when we enter the workplace, we bring ourselves in all our dimensions, and the private becomes public as we interact with others.

Organic organizations allow for grieving when needed, engage fear and anger when they occur, and attract people who love their work. A friend of mine often asks his colleagues," If you won a million dollars tonight, would you show up for work tomorrow?" He told me that if anyone hesitates even for a few seconds, he responds, "Then you should not be working here." Enthusiasm, even passion, is vital to organizational health. Once again, "know thyself" is as vital as the mission statement of any organization.

PEOPLE IN HEALTHY ORGANIZATIONS KEEP AGREEMENTS

What is an agreement? Most people immediately think of legal contracts, which of course are one form of agreement. But if we stop to think about this question for a time, it soon becomes apparent that there are many other types of agreements that weave through our daily lives. Making an appointment to see someone at eleven o'clock is an agreement, as is charging gas on a credit card. Parents promise to pick up children at a certain time and place, workers agree to certain tasks, companies promise to deliver goods and services in exchange for payment, and adults make an all-encompassing agreement we call marriage. Some agreements are explicit, such as contracts or marriage certificates, and some are implicit, such as the agreements parents make to raise, clothe, feed, and educate their children. We make some agreements consciously, while others creep up on us, and we become aware of their full impact only later.

Broken agreements are a great source of stress and frustration in the workplace. When one party to an agreement falls down, it affects the others. If a report is not completed on time or a key person forgets to attend a crucial meeting, the productivity of everyone is affected. When called in to work with conflict, I often find that the root cause of the difficulty rests with one form or another of broken agreements. People remember even minor injustices, and over time they can build into serious organizational issues. Some of the causes of broken agreements may be rooted in inconsequent child rearing, a history of broken promises, or an organizational culture that condones irresponsibility. As iron filings are drawn to a magnet, so people tend to find their way to organizations that allow them to perpetuate their shortcomings; for change is often difficult if not painful, and most people avoid pain. Broken promises may also be due to organic reasons, as discussed in an earlier chapter on the liver. Often people have the best of intentions, but are just not able to follow through on what they have promised.

A healthy organization makes agreements with as much consciousness as possible. This involves looking at several key questions:

1. Who has to be party to this agreement? Not everyone need be part of every agreement, and misunderstandings about who is a "player" can cause hurt feelings at the least. Depending upon the issue or the task, different people in an organization need to be party to an agreement. A driver's license is between a person and the state, whereas a doctor's appointment is between two people. Other agreements, such as new employment, may involve several parties.
2. What will be different before and after the agreement? Often people rush into agreements and then have to spend

much time amending or even redoing the agreement. More time needs to be spent ahead of time looking at the various factors that need to be taken into account. My image of this is of a funnel with the opening at the top for the beginning of the process. Be as inclusive as possible at the start, and clearly delineate the timeline, and who will be party to the final agreement, the spout of the funnel.

3. Who is responsible for the process? Someone needs to attend to the navigation of the steps toward an agreement, and it helps if it is not one of the principles; good facilitation means to guard the process without any personal benefit from the eventual outcome. As a sidebar, I have increasingly found self-appointed process junkies who continually hold things up in the name of "process." Often, it is a thinly veiled ruse for power and influence. Only one objective process facilitator is needed; too many chefs in the kitchen can spoil the cake.

4. What information is necessary before we make an agreement? Often people stumble into an agreement because of the urgency of the situation only to find some crucial piece of information afterward that sets everything on end. When an organization is continually recasting agreements it often means that they are not working with the right information to begin with. It is always helpful to ask: What else do we need to know? Who can help us see the picture more fully?

5. In the final stages of forming an agreement, it is often helpful for each person to ask: What do I really want? What can I give up? Both are present in every agreement. Moreover, it seems to me that a lopsided agreement is more likely to fail. There has to be a sense of "rightness" all around, otherwise the undermining of the agreement will set in almost immediately.

6. Finally, all agreements should include the possibility for periodic review, not so that people can bail out, but so that life experience can be brought to bear and improvements can be incorporated. If people know that there will be opportunities for review they are less likely to sabotage the agreement along the way.

The issue of enforcement of agreements comes to meet me repeatedly in my consultations. Groups are frustrated by those who break agreements, those who honor the "letter of the law" but violate the spirit of the agreement, and by the sense of betrayal that arises when people don't do what they say. At times, accusations of being "stabbed in the back" poison the workplace. One school had a few teachers taking advantage of the "sick leave" policy to the extent that those who were substituting refused to do so anymore. This became especially hurtful when it was discovered that some that had called in sick were seen shopping at the mall that very afternoon. When confronted, the nonchalant reply was, "I am feeling better now." Some people seem to lack social intelligence, not to mention the personal responsibility that glues agreements. Rather than blaming, however, one can use some of the resources mentioned in earlier chapters. One can ask: Is this a liver issue or trace metals? Is there too little "iron" or planets? Is this a self-conscious type? These tools are useful for looking beyond the immediate issues to see the underlying causes.

So what really is an agreement? In forming an agreement one consciously gives up some of one's freedom, as all parents know too well. Yet one makes the agreement out of a sense that higher aims can be realized, like bringing into the world some wonderful children. In making an agreement one places a higher goal above lesser goals, and one agrees to strive toward fulfillment. Those making an agreement are equal in every respect. If I make an appointment to see a student in my office at Antioch University, I am equally bound by that appointment and have no more right to brush it off than does the student. Position, rank, and salary do not excuse a lapse of an agreement, and when people in positions of responsibility disregard agreements, they are eventually toppled, as we saw with President Nixon and with the top management at Enron. An agreement is a sacred pact between two or more people and to honor it means to create conditions of health throughout the organization or group. Agreements are the fabric that holds people together.

When agreements are habitually broken, I often suggest that rather than appointing a "policeman," the organization build a web of mutual accountability, beginning with a buddy system for check-ins, some small-group coaching, clear assignment of tasks with frequent reporting, and a manageable period that allows for success. Like weaning a child from the bottle, some people need many baby steps toward wholeness in holding to agreements.

Human Beings are Resources, not Commodities

This topic has been discussed a great deal, and much could be said. To add one more cogent example, some years ago my brother gave me a book by John Abrams called *The Company We Keep: Reinventing Small Business for People, Community, and Place.* I have dabbled in this wonderful story of entrepreneurship that takes place on Martha's Vineyard, and I have enjoyed the many gems shared by Abrams. The essential story is of a successful cabinetmaker and his carpenter friends who one day back in 1986 decided to change from a sole proprietorship to a worker owned cooperative corporation, the South Mountain Company. Abrams first transferred his ownership to a group of three and soon to sixteen worker-owners. After five years, new employees could also expect to become eligible for owner status. The business has grown, yet they have been able to live their values, some of which are expressed early in the book:

> cultivating workplace democracy
> challenging the gospel of growth
> balancing multiple bottom lines
> committing to the business of place
> celebrating the spirit of the craft
> advancing 'people conservation'
> practicing community entrepreneurism
> thinking like cathedral builders[5]

Rather than practice wage servitude and environmental recklessness, the members of the South Mountain Company brought their values into alignment with their business practices. Each of the stated underpinnings could be developed further, but I would like to focus here on the notion of "people conservation."

Abrams shares many stories about meeting extraordinary people who have housing needs and ideals. Beginning with a small house his company built for a widow who could not afford even $50,000 and ultimately creating a co-housing project on the island that led to similar projects elsewhere, The South Mountain folks practice their values in their community work as well as their internal governance. This congruence of values and practices is inspiring wherever one meets it, and it starts by putting human beings first. This means caring for others beyond the terms of employment and it means treating others as resources waiting to be discovered.

This example leads into the point I wish to make: Organic organizations look at their compensation policies to see whether more can be done to meet *needs* rather than merely compensate as entitlement. For example, expenses for parents raising children are naturally higher, yet few organizations recognize this. Some organizations have finally shifted to flex time and a few provide quality day care, but in most instances, organizations have an attitude of "children are your problem." However if you talk with moms and dads, you find that child-rearing issues are front and center. Why not consider a dependent care allowance as seriously as retirement plans? Why can't our organizations become more child-friendly?

People conservation in human resource management also involves the whole notion of time. Rigid organizations pay by the hour; even those who are on salary often are expected to quantify work done. How does one measure a good idea, a well-placed phone call, or a conversation that turns a situation around? I suggest that we need to look at our evaluative and compensation practices to see if they fully reflect our values. Some of the tools found in this book, such as the planetary types, geometry of groups and the language of the organs can inform us in establishing evaluative procedures that use dialogue, portfolio assessment, and self-assessment as opposed to the more rigid performance evaluation check lists.

Diversity, Gender Equity, and Differing Perspectives Are needed for Sustainability and Organizational Health.

Much has been developed in a vast literature, and I will not attempt to repeat what others have already articulated on this subject—except to say that, in particular, I have appreciated Sonia Nieto's work on multiculturalism. My main point that is that issues of inclusion matter not just in terms of race, gender, and ethnicity, but also in how people work together in groups. Frequently, patterns that show up on a macro level as race issues are also found on a micro level, in peoples' daily inter-actions regardless of their backgrounds. In a healthy organization all people are valued and respected, not just for their skills, but also for their human capacities, their temperaments, planetary types, feelings, thoughts, and initiatives. Keeping in mind different types of people, as discussed in earlier chapters, will assist leaders and individuals in orga-nizations to keep objective viewpoints in working with one another.

Meetings are Short, Efficient, and Regular

Where did meetings come from? Who was the fool, who first said, "Let's sit down and talk about this?" From what may have been humble beginnings, we now have Meeting Monsters that suck precious time and energy into their hungry jaws. The *New York Times* recently stated that "of those workers who attend meetings each week, fully seventy-five percent say that those gatherings could be more effective." That means a lot of unproductive time occurs because 91,000,000 workers spend time in meetings each week. For most, it is one to eight hours, but a hardy eleven percent of men (who are more meeting-prone than women) somehow survive thirteen or more hours of meetings a week."[6] If occasionally you were to count the number of people in a meeting and multiply it by the number of hours spent there, multiplied again by the average hourly compensation, you would be astounded at the pure financial cost of all those meetings.

I am not opposed to meetings per se, but only to the quantity and length of many of them. I have found that a healthy organization has regular meetings with those who need them, and that the members reg-ularly ask: Do we need to this together, or can someone else or a com-mittee do this for us? Healthy organizations use the heart as a template for circulation from committees—the farther extremities—toward the center. Wherever there is good flow, there is also less need for meet-ings that include everyone. Using the information from the section on organs, the wisdom of the heart can speak to our meeting practices.

Financial Health

Many other sources can benefit organizations through sound finan-cial practices, but here I would like to observe that, when the finances are in order, it is very likely that the rest of the organization is healthy. Finances reflect human activity, and when the internal and external dynamics are working well, the finances usually reflect that. Exceptions to this do occur, however, in instances of calamities such as hurricanes or other unforeseeable events. Although I am not a banker, I tend to ask a few questions in this area, which helps me determine how other parts of the organization are working.

1. When looking at a non-profit, is there a balanced budget? What is the historical picture? When looking at a for-profit, what is the rate of return on shareholder equity?

2. If there is debt, what kind is it and does debt service, including mortgages, exceed more than thirty- five percent of operating income? Paying back a loan for a building is perfectly normal, but I am particularly sensitive to accumulated operating debt that is simply rolled over into the next fiscal year.

3. What percentage of the operating budget is used for personnel, and in what categories? Although seventy percent is the norm in the non-profits that I work with, I look especially for excesses in one department or another. This often speaks to failed oversight or undue influence in one group or another. Is the yearly budget a true "footprint" of the intentions of those guiding the strategic vision?

4. To what extent are personnel subsidizing the operating budget through salaries that are lower than they should be? While this human resource subsidy can work for a while in a pioneering organization, it becomes a trap over time and the best talent tends to depart prematurely.

5. Moving slightly beyond the finances, I also look to see how problems are dealt with when they come up and whether people are willing or able to ask for timely help. Do they consult others outside their organization? Are they part of a professional network that can lend support? Are people improving their skills? Degrees are, in my opinion, not as important as finding the right people from whom we can learn the lessons of life. We all need and deserve mentors.

QUALITY VS. MEDIOCRITY

Although this might seem to be a simple choice, I am surprised how often organizations choose the latter. Sometimes people are afraid of "looking bad" by having to hire talent, or else they rationalize that they can save money—usually only in the very short term. Sometimes there are deep-seated prejudices that prevent good hiring. Whatever the reason, there is no surer sign of a failing organization than one that goes for mediocrity over talent and then fails to mentor or evaluate, thus perpetuating mediocrity.

For those who want some solid examples of how important it is to get the right people "on the bus," even if you don't know at first just where everyone will sit, I recommend Jim Collins's book *Good to Great: Why Some Companies Make the Leap...and Others Don't*. If you can attract the very best people available, many other things will gradually sort themselves out. Reviewing the chapter on planetary types is also a good tool for organizations when considering personnel choices.

SHARED VISION

Strategic planning is quite common these days, yet I find that when people use that term they mean all sorts of different things—from simple goal setting, to mission statements or practical budget setting. I have found it instructive to inquire if an organization has a shared vision and if so how they achieved it. The most common failure I have seen of late is that, whereas there may be a mission statement "in writing," and whereas some in the organization may espouse a vision, it is not always shared by all the parts and subgroups. This often occurs because the vision was achieved behind closed doors by only part of the organization. In this case, the vision does not truly resonate through the organism, and progress may be limited or bound to the participation of just a few key individuals.

Some years ago I did the "Future Search" training with Sandra Janoff and Marvin Weisbord. I was impressed with how they work with large groups to achieve a shared vision. More than sixty participants with varying agendas were present, yet Janoff and Weisborg guided us through a three-day sequence that really brought people together. I have since adapted some of their techniques found in their book *Future*

Search. I have found the techniques to be helpful in settings such as back-to-school retreats and whole-systems strategic planning. I suggest their book as a tool to assist in creating organic organ-izations.

In addition to the "big picture" work of shared visioning, there is of course value to yearly goal setting. For schools I recommend late summer retreats with faculty, administration, board and lead parents to review the shared vision, set practical goals, and work on "follow-ership" skills. There is much literature on effective leadership, but if everyone leads, one simply has a lot pushing and shoving. The culture of an organization is enhanced when a group can enumerate expectations of its members, especially in relation to the goals set for the year ahead. Those who are then charged with responsibility can be assured that they will not work in a vacuum, but will in fact have resources and encouragement along the way.

MAINTENANCE

Finally, a word on the care of an organization's physical plant. When things are clean and well maintained, it speaks volumes about how people relate to one another and the organization of which they are a part. Even if the buildings are modest and the budget limited, there is no reason rooms cannot be cleaned and simple repairs made in a timely way. When people respect their work environment they may be somewhat more likely to respect each other. Maintenance also implies the care of group process and respect for the needs of the individuals within our organizations. Just as plants need watering, so attention needs to be given to such mundane matters as the chairs folks are asked to sit in, the circulation of air and the quality of light. On another level, this maintenance work is part of the "copper" motif mentioned earlier in the chapter on trace metals, the relationships between people in the workplace and their connections. The care and maintenance functions in an organization reveal what we value. We see that by examining the human organism and its parts and relating them to organizations we have arrived at a picture of the organic organ-ization. The above attributes are the outer images of the fruit that is borne by working toward these ideals in organic organ-izations.

20. THE CONSULTATION PROCESS

ONE OF THE final points of the last chapter involved asking for help. With organizations, this frequently involves bringing in an outside consultant. Whereas most of the preceding chapters have advocated for what might be called internal consulting, or self-help within an organization, in this chapter we will look at some of the necessary stages in an external consultation process.

There are so many "consultant stories" floating around that I could not resist telling one here as preamble to this chapter on change efforts.

A sheepherder was tending his flock in a field at the edge of a country road in rural Wyoming. A brand new SUV came flying down the road and screeched to a halt, and the driver—dressed nattily—hopped out and approached the shepherd. He looked at the flock and said, "If I can guess the exact number of sheep here, will you give me a young lamb?"

The shepherd looked over the sprawling herd, stroked his chin, and said, "Sure, give it a whirl."

The young man connected his notebook and wireless modem, did some computer acrobatics, turned to the shepherd, and said, "Looks like 1,586 sheep are here."

The herder said, "Whoa! You hit it right on the nose. Unbelievable! Take your pick."

As the man picked up a young lamb and turned to go, the shepherd said, "Wait a minute, son. If I can guess your profession, will you give me back my lamb?"

"Sure," the young man said.

"You're a consultant."

"Exactly! How did you know?"

"It's pretty simple. You came here uninvited and charged me a fee to tell me something I already knew."[7]

This story, while humorous, reveals some of the dissatisfaction people have with consultants. While not usually "uninvited," they do have a way of showing up when only a part of an organization has extended the invitation—perhaps the leadership or a disenfranchised group that feels it has lost its voice. An extreme example for me was the time a school invited me, through its administration and board, to visit at the end of the summer. I traveled three thousand miles and showed up at the first meeting, only to have the group ask, "What are you doing here?" It turns out they'd had elections the previous night, and an entirely new board had been chosen, none of whom knew of my engagement and previous phone conversations. We worked it out, but it was an awkward beginning.

I have found that no matter how much some folks complain about consultants and their fees, if organizations cannot solve their problems themselves they inevitably turn to outside help. Moreover, for every horror story of a failed consultation that I have heard, I can cite an equal number of successful turnarounds that are remembered even years later as pivotal in the health and growth of the organization. We all need help from time to time. The real questions are: How do we work with setting expectations? What consultation process is most helpful? What are the best practices to be learned and the common pitfalls to be avoided? How can an organization go through change in a way that leads to growth and future success?

When my phone rings or the e-mail goes "ping," I often hear from someone who is distraught, has had experiences that point to organizational dysfunction, and has just had enough. Sometimes that person is in a position of responsibility, other times there is a more peripheral relationship. I try, in the initial minutes to listen with empathy, ask a few questions to clarify and help the person focus on the core issues. All the while, I repeat silently to myself, "This is just one person in that organization, and what I am hearing is a semblance of the problem; I will need to look further." At some point in this initial conversation I usually mirror back what I have heard and describe a typical consultation process, which follows.

ASSESSMENT

The consultation process I have developed is a classic instance of the threefold method of inquiry used throughout this book. The first step is to collect the relevant "facts" through interviews, group meetings, and review of pertinent documents. That is not enough, however.

I need to know how things sit with those concerned and get their feelings and impressions on the issues. Then, with time and often upon my return home, I try and access the "essence" of the need, the core issues. Fact, feeling, and essence become mutually supportive steps in the consultation process.

Over the years I have gradually gained great respect for the importance of inquiry—asking questions and doing a complete assessment before starting the change process. One needs to do this thoroughly, and not succumb to the temptation to accept at face value the "presenting problem." Otherwise, part way through the consultation, when new information surfaces—and it always does—one has to backtrack and begin again. Therefore, I do an extensive assessment, which usually includes reading relevant documents: recent minutes of meetings, long-range plans, reports to other entities, news articles, and even budget summaries. I also hold large group meetings and conduct individual interviews. In the large groups I get an overview of the key issues and can assess the "temperature" around them. In the individual interviews—as many as forty or fifty—I probe deeper, examine relational issues, test leadership responses, and even test "trial balloons"—possible outcomes of the consultation process. Many times, the individuals interviewed feel better just by having a place to share and unburden. In one case I had already completed the interviews when one more person ran up to me and said, "I need to talk with you even though you already have a full picture of the situation. I just need a chance to talk about things that have not been possible anywhere else." Indeed, in most instances people feel a lift from not only the sharing but also the sense that finally something is being done about the problem.

The assessment culminates in a report of "findings and recommendations." I have tried various ways of communicating the report, from just sending it in, to presenting it in person with handouts available at the end of the meeting. Sending it in is cost effective and has the advantage of getting people to think about it before they respond at my next visit. The downside is that misunderstandings can flourish and despite requests not to, small groups tend to talk about the report, thus creating new realities of interpretation. The advantage to sharing the report initially in person is that I can calibrate my presentation to take advantage of the setting, the particular questions of those in attendance and field any misunderstandings immediately. Organizations also tend to want begin the change process right away, and it is often frustrating for them to wait until my next visit, which sometimes happens months after the assessment.

In the years ahead, I plan to add a new component to the assessment process, namely the physiological "lenses" described in this book. Using the tools described in various chapters, I hope to be able at least to pose a hypothesis or two regarding the overall gestalt of the school. Do the phenomena assessed describe a "heart" or a "lung" organization? Is there a whole-systems approach to problem solving or not? How do leaders score on the leadership inventory? These are only a few of the practical applications possible indicated by the research now completed.

THE CHANGE EFFORT

This second stage of the consultation can last as much as a year. It can represent just a few visits with the organization doing "homework" in between, or it can involve many visits and conference calls in between. This is the stage when we take one recommendation after another and begin to do the work. It is highly collaborative and takes much good will on all sides. I have learned to consider carefully the sequence of changes, as they tend to influence one another; when successful, one positive development can be leveraged to support others.

Usually part way through this stage we come up against the big "R," otherwise known as resistance. Most people see the need for change, especially after the assessment, but actually doing what it takes is another story. Usually there are hot issues with a history, personal grudges and interests that surface to try and block change. Sometimes this is overt, as in outspoken criticism in meetings, but more often it is subtle, such as politicking between my visits, off-the-cuff comments or nonattendance at meetings. I have been particularly aware of the "passive-aggressive" pattern in which a person refuses to engage fully when I am on site but then lashes out at those who are carry the change effort forward in my absence. Often this is where the issues of fear, anger, and personal lack of fulfillment come into play, yet since they have been neglected for so long, they come out as projections and resistance to the change process itself.

Another frequent challenge is that when things get better in an organization, people are often so relieved that they are willing to drop the rest of it and go back to life as usual. "I am no longer so frustrated with our meetings, so we don't need to do all the rest of this stuff now." When organizations drop things at the "somewhat better" stage, they do so at their peril, for it is highly likely that the previous symptoms will return in time. When the root causes are not addressed, organizations tend to live in cycles—boom and bust, crisis and relative calm. I am also amazed at how resilient people become in that they have learned to live with a certain level of dysfunction and can now tolerate more than is good for them or the group. Part of the point of the change process is to lift the general level of work so that those involved experience a new way of doing things. To this end, the consultant has to try to model what he or she would like to see others doing. It is usually not enough to just effect structural changes, one needs to change the patterns of behavior within the structure.

This brings me to another central dilemma. It is often not clear as to whether to try and change the culture and ways of working between people first, or to make structural changes that can serve as scaffolding for the rest of the organization. Neglecting one or the other usually comes back to haunt me. So generally, I end up doing some of both. When there is a serious crisis that threatens the existence of the organization, I tend to lean more toward structural and leadership change; when there is time, I do more in the interpersonal realm first and then enlist their help in making the structural changes. It is all a matter of the amount of time and resources available to do what needs to be done.

Review

When the change effort is complete, it is a natural tendency just to go on with life. In recent years, however, I have insisted on a final, follow-up visit to review, reassess, and do some fine-tuning if needed. It is good for organizations to be reflective at times and sitting back to talk about how it has been the past six months can be a learning experience for all concerned. This is consistent with the Saturn and Moon influences from the chapter on planetary types. With a review, one also models accountability, even for the consultant. Much of my learning has come from groups telling me what has worked and what could have been better. There is also a need to bring closure to a process. Organizational health can be enhanced when beginnings and endings are honored, and when people can experience the potency of their efforts at change. One hopes that participants in an organization have learned new skills which then can be applied earlier next time, and that there would in the future be an array of "internal consultants" available to meet future challenges.

Not every consultation need be so involved. For example, as mentioned earlier, I have found whole-systems retreats to be of great value. In this scenario, all the main constituent groups gather in one place for one to three days to work together. This is especially helpful in establishing one coherent picture of the mission of the organization, specific goals for the years ahead, and coordinating the efforts of the individual committees and working groups. Often too little time is spent on the "umbrella," the overarching vision that can hold everything together when external challenges arise. A retreat helps people get on the same page, while at the same time individuals get to know one another better, relationships are cultivated, and interest in mutual tasks can be awakened.

I would like to end this chapter with a metaphor. A midwife or nurse serves a real need. She will be there at crucial moments to coach, assist, and bring something entirely new into the world. When the work of birthing is done, she cleans up and leaves. The midwife is neither the parent nor the child, but her assistance can be crucial. I like to think of a consultant as a midwife, someone who assists with new birth while making sure that ownership of the identity of an organization is held by those whom will be together for years to come. When done well, consulting is a selfless task with outcomes that cannot be predicted. With an open heart, some helpful skills, and an abiding belief in the essential goodness that emerges from people when they engage in renewal, a consultant can facilitate the changes that long to happen. There is no experience greater in this world than the miracle of birth.

21. THE LILY AND THE ROSE

IN MANY WALDORF schools, the school year begins and ends with the "rose ceremony." At the start of their journey, first graders and their new teacher are each given a rose by an eighth grader. The little ones walk across the stage to receive a rose and then stand with their partners until an entire semicircle of pairs stretches across the stage. At the end of the year, the first graders each give a rose to one of the graduating eighth graders. The other students and teachers, as well as many of the parents attending these events, are often moved by the simple yet profound experience. Over the years, this rose ceremony enters the consciousness of all the students, and the archetypal act of the "passing on" of the rose is remembered forever.

When our daughter Louisa graduated from eighth grade, she received not just a rose, but also an entire bush. A few days later I planted it along our split-rail fence in the backyard, where it joined a few other rose bushes. To make room, however, I had to thin out some of the day lilies that had taken over, and that got me thinking about roses and lilies.

As I was reminded when planting Louisa's bush, the rose has a hard stem and numerous thorns. This part of the rose plant has a wooden, earthlike aspect. Both in coloration and in texture, one senses that the rose follows the hard path, the journey down into darkness. Then you gaze at the flower, and you see richness, color, and enclosed light. The rose has something sacred about it, regardless of color. The deep red rose always moves me more than the others, with the blood red petals opened to the surrounding world. A wise Sufi teacher once comforted me in a moment of personal grief by suggesting I inwardly place myself inside the rose bud and experience its gradual opening. She suggested that I would experience the fear and uncertainty that comes with grief, but also the courage to open once again to the surrounding world.

Sacred traditions throughout time have used the rose symbolically. Films, from *Beauty and the Beast* to the *Da Vinci Code,* utilize the rose, although many today do not understand its significance. The Rosicrucians, a spiritual order originating in the Middle Ages, used the rose for some of their most striking meditations, and "under the Rose" means to take an oath of silence. Indeed, one can best experience the divine when the earthly senses are silenced and overcome. The rose calls on us to transform the earthly into what lives in sunlight and wisdom.

As I discovered again recently while transplanting, the lily, is much more juicy, fluid in movement, and leafy to the point of being mostly leaf. Its gesture is expansive and gracefully adorns our New England rock walls. Without much care, they bloom profusely all summer. While the rose points to the hard path of life experience, the lily indicates mercy and unexpected blessing. It is the flower of the annunciation. In fact, the daylily, or *hemerocallis,* is not the same plant as the lily, or *lilium,* which has a stem with smaller leaves attached in a different gesture. The *lilium* is the flower of the annunciation.

Both the rose and the lily, as *gestures,* are needed in healthy organizations. If we try to be all smiles, always joyful, expansive, and friendly, we risk superficiality. If we focus singly on the challenges and obstacles, we can become too serious. Together, the rose and the lily are the pillars needed to herald birth. The rose is closest to the path taken by the will—of hard work, overcoming countless challenges, and bringing forth patience in response. The lily expresses those moments when an unexpected and kind gift comes your way, and shows the path that leads human beings to their own special relationship to both the heavens and the earth. We all pass through the portal of birth and grow through a series of developmental stages, and organizations follow a similar path of incarnation.

This rainbow bridge leads in stages from the expansive vision of the entrepreneur to concrete goals and practical tasks. To "incorporate" means to find a body, a vehicle that will serve the mission of the organization. The incarnation path of an organization is much more than filing legal papers. Incorporation is a process of vision, finding a relationship to the environment and developing practices that work. This is a unique practice for each organization. For example, Ben and Jerry like to tell how they experimented with creating flavors of ice cream. Jerry mixed and then had Ben do the tasting. He always asked for more flavor. Much later they found out that Ben had limited smell and taste senses; thus the company ended up with extra strong flavors. The incarnation path of an organization defines its unique character.

One can distinguish at least three major stages in organizational development: the founding phase, a stage of differentiation, and a phase of integration. Bernard Lievegoed and others have described these stages in more detail than I can here, but for the purposes of healthy organization; I want to mention a few characteristic aspects.[8]

The founding stage of a successful organization has a charmed quality; people and resources come together in ways governed more by synchronicity than strategic planning. There is magic to the way in which wonderful things happen between people, their enthusiasm, and long hours. At this stage one sees much initiative, and the founders carry largely unquestioned authority. Decisions are based on the capacities of the founders; indeed, there is little formal organizational structure. For the first seven years or more, events, people, and resources seem to flow together as if by divine plan. Despite the long hours, participants are often reenergized by the tremendous progress they experience in such a short time.

The danger occurs when the pioneering phase is carried over too long, and the informal leadership style of the founders is perpetuated over time. I have found that even when the early founders retire, some organizations try and keep going without entering the next stage and they either place "puppets" in leadership roles or learn to work with a leadership vacuum, to the detriment of organizational sanity.

For what should happen next is a stage of differentiation in which responsibilities are clarified, job descriptions are created, tasks are divided up and decision-making is examined. Some organizations move into a typical hierarchical structure at this time, others remain horizontal with myriad committees. With the potential veto of the founders no longer present, there is much sorting out and shifting of responsibilities at this stage. If the first stage is characterized by sentient-soul-like enthusiasm, this next stage tends to be more like the intellectual soul in its abstractions and delineation of tasks. A certain amount of rigidity can set in during this second stage, and people can start to feel that they work "for" rather than "with."

In the next phase of integration, there is usually a concerted attempt to bring together all the constituent parts into one dynamic "whole." In a school setting, somewhat as a vestige of the founding stage, this can mean establishing a PTO to work alongside the board and the faculty. In the third stage, the attempt is made to achieve not cooperation but a degree of collaboration in which each part can act singularly while all have the same vision of the future of the organization.

Throughout these stages, the people within an organization can either create or remove hindrances to its development. In this book, we have explored human physiology as a guide to healthy organizations. With the tools given here and by using the map of human physiology, one can test for organizational health by asking key questions:

1. What attitudes and practices do people in this organization have toward the essential nature of the human being?

2. What is the "temperature," the warmth factor here?

3. Are there blockages or is there a healthy circulation between the groups? (heart)

4. Is there a balance between differentiation and integration? (kidney)

5. Do people do what they said they would do? Are agreements honored? (liver)

6. How strong is the immune system? (Does the organization jolt from crisis to crisis, overreacting to small external and internal changes?)

7. What is the level of activity—hyperactive or lethargic? (thyroid and other glands)

8. What "metal" of leadership shows itself in this organization?

9. Are differing points of view welcomed and used to build lasting solutions? (planets)

10. Are key players able to see beyond the "parts" to encompass a whole-systems approach?

11. Are outside visitors welcome?

12. If this is a nonprofit, is the budget balanced?

13. What is the quality of group work?

14. Is there transparency behind decision making?

15. Is this a "sensible organization" i.e., do leaders gather information from many sources and connect "the dots."

16. Are there unresolved issues of power and control? (lung)

17. Is there a rhythm to organizational processes? (heart, spleen)

18. Are assumptions tested and do leaders allow for unusual questions?

In his seminal work *Images of Organizations*, Gareth Morgan said, "Organizations, like organisms, can be conceived of as sets of interacting subsystems.... The open-systems approach encourages us to establish congruencies or 'alignments' between different systems and to identify and eliminate potential dysfunctions."[9] In the language of this book, this means that when something is alive, such as the human body, it has numerous interacting subsystems, like circulation and respiration and others that tend to self-correct on a daily basis. Rather than form abstractions about organizational tasks, it is far more helpful to attend to the basic functioning of whole systems, which often self-maintain without human interference. Rather than just tinker with the parts, trying to direct how each person should perform each task, it is far better for leaders to attend to the processes described here while trusting their basic wisdom. Despite billions spent each year in the medical industry, one human body is wiser than all the doctors and hospitals put together. Likewise, the more we tinker with organizations and focus on work outcomes in the name of productivity, the more we actually inhibit the very life systems that are needed for success.

More than ever before in human history, we need to see the whole before the parts. In fact, as shown in the chapters on the skeleton and the organs, we can even see the whole in the parts. When we do this then we are working with living systems that sustain life, promote initiative, and unleash human creativity. All it takes is one invention, one flash of human potential, and the world is changed. Let us never underestimate the human being in all dimensions. Moreover, let us use a methodology such as the threefold method of research involving fact, feeling, and essence, which allows for true learning.

A tree is a fact, whether oak, pine, or maple. One has only to spend time with just one of these trees to develop feelings about the colorful maple, the evergreen pine, or the sturdy oak. Then, with the passage of time, one begins to glimpse the essence, the true being of the tree; one begins to wonder what it is like to be an oak or a pine. At this third stage, one joins in the essence of the phenomenon that started out as a mere fact.

Thus it is with the organs and the human body. I have shared a few facts without getting too technical, surfaced some relational aspects without getting carried away in feelings, and then indicated a few of the essential qualities that pertain to living systems. I am not finished, yet I have recognized that this, too, is a feature of organic organ-izations. I have taken a few risks in these chapters, but I could not really do otherwise if I am to promote reexamination of how we choose to work together in the years to come.

At a recent graduation ceremony at the High Mowing School in Wilton, New Hampshire, two seniors stood up to read a few words from an anonymous source that captured their feelings of the day and serve as a fitting conclusion to this work on organizational health:

> "To laugh is to risk appearing the fool
> To weep is to risk appearing sentimental
> To reach out to another is to risk involvement
>
> To try is to risk failure
> To hope is to risk despair
> To live is to risk dying....
>
> But risks must be taken for the greatest hazard
> in life is to risk nothing
> The person who risks nothing, does nothing, has nothing,
> and is nothing
>
> They may avoid suffering and sorrow, but they cannot learn,
>   feel, change,
> grow, love, live....
> Chained by their attitude, they are a slave, they have forfeited
>   their freedom.
>
> Only the person who risks is free.
>   —ANONYMOUS

APPENDICES

TESTING YOUR LEADERSHIP METAL

AN INVENTORY DEVELOPED BY TORIN FINSER BASED UPON STUDY OF THE METALS IN ORGAN-IZATIONS

THIS IS A leadership inventory of the metals in which individuals can respond to key descriptors and then rate themselves on a score sheet. The groupings end up in the seven basic metals. For each statement consider how well it applies to you and circle a number 1 to 5, with 1 being "least like me" and 5 being "very much me." Then turn over the page and enter your scores for each item.

1. When something needs doing I prefer to jump in and do it rather than sit around talking about it.
   1 2 3 4 5

2. I enjoy connecting with other people.
   1 2 3 4 5

3. Nowadays one needs to protect and guard oneself against crazy ideas and suggestions.
   1 2 3 4 5

4. Flexibility is important.
   1 2 3 4 5

5. When things become scattered & dispersed, I like to bring ideas and people back together again.
   1 2 3 4 5

6. Meetings need form and structure.
   1 2 3 4 5

7. Things usually turn out all right in the end.
   1 2 3 4 5

8. I admire strength and courage in others and I try and emulate these qualities whenever I can.
   1 2 3 4 5

9. People need to be supported with warmth.
   1 2 3 4 5

10. Once something has been decided one must stick to it.
    1 2 3 4 5

11. I am able to reflect what other people say and mirror it back to them.
    1 2 3 4 5

12. Life is full of give and take—trade-offs are necessary to get what you want.
    1 2 3 4 5

13. I admire consistency and steadiness.
    1 2 3 4 5

14. We need to simply encourage people to do their best and they will.
    1 2 3 4 5

15. In our complex world we need practical advice and tools to get things done.
    1 2 3 4 5

16. In confrontation, it is best if each person can adapt and compromise a bit.
    1 2 3 4 5

17. There are things one can do and things one cannot do---one
has to be realistic.
1 2 3 4 5

18. I don't ask much for myself.
1 2 3 4 5

19. I often find myself in the role of messenger.
1 2 3 4 5

20. I like to know the agenda ahead of time.
1 2 3 4 5

21. If you stay true to your heart you will know what to do.
1 2 3 4 5

22. Adversity forms character.
1 2 3 4 5

23. When people are held and supported they can do more.
1 2 3 4 5

24. To understand things correctly sometimes one has to take
things apart and examine ideas sentence by sentence.
1 2 3 4 5

25. I love gazing at a full moon on a clear night.
1 2 3 4 5

26. I like moving between groups, listening in on good conversations and making a little contribution here and there.
1 2 3 4 5

27. People have to set personal and professional boundaries.
1 2 3 4 5

28. A good deed goes a long way.
1 2 3 4 5

29. Getting anywhere in life requires hard work, effort and inner strength.
    1 2 3 4 5

30. The health of the group is very important to me.
    1 2 3 4 5

31. Tasks need clarity and definition.
    1 2 3 4 5

32. Things in this world are always moving and changing; just go with the flow.
    1 2 3 4 5

33. I like connecting people with each other.
    1 2 3 4 5

34. One cannot just be "open" to what happens; you need to discern what is right and appropriate
    1 2 3 4 5

35. It is essential to strive for harmony.
    1 2 3 4 5

36. I like to be engaged, active, and even assertive.
    1 2 3 4 5

37. I value good listening and communication.
    1 2 3 4 5

38. Too much going on at once gives me a headache.
    1 2 3 4 5

39. Sometimes I daydream.
    1 2 3 4 5

40. Life is full of variety and joy.
    1 2 3 4 5

41. I am who I am.
   1 2 3 4 5

42. Our conscience is an inner compass that needs to be consulted in making decisions.
   1 2 3 4 5

43. Follow-through is important.
   1 2 3 4 5

44. Connecting ideas is fun.
   1 2 3 4 5

45. We need to define what we mean.
   1 2 3 4 5

46. Brainstorming is great; lets see what happens.
   1 2 3 4 5

47. Borrowing ideas is okay at times.
   1 2 3 4 5

48. Do what you said you would do.
   1 2 3 4 5

49. We need to praise and acknowledge people more.
   1 2 3 4 5

SCORE SHEET

Find your question number below and next to it write the number you selected from 1 to 5. Then add up each group to find your leadership preference. Each group is meant to be a different metal, so your highest scores will be your preferred metal with attendant leadership characteristics described in chapter 4.

Group I

Items	Your Score
1	
8	
15	
22	
29	
36	
43	
Total:	

Group II

Items	Your Score
2	
9	
16	
23	
30	
37	
44	
Total:	

Group III

Items	Your Score
3	
10	
17	
24	
31	
38	
45	
Total:	

Group IV

Items	Your Score
4	
11	
18	
25	
32	
39	
46	
Total:	

Group V			Group VI		
Items	Your Score		Items		Your Score
5			6		
12			13		
19			20		
26			27		
33			34		
40			41		
47			48		
	Total:			Total:	

Group VII	
Items	Your Score
7	
14	
21	
28	
35	
42	
49	
	Total:

Appendix B

By Kim John Payne m.ed

Moon
Physical Body

Metal: Silver
Color: Violet
Bodily: Reproductive Organs
           Skin
           Brain
           Cell division

Qualities of Soul:

The Romantic Type
    Inner world dominates
    Conservers
    Mirror consciousness
    Recapitulation
    Abstraction
    Details
    Reflective preservers
    Ritual in thinking , feeling and action
    Inflexibility
    Followers
    Planners
    Traditionalist
    Fact over fiction
    Love of statistics and formula
    Step-by-step process
    Love of specifics, clarity

Selfless
Form receiving
The archivist

Questions for the teacher:

What am I teaching?
Is it in the right place and time?
Have I been clear with the schedulers?
Why am I teaching this subject in this way?
What is it I can do to encourage the students to reflect?
Have I reflected deeply on my own practice?
Have I incorporated an identifiable process?
Am I able to summarize the major points?
Have I done enough preparation?
Have I done too much preparation?
Am I feeling well?
Am I taking care of my health?
Are my appearance, clothing and hygiene good?

SATURN
EGO

Metal: Lead
Color: Midnight/Dark blue
Bodily: Skeleton
            Bone marrow
            Spleen
            Immune system
            Pineal gland

Qualities of Soul:

The Aesthetic Type
    Outer world dominates
    Essential from the non-essential
    Investigator

Judgment out of sympathy/antipathy
Defining
Focusing
The Researcher
Weighing up
From the far past to the far future
From cosmic to individual memory
Radical
Not interested in traditions
Metamorphosis
From crisis to new possibility

Questions for the teacher:

Can I set defined goals and achieve them?
Do I remain focused?
Am I able to hear the essence of a question and respond
appropriately?
Am I able to make clear transparent judgments?
Do I become overly critical of students and colleagues?
Am I sensitive in my feedback/reflections to students and
colleagues?
Have I gone deep enough in my research and presentation?
Do I encourage the students to go ever deeper?
To interact with lead it has to be warmed...Have I warmed the
students?

MERCURY
ETHERIC BODY

Metal:	Quicksilver
Color:	Yellow
Bodily:	Lymph glands
	Lung

Qualities of Soul:

> The Mobile Type
> Inner and outer world in balance
> Adaptive
> Inventive
> Love of new discovery, new tasks, and new environments
> Experimentation
> Constant movement
> God of merchant, thieves and healers
> The motivator
> Asymmetry
> Chaos
> Busy

Questions for the teacher:

> Do I flow easily through the material?
> Do I get stuck and spend too long on one aspect?
> Do I motivate the class?
> Can I adapt to unexpected and unplanned changes and input?
> Do I encourage experimentation and projects?
> Do I inspire original ideas?
> Do I leave open spaces and possibilities for students to
>   inspire each other?
> Do I involve movement in the lesson?
> Can I allow chaos and brainstorming?
> Is there something new in each lesson?
> Do I allow the students to make their own discoveries or
>   do I over-teach?

JUPITER
INTELLECTUAL/MIND SOUL

Metal:	Tin
Color:	Orange
Bodily:	Liver
	Muscle

Qualities of Soul:
    The Dominant Type
        Inner and outer world balance
        The present
        Forming
        Rounding off
        Sculpting
        Symmetry
        Living thinking
        Understanding
        Beauty
        Wisdom
        The archetype
        The overview

Questions for the teacher:

        Have I brought enough breadth to my lesson?
        Did I give a full picture, an overview?
        How does the content of my lesson fit with the whole course?
        How does the course relate to the whole picture of
            adolescent development?
        Am I relating this content to the lives of the students?
        Is it relevant?
        Do the students have an understanding of the couse process,
            the steps we are taking and why?
        Do my assignments have enough breadth in them?
        Do I have enough form in the lesson and course?
        Does the lesson have a well-defined beginning and end?
        Am I being overly structured?
        Do I care as much for the process as for the outcome?

VENUS
ASTRAL BODY

Metal:	Copper
Color:	Green
Bodily:	Kidney
	Eye

Qualities of Soul:

The Self-conscious Type
    Inner world dominates
    Dreamy nurturer
    Supporting
    Listening
    Non-judgmental
    Accepting
    Receptive
    Illuminates
    Detachment from materialism
    Creates space where an impulse can manifest
    Care of others
    Care of the environment
    Care of relationships

Questions for the teacher:

Have I encouraged all the class to enter into the lesson?
Do I notice and help students who are struggling?
Do I listen and encourage others to listen?
Do I create a safe place for students to express their
    vulnerabilities?
Do I encourage the quieter students to contribute?
Do I talk too much?
Am I too quick to judge?
Am I aware of the subtleties of the class's social dynamic?
Do I strive to see the individual needs of the students?
Am I overly familiar with the students?
Do I draw on the students' feelings in my classes?
Do I contribute to keeping the classroom beautiful?
Do I encourage peer support where a stronger student can
    assist a weaker one?
Do I relate the content to the students' feeling life?

MARS
SENTIENT SOUL

Metal: Iron
Color: Red
Bodily: Gall

Qualities of Soul:

 The Aggressive Type
  Outer world dominates
  Little contact with inner process
  Overcoming
  Conquering
  Building
  Initiative
  Conviction
  Creativity
  Honesty
  Frankness
  Fairness
  Speaking
  Debating
  Courage to confront issues
  Change
  Transformation
  Future
  Needs resistance

Questions for the teacher:

  Do I take initiatives?
  Am I willing to take risks?
  Can I make appropriate challenges?
  Can I be frank without being insulting or insensitive?
  Do I know when I have been insensitive?
  Am I open to feedback from colleagues and students?
  Is there a clear purpose to the lesson?
  Is my speech clear?

Can I instill a sense of purpose in my students?
Do I set clear objectives and encourage student follow-through?
Do I keep to deadlines?
Do I create space for debate and questioning in my classes?
Do I encourage student-initiated change in my lessons and
within the school?

SUN
CONSCIOUSNESS OF SELF

Metal:	Gold
Color:	White
Bodily:	Heart

Qualities of Soul:

The Radiant Type
Balance between:
Point and Periphery
Substance and Spirit
Self-development and Social development
Tension and release
Individual and Group
Today and Future
Harmony
Certainty
Cooperation
"A place for everything under the Sun."
Warmth
Comfort
Belonging
Attentive
Loving

Questions for the teacher:

Have I balance in my teaching between:
Information and research?
Talking and listening?

Individual and group work?
Silent and conversation-based working?
Movement and stillness?
My speaking and student contribution?
Dictation, copying and original work?
Humor and seriousness?
Concentrated work and relaxation?
Seeing the needs of the individual and the group?
The social life of the class/individuals and academics?
Cognitive, expressive and action-based work?
Sympathy and antipathy?

THE ROMANTIC TYPE

Qualities:

I am more interested in understanding my feelings and thoughts.
I can be contemplative.
I like to collect things.
I can reflect back to others how they are feeling.
I can sum up a situation.
I can think in abstraction.
I have a love for details.
I don't like change for the sake of change. It must have a reason.
I relate well to tradition and ritual.
I do not change views quickly.
I do not like to be in the spotlight.
I enjoy making plans.
I do not reject customs and tradition just because they are old.
I prefer fact over fiction.
I relate to statistics and formula.
I enjoy a step-by-step process.
I have a love of specifics and clarity.
I really dislike waffling, not getting to the point.
I think I am fairly selfless.
I am particularly loyal to friends.
I don't tend to make waves and will generally go along with the
    crowd.
I could be described as an archivist.

Questions to engender this quality:

> What am I doing in this situation?
> Is it in the right place and time?
> Have I been clear?
> Why am I engaging in this subject?
> What are people really asking of me?
> I wonder why I do what I do?
> Have I understood the process of what is happening?
> Am I able to summarize the major points?
> Am I prepared for what is happening?
> Am I feeling well?
> Am I taking care of my health?
> Are my appearance, clothing and hygiene good?

THE AESTHETIC TYPE

Qualities :

> I am more interested in what's going on around me than asking how I feel about it.
> I like to work out what is essential from the non-essential.
> I don't like clutter.
> I like to investigate and find out for myself.
> I make judgments after thinking it out.
> I like to define meaning.
> I can stay focused.
> I enjoy research and finding out what makes people do the things that they do.
> I weigh up a situation before getting involved.
> I take the long view and can look back to how things were and forward to how they will be.
> I can be radical and not bound by tradition.
> I like to see things change and transform.
> I am not afraid of crisis as this usually leads to new possibilities.

Questions to engender this quality:

> Can I set defined goals and achieve them?
> Do I remain focused?

Am I able to hear the essence of a question and respond
   appropriately?
Am I able to make clear transparent judgments?
Do I become overly critical of others?
Am I sensitive in my feedback/reflections to others?
Have I gone deep enough in my research and presentation?
Do I encourage the others to go ever deeper?
Have I warmed the others to the process?

THE MOBILE TYPE

Qualities:

I am as interested in the world around me as I am in my own
   inner processes.
I adapt to new situations.
I am inventive.
I love new discovery, new tasks, new environments.
I enjoy experimentation.
I am constantly on the go.
I can motivate myself and others.
I can live with contradictions.
I can handle certain amounts of chaos.
I am always busy.

Questions to engender this quality:

Do I flow easily through the material?
Do I get stuck and spend too long on one aspect?
Do I motivate the group?
Can I adapt to unexpected and unplanned changes and input?
Do I encourage experimentation and projects?
Do I inspire original ideas?
Do I leave open spaces and possibilities for participants to
   inspire each other?
Do I involve movement in the lesson/session?
Can I allow chaos and brainstorming?
Is there something new in each lesson/session?
Do I allow the others to make their own discoveries or do I over
   teach?

THE GOVERNING TYPE

Qualities:

I am equally interested in the world around me as well as my own inner processes.

I particularly relate to the present.
I enjoy bringing form and order to a situation.
I don't like leaving things half-done. I enjoy rounding off.
I enjoy knocking things into shape, sculpting situations.
I like things to line up both in practice and in my thinking. I love symmetry.
I like it when I can put my ideas into practice.
I am understanding.
I like to be surrounded in beauty.
I relate to people who seem thoughtful and wise.
I see and look for who a person really is.
I tend to be objective and see the big picture.

Questions to engender this quality:

Have I brought enough breadth to my approach?
Did I give a full picture, an overview?
How does the content of my session fit with my plans for where we are going?
Am I taking into account the age of the participants?
Am I relating this content to the lives of the students/participants in a relevant way?
Do the students/participants have an understanding of process of the course, the steps we are taking and why?
Do my assignments have enough breadth in them?
Do I have enough form in the lesson and course?
Does the lesson/session have a well-defined beginning and end?
Am I being overly structured?
Do I care as much for the process as for the outcome?

The Receptive Type

Qualities:

I am more interested in staying true to my feelings than being
    influenced by others.
I can be dreamy.
I am often seen as a nurturer.
I naturally support others.
I tend to listen more than I speak.
I am slow to form opinions and can be non-judgmental.
I am generally accepting of other people's ways.
I often help other people see where they are coming from.
I don't need a lot of material things in my life.
I can help create space where an impulse can manifest.
I take care of the environment in which I live.
Caring for relationships is a higher priority for me than getting
    the task completed.

Questions to engender this quality:

Have I encouraged the entire group to enter into the
    lesson/situation?
Do I notice and help participants who are struggling?
Do I listen and encourage others to listen?
Do I create a safe place for the participants to express their
    vulnerabilities?
Do I encourage the quieter people to contribute?
Do I talk too much?
Am I too quick to judge?
Am I aware of the subtleties of the class's social dynamic?
Do I strive to see the individual needs of everybody?
Am I overly familiar with the students?
Do I draw on the participants feelings in my classes?
Do I contribute to keeping the classroom beautiful?
Do I encourage peer support where a stronger student can assist
    a weaker one?
Do I relate the content to the students feeling life?

The Assertive Type

Qualities:

> I am more interested in what's going on around me than I am in asking how I feel about it.
> I don't like to sit around too long and think about things.
> I enjoy overcoming problems.
> I like taking initiative.
> I don't do things halfway.
> I have the conviction to follow my principles.
> I enjoy the creative process.
> I am honest and frank even if makes people uncomfortable.
> I speak out if things don't seem fair.
> I am not overly bothered by public speaking.
> I am willing to debate a point if needed.
> I will confront issues.
> I like to transform old ways.
> I look mainly to the future.
> I like it when people challenge my ideas. It makes me work harder.

Questions to engender this quality:

> Do I take initiatives?
> Am I willing to take risks?
> Can I make appropriate challenges?
> Can I be frank without being insulting or insensitive?
> Do I know when I have been insensitive?
> Am I open to feedback from colleagues and students?
> Is there a clear purpose to the lesson/course?
> Is my speech clear?
> Can I instill a sense of purpose in the participants?
> Do I set clear objectives and encourage everyone to follow through?
> Do I keep to deadlines?
> Do I create space for debate and questioning in my work?
> Do I encourage participant-initiated change in my sessions and within my community?

THE RADIANT TYPE

Qualities:

> I enjoy both social activity and being alone.
> I feel spiritual values are as important as practical daily life.
> I like to work hard and completely relax.
> I give as much attention to the individual as I do the group.
> I am interested in what's going on around me as much as I am in the future.
> I don't do well when there is uncertainty.
> I can often bring people together and help them cooperate.
> "A place for everything under the Sun."
> I am warm towards people and make them feel comfortable.
> I am a fairly secure person and have a sense of being in the right place wherever I am.
> I am usually attentive to situations and other people.
> I think I could honestly say I am a loving person.

Questions to engender this quality:

> Have I balance in my leadership between:
>> Information and research?
>> Talking and listening?
>> Individual and group work?
>> Silent and conversation based working?
>> Movement and stillness?
>> My speaking and student contribution?
>> Dictation, copying and original work?
>> Humor and seriousness?
>> Concentrated work and relaxation?
>> Seeing the needs of the individual and the group?
>> The social life of the group/individuals and the academics?
>> Cognitive, expressive and action-based work?
>> Sympathy and antipathy?

Appendix C

Element	Human	Physiology	Senses	Types of Ether-Life Forces
earth	physical body	physical skin / bones	touch	chemical, formative
water	etheric	lymph	life sense	life ether, sound
air	astral	nerves	movement	air and light ether
fire	ego	blood	balance	warmth ether

APPENDIX D
QUESTIONNAIRE OF JULY 2006

DESIGNED BY TORIN FINSER FOR PURPOSES OF ORGANIZATIONAL RESEARCH

1. Reflecting on your work experiences, what do healthy organizations look like?

2. When you are in a group that is working well, what are the qualities of interpersonal interaction that make for a successful experience?

3. In your experience working in groups, what have been the most frequent challenges?

4. What issue or issues have most challenged your organization as a whole this past year?

5. Knowing what you do of human physiology, would you say your organization works mostly out of the heart, lung, liver, spleen or kidney? (Circle one of the above.)

6. When you are in a small working group, what size have you found to be most successful? Circle one: 3 4 5 6 7

7. At your place of work this past year, do you feel people think mostly of:
   1. Their particular job.
   2. The needs of the whole.

8. In your organization, are agreements:
   1. Clearly articulated and adhered to or,
   2. Vague and not often followed. (Select one.)

9. Choose one word or phrase that describes leadership in your place of work.

NOTES

PART I: FOUNDATION STUDIES IN ANTHROPOSOPHY

1. Rudolf Steiner, *Theosophy*, p. 24.
2. Ibid., p. 30.
3. Ibid., p. 46.
4. Ibid, p. 47.
5. Ibid., p. 48.
6. Rudolf Steiner, *A Psychology of Body, Soul, Spirit*, p. 43.
7. Rudolf Steiner, *Theosophy*, p. 66.
8. Ibid., p. 85.
9. Steiner gave many lectures on reincarnation and karma, including an eight-volume series of lectures entitled *Karmic Relationships*. See www.steinerbooks.com.
10. Rudolf Steiner, *Vocation*, p. 99.
11. Rudolf Steiner, *Reincarnation and Karma*, p. 18.
12. Karl Konig, *Living Physiology*, p. 47.
13. Rudolf Steiner, *Esoteric Science*, p. 199.
14. Ibid., p. 199.

PART II: ORGANS AND ORGAN-IZATIONS

1. Walter Buhler, *Living With Your Body*, p. 45-46.
2. Ibid., p. 49.
3. Rudolf Steiner, *Spiritual Science and Medicine*, p. 24.
4. Karl König, *The Temple*, p. 55.
5. Friedrich Husemann , *The Anthroposophical Approach to Medicine*, p. 333.
6. Rudolf Steiner, *The Four Temperaments*.
7. The reader will note that there are distinctions in the Anthroposophic definition of ego from that used in 20th century psychology.

8. Holtzapfel, *The Human Organs*, p. 71.
9. Friedrich Husemann, *The Anthroposophical Approach to Medicine*, p. 335.
10. Holtzapfel, *The Human Organs*, p. 54.
11. Friedrich Husemann, *The Anthroposophical Approach to Medicine*, p. 296.
12. Ibid,. p. 298.
13. Friedrich Husemann, *The Anthroposophical Approach to Medicine*, p. 302.
14. Victor Bott, *An Introduction to Anthroposophical Medicine*, p. 138.
15. Friedrich Husemann, *The Anthroposophical Approach to Medicine*,p. 303.
16. Victor Bott, *An Introduction to Anthroposophical Medicine*, p. 121.
17. Holtzapfel, *The Human Organs*, p. 120.
18. Ibid., p.25.
19. Giovanni Maciocia, *The Foundations of Chinese Medicine* , p. 81.
20. Rudolf Steiner, *Curative Education*, p. 27.
21. Giovanni Maciocia, *The Foundations of Chinese Medicine* , p. 81.
22. Ibid. , p. 79.
23. Friedrich Husemann, *The Anthroposophical Approach to Medicine*, p. 308-309.
24. Ibid, p. 310.
25. Giovanni Maciocia, *The Foundations of Chinese Medicine*, p. ?.
26. Rudolf Steiner, *An Occult Physiology*, p. 65.
27. Giovanni Maciocia, *The Foundations of Chinese Medicine*, p. 90.
28. Ibid., p. 91.
29. Holzapfel, *The Human Organs*, p. 35.
30. Ibid., p. 39.
31. Ibid., p. 41.
32. John J. Ratey, M.D., *The User's Guide to the Brain*, p. 53.
33. Holzapfel, *The Human Organs*, p. 42.
34. Friedrich Husemann, The *Anthrosophical Approach to Medicine*, p. 322.
35. Friedrich Husemann , *The Anthrosophical Approach to Medicine*. p. 232.
36. Ibid, p. 324.
37. Friedrich Husemann, *The Anthrosophical Approach to Medicine,* p. 325.
38. Rudolf Steiner, *Foundations*, p. 39-41.
39. Holzapfel, *The Human Organs*, p. 32.
40. Margaret Wheatley, *A Simpler Way*, p. 26.
41. Ibid, p. 82.

42. Friedrich Husemann, *The Anthrosophical Approach to Medicine*, p. 111.
43. Ibid., p. 112.
44. M. Kendall, "The Cells of the Thymus," p. 63-83.
45. Andra Munger, "The Thymus and the Forces of the Cosmic Ether," p?.
46. A. J. T. George, and M. Ritter, "Thymic Involution with Aging: Obsolescence or Good Housekeeping?" pp 267–272.
47. Carla Hannaford, *Smart Moves*, p. 90.
48. Ibid., p. 91.
49. Ibid., p. 59.
50. Rudolf Steiner, *Knowledge of Higher Worlds* and study notes from Rudolf Steiner House.

PART III: OTHER ASPECTS OF HUMAN PSYCHOLOGY

1. L. F. C. Mees, *Secrets of the Skeleton*, p. 26.
2. For a more thorough explanation of framing issues see *School Renewal*, Chapter 7.
3. Torin Finser, Research, AWSNA Publications, Fair Oaks, CA, 1995.
4. Albert Soesman, *Our Twelve Senses*, p. 142.
5. John J. Ratey, M.D., *The User's Guide to the Brain*, p. 77.
6. Albert Soesman, *Our Twelve Senses*, p. 17.
7. John J. Ratey, M.D. *The User's Guide to the Brain*, p. 172
8. Carl Honore, *In Praise of Slowness*.
9. Wayne Muller, *The Sabbath*, p. 6.
10. Felix Marti-Ibanez, M.D.,*The Epic of Medicine*, p. 37.
11. John J. Ratey, M.D., *The User's Guide to the Brain*, p. 64.
12. Albert Soesman, *The Twelve Senses*, p. 75.
13. Ibid., p. 76.
14. John J. Ratey, M.D., *The User's Guide to the Brain*, p. 69.
15. Albert Soesman, *The Twelve Senses*, p. 96.
16. Friedrich Husemann, *The Anthroposophical Approach to Medicine*, p. 60.
17. Theodore Schwenk, *Sensitive Chaos*, p. 87.
18. Albert Soesman, *The Twelve Senses*, p. 114.
19. John J. Ratey, M.D., *The User's Guide to the Brain*, p. 163.

Part IV: Leadership

1. Wilhem Pelikan, *Secrets of Metals*, p 111.
2. US Geological Survey, "Minerals Information," internet site
3. Wilhem Pelikan, *Secrets of Metals*, p. 83.
4. Ibid., p. 86.
5. US Dept of Interior, US Geological Survey, internet site
6. Wilhem Pelikan, *Secrets of Metals*, p. 113.
7. Rudolf Hauschka, *The Nature of Substance*, p. 164.
8. Wilhem Pelikan, *Secrets of Metals*, p. 115.
9. L. F. C. Mees, *Living Metals*, p. 24.
10. US Dept of the Interior, US Geological Survey, p. 96.
11. Wilhem Pelikan, *Secrets of Metals*, p. 28.
12. Ibid., p. 36.
13. Rudolf Hauschka, *The Nature of Substance*, p. 172.
14. Ibid., p. 171.
15. Ibid., p. 195.
16. Wilhem Pelikan, *Secrets of Metals*, p. 33.
17. Ibid., p. 42.
18. US Geological Survey, p. 177.
19. Rudolf Hauschka, *The Nature of Substance*, p. 167.
20. L. F. C. Mees, Living Metals, p. 47.
21. Rudolf Hauschka, *The Nature of Substance*, p. 169.
22. *Wall Street Journal,* April 12, 2006, p.1.
23. US Geological Survey, p. 74.
24. Wilhem Pelikan, *Secrets of Metals*, p. 87.
25. Ibid., p. 95.
26. Ibid., p. 101.
27. Edith Hamilton, *Mythology*, p. 24.
28. Ibid., p. 34.
29. Ibid., p. 30.
30. Ibid., p. 32.
31. Wilhem Pelikan,*Secrets of Metals*, p. 39.
32. Rudolf Steiner, *Anthroposophical Medicine*, p. 94.
33. Max Stibbe, *The Seven Soul Types*, p.28.
34. Ibid, p. 52.
35. Ibid., p. 37.
36. Interview with Jamie York.
37. Rudolf Steiner, *Cosmosophy*, p. 149.

38. Jamie York, *Making Math Meaningful*, p. 175.
39. From notes taken in conversation with Jamie York.
40. John Neinhardt, *Black Elk Speaks*.
41. Much of the Native American information here came from one of my Antioch students, Angela Wilder-Linstrom.
42. Peter M. Senge, *The Fifth Discipline*, p. 69.
43. Andrew Weil, M.D., *Eight Weeks to Optimum Health*, p. 17.
44. Peter M. Senge, *The Fifth Discipline*, p. 71.
45. Ibid., p. 73
46. Rudolf Steiner, *Anthroposophy and Everyday Life*, pp 67–81.
47. Felix Marti-Ibanez, M.D., *The Epic of Medicine*, p. 67.

PART V: HEALTHY ORGAN-IZATIONS

1. Mattias Karutz, "Forming School Committees," p. 17
2. Georg Kühlewind, *Journal for Anthroposophy,* vol. 55, fall 1992, p. 67.
3. I am indebted to my colleague Kim John Payne for his lecture notes on this subject.
4. Georg Kühlewind, *Journal for Anthroposophy,* vol. 55, fall 1992, p. 67.p. 63.
5. John Abrams, *The Company We Keep*, p. 16.
6. *New York Times,* Sunday June 18, 2006, p. 2.
7. John Abrams, *The Company We Keep*, p. 202.
8. *Journal of the Pedagogical Section at the Goetheanum,* summer 2006, p. 13.
9. Gareth Morgan, *Images of Organizations*, p. 43.

Bibliography

Books

Abrams, John. *The Company We Keep*. Brattleboro, VT: Chelsea Green Publishing, 2005.

Aeppli, Wille. *The Care and Development of the Human Senses*. Sussex, UK: Steiner School Fellowship, 1993.

Albrecht, Karl. *Social Intelligence: The New Science of Success; Beyond IQ Beyond EI, Applying Multiple Intelligence Theory to Human Interaction*. San Francisco, Wiley, 2006.

Baur, Alfred. *Healing Sounds*. Fair Oaks, CA: Rudolf Steiner College Press, 1993.

Bittleston, Adam. *Then Seven Planets*. Edinburgh: Floris Books, 1985.

Bolen, Jean Shinoda M.D. *God in Every Man*. New York: Harper & Row, 1990.

Bott, Victor. *An Introduction to Anthroposophical Medicine*. London: Sophia Books, 2004.

Buhler, Walter. *Living With Your Body*. London: Rudolf Steiner Press, 1979.

Collins, Jim. *Good to Great: Why Some Companies Make the Leap...and Others Don't*. New York: Harper Collins, 2001.

Glasl, Friedrich. *Confronting Conflict*. Stroud, UK: Hawthorn Press, 1999.

Hamilton, Edith. *Mythology* New York: Mentor Books, 1942.

Hannaford, Carla, PhD. *Smart Moves - Why Learning is not All in Your Head*. Salt Lake City: Great River Books, 2005.

Hauschka, Rudolf. *The Nature of Substance*. London: Rudolf Steiner Press, 1983.

Holdrege, Craig. *The Dynamic Heart and Circulation*. Fair Oaks, CA: AWSNA, 2002.

Holtzapfel, Walter, *The Human Organs: Their Funtional and Psychological Significance*. The Lanthorne Press, Cornwall, 1993.

Honoré, Carl. *In Praise of Slowness: Challenging the Cult of Speed.* New York: HarperCollins, 2004.

Husemann, Armin. *The Harmony of the Human Body.* PLACE: Floris Books, 1994.

Husemann, Friedrich and Otto Wolff. *The Anthropological Approach to Medicine: An Outline of a Spiritual Scientifically Oriented Medicine.* vol. 1. Great Barrington, MA: SteinerBooks, 1996.

Jocelyn, John. *Meditations on the Signs of the Zodiac.* San Antonio, TX: Naylor,1966.

Kempter, Friedrich. *Rudolf Steiner's Seven Signs of Planetary Evolution.* Spring Valley, New York: St. George Publications, 1980.

Kendall, Marion D. "The Cells of the Thymus"; *The Thymus Gland,* M. Kendall, ed. London: Academic Press, 1981.

Klocek, Dennis. *Seeking Spirit Vision.* Fair Oaks, CA: Rudolf Steiner College Press, 1998.

König, Karl. *My Earth Man.* Rhode Island: Bio-Dynamic Literature, 1982.

Kranich, Ernst Michael. *Planetary Influences Upon Plants.* Rhode Island: Bio-Dynamic Literature, 1984.

Lievegoed, Bernard C. J. *The Developing Organization.* New York: Harper & Row, 1973.

―――. *Man on the Threshold: The Challenge of Inner Development.* Stroud, UK: Hawthorn Press, 1985.

Maciocia, Giovanni. *The Foundations of Chinese Medicine: A Comprehensive Text for Acupuncturists and Herbalists.* Livingstone, NY: Churchill, 1989.

Marti-Ibanex, Felix, M.D. *The Epic of Medicine.* N. Potter, NY: Clarkson, 1962.

McManus, Chris. *Right Hand left Hand, the Origins of Asymmetry in the Brains, Bodies, Atoms, and Cultures.* Cambridge, MA: Harvard University Press, 2002.

Mees, L. F. C. *Living Metals.* New York: Regency Press, 1974.

―――. *Secrets of the Skeleton.* Great Barrington, MA: SteinerBooks, 1984.

Moore, Richard D. M.D., Ph.D. *The High Blood Pressure Solution.* Rochester, Vt: Healing Arts Press, 2001.

Morgan, Gareth. *Images of Organization.* London: Sage Publications, 1997.

―――. *Images of Organization.* London: Sage Publications, 1998.

Muller, Wayne. *The Sabbath: Restoring the Sacred Rhythm of Rest.* New York: Bantam, 1999.

Murray, MacKay M.D. *Human Anatomy Made Simple*. New York: Doubleday, 1969.

Neihardt, John G. *Black Elk Speaks*. Lincoln: University of Nebraska Press, 1961.

Pelikan, Wilhem. *Secrets of Metals*. Great Barrington, MA: SteinerBooks, 2006.

Priever, Werner, M.D. *Illness and the Double*. New York: Mercury Press, 1984.

Ratey, John J., M.D. *A User's Guide to the Brain: Perception, Attention, and the Four Theaters of the Brain*. New York: Vintage, 2002.

Schwenk, Theodore. *Sensitive Chaos: The Creation of Flowing Forms in Water and Air*. London: Rudolf Steiner Press, 2001.

Senge, Peter, M. *The Fifth Discipline: The Art & Practice of The Learning Organization*. New York: Currency and Doubleday, 1990.

Soesman, Albert. *Our Twelve Senses, Wellsprings of the Soul*. Stroud: Hawthorne Press, 1999.

Steiner, Rudolf. *Anthroposophy in Every Day Life*. Hudson, NY: Anthroposophic Press, 1995.

———. *Cosmosophy,* vol 2. lecture 8, Dornach, November 1921.

———. *Curative Education*. London: Rudolf Steiner Press, 1972.

———. *Eine Okkulte Physiologie*. Dornach, Switzerland: Verlag der Rudolf Steiner-NachlaBverwaltung, 1957.

———. *Evolution in the Aspect of Realities,* Blauvelt, NY: Garber, 1989.

———. *Feverish Pursuit of Health*. New York: Anthroposphic Press, 1969.

———. "The Four Temperaments." New York: Anthroposophic Press, 1980; also contained in *Anthroposophy in Everyday Life.*

———. *Geistige ZusammenHange in der Gestaltung des menschlichen Organismus*. Dornach, Switzerland: Philosophisch-Anthroposophischer, 1945.

———. *Health and Illness*. New York: Anthroposophic Press, 1983.

———. *Introducing Anthroposophical Medicine*. Hudson, NY: Anthroposophic Press, 1999.

———. *Lectures to the Workers*. New York: Anthroposophic Press, 1989.

———. *Man's Life on Earth and in the Spiritual Worlds,* lecture 2, "The Cosmic Origin of the Human Form." lecture in Oxford, August 22, 1922, Mokelumne Hill, CA, 1960.

———. *Nutrition and Health*. New York: Anthroposophic Press, 1987.

———. *An Occult Physiology*. London: Rudolf Steiner Press, 2005.

———. *The Occult Significance of Blood, Occult and Modern Thought.* New York: Book Centre, 1912.

———. *A Psychology of Body, Soul, and Spirit: Anthroposophy, Psychosophy, and Pneumatosophy.* New York: Anthroposophic Press, 1999.

———. *Spiritual Science and Medicine.* London: Rudolf Steiner Press, 1975.

———. *Theosophy: An Introduction to the Spiritual Processes in Human Life and in the Cosmos.* Hudson, NY: Anthroposophic Press, 1971.

———. *Therapeutic Insights Earthly and Cosmic Laws.* Spring Valley, NY: Mercury Press, 1984.

———. *The Work of the Angels in Man's Astral Body.* London: Rudolf Steiner Press, 1972.

Steiner, Rudolf and Wegman, Ita. *Extending Practical Medicine.* London: Rudolf Steiner Press, 2000.

Silbernagl, Stefan and Florian Lang. *Color Atlas of Pathophysiology.* New York: Thieme, 2000.

Stibbe, Max. *Seven Soul Types.* Stroud, UK: Hawthorn Press, 1992.

Spock, Majorie. *In Celebration of the Human Heart.* Spring Valley, NY: St. George Publications, 1882.

Treicher, Rudolf. *Soulways: Development, Crises, and Illnesses of the Soul.* London: Hawthorn Press, 1982.

Twentyman, Ralph. *The Science and Art of Healing.* Edinburgh: Floris Book, 1989.

U.S. Geological Survey, Minerals Site, internet.

Verhulst, Jos. *Developmental Dynamics in Humans and Other Primates.* Ghent, NY: Adonis Press, 2003.

von Goethe, Johann Wolfgang. *Fairy Tale of the Green Snake and the Beautiful Lily.* Great Barrington, MA: SteinerBooks, 2006.

von Mackensen, Manfred and Claudia Allgower and Andreas Bienfeld-Ackermann. *Uprightness, Weight, and Balance.* Fair Oaks, CA: AWSNA, 2003.

Weihs, Thomas J. *Embryogenesis in Myth and Science.* New York: Anthroposopic Press, 1986.

Weisbord, Marvin R. *Discovering Common Ground.* San Francisco, CA: Berrett-Koehler, 1992.

Weil, Andrew, M.D. *Eight Weeks to Optimum Health.* New York: Random House, 1997.

Weisborg, Marvin & Sandra Janoff. *Future Search: An Action Guide to Finding Common Ground in Organizations & Communities.* San Francisco, Berrett-Koehler, 2000.

York, Jamie. *Making Math Meaningful.* Denver, CO: Whole Spirit Press, 2004.

Zimmerman, Jack M. and Virginia Coyle. *The Way of Council.* Putney, VT: Bramble Books, 1996.

ARTICLES

George, A. J. T. and M. Ritter. "Thymic Involution with Aging: Obsolescence or Good Housekeeping?" *Immunology Today,* (1996): 17:6.

Grohman, Gerbert. "Drawing: From First Grade to High School." *Education as an Art* Rudolf Steiner School Association (1959): spring.

Munger, Andra. "The Thymus and the Forces of the Cosmic Ether." Woodlands, TX: nd.

———. 'Supersensible Physiology in Education." Stuttgart, September 21, 1920; private manuscript for members of the Anthroposophical Society. 16 lectures in Dornach, April–May 1920.

Journal of Anthroposphic Medicine (fall 1991), vol. 8.

Journal of Anthroposphic Medicine (summer 1992), vol. 9.

Journal of Pedagogical Section at the Goetheanum. (mid-summer 2006)

Waleda News. (November 1980)

Antioch University New England OFFERS GRADUATE AND CERTIFICATE PROGRAMS IN EDUCATION, ENVIRONMENTAL STUDIES, MANAGEMENT, AND PSYCHOLOGY THAT REFLECT A DEDICATION TO ACTIVISM, SOCIAL JUSTICE, COMMUNITY SERVICE, AND SUSTAINABILITY. PROGRAMS INCLUDE:

Waldorf Teacher Education Program

AWAKEN YOUR COMPASSION IN A POWERFUL MED PROGRAM THAT HELPS YOU REALIZE YOUR TEACHING POTENTIAL. THE FULLY ACCREDITED, FIVE-SEMESTER PROGRAM OFFERS LIVELY COURSES IN THE ARTS, ANTHROPOSOPHY, AND A CHILD-CENTERED CURRICULUM. A SUMMER SEQUENCE PROGRAM IS ALSO OFFERED.

Collaborative Leadership Program

THIS SERIES OF INSTITUTES STRENGTHENS ORGANIZATIONAL LEADERSHIP AND THE WORKING RELATIONSHIPS OF PARENTS, TEACHERS, ADMINISTRATORS, AND BOARD MEMBERS IN A WALDORF SCHOOL COMMUNITY.

MBA in Organizational and Environmental Sustainability (Green MBA)

A FULL-TIME PROGRAM WITH A PART-TIME, WEEKEND DELIVERY, THE GREEN MBA COVERS WHAT YOU'D EXPECT IN AN MBA PROGRAM, PLUS THE UNEXPECTED—A CURRICULUM THAT CONSIDERS NOT ONLY SUSTAINABLE BUSINESS PRACTICES, BUT ALSO ENVIRONMENTAL STUDIES, AND BEHAVIORAL AND SOCIAL SCIENCES.

ANTIOCH
UNIVERSITY
NEW ENGLAND

Because the world needs you now.

www.antiochne.edu

MONEY CAN HEAL

EVOLVING OUR CONSCIOUSNESS –
THE STORY OF RSF AND ITS
INNOVATIONS IN SOCIAL FINANCE

BY SIEGFRIED E. FINSER

EXPLORING THE WONDERS of every kind of monetary transaction, Siegfried Finser reveals how all transactions interact with the human psyche. Having evolved through the ages, money is no longer an object so much as it has become a "worldwind" of circulation, moving at various speeds and achieving a myriad of results.

Our human intentions give money its qualities and determine its speed and its effect on people everywhere. From object to pure movement, money is now poised to serve our highest goals. As we have nurtured money in its evolution, we must now take responsibility for directing its great potential in transforming social life, thereby bringing healing to the world. The author gives RSF Social Finance as an example of an organization working to heal our social life.

Money Can Heal shows a way beyond money as "a thing one acquires" toward money as "movement" among human souls. You'll never see money the same way again.

SIEGFRIED FINSER was a Waldorf schoolteacher, managed a division of Xerox, and was Director of Executive Development worldwide for ITT. He has consulted with many large corporations and was president of the Threefold Educational Foundation, treasurer of the Anthroposophical Society in America, and founder of the Rudolf Steiner Foundation (RSF), where he continues on the Board of Trustees. He has a BA from Rutgers University and an MA in Educational Psychology from New York University. He frequently lectures on the nature of money and the healing potential in monetary transactions.

Paperback • 248 pages • $25.00 • ISBN: 9780880105736